**Diana Stephenson** was formerly a researcher for the University of Strathclyde and many international organisations; also a member of the European team which compiles the Clarendon Reports.

For this fourth edition of what started as 'The Bookshops of Inner London' she has made a great many updatings and new entries.

## Preface

Much as we would like to claim the idea for this book we must acknowledge that it stems from a range of publications published in Australia by Tom and Wendy Whitton of Second Back Row Press, Sydney. This book is published with their blessing and we hope it measures up to the standards that they set.

Reference books tend to improve in successive editions and 'Bookshops of London' is no exception.

In this edition, we have added some shops which somehow escaped the net of research last time and we have made numerous amendments to 3rd edition entries.

For the present we are keeping to moderate print runs in order that revision frequency can be maintained at a high level.

While every effort has been made to give accurate information and descriptions of the shops listed, we must disclaim responsibility for any errors.

The publisher welcomes written information or suggestions which might make the next edition even better.

We have tried to include all shops retailing books. If we have omitted any, please let us know. Note the paragraph on 'Exclusions' below before doing so.

## Explanations

**Sequence Adopted.** Shops have been grouped by postal district and are in fact listed in post code order. This has been done largely for the convenience of publishers and their representatives — amongst the principal users of this book.

**Shop Index.** The alphabetical shop index will assist those readers who may not know the postal district system of London.

**Subject Index.** Booksellers with any degree of specialisation are listed by number in the Subject Index which will be found at the back of the book.

**Exclusions.** This book does not include bookshops specialising in pornography, nor does it include newsagents whose stock is non-book by nature. We have also excluded minor shops of the major chains as these also are principally retailers of magazines and stationery.

Dealers in books who are not retailers to the public have also been excluded as have those retailers who are open only on two or three days a week.

# Bookshops
## of London
### Diana Stephenson

**New, second hand and antiquarian books
Specialised and general booksellers**

> "The Booksellers are generous,
> liberal minded men."
> *Dr. Johnson*

**Roger Lascelles,** Cartographic and Travel Publisher
47 York Road, Brentford, Middlesex TW8 0QP   Telephone: 01-847 0935

# Publication Data

| | |
|---|---|
| **Title** | Bookshops of London |
| **Typeface** | Phototypeset in Compugraphic Times |
| **Printing** | Kelso Graphics, Kelso, Scotland. |
| **ISBN** | 0 903909 43 x |
| **Edition** | First, October 1981.   Third, July 1984.<br>Second, February 1982.   This Fourth June 1985. |
| **Publisher** | Roger Lascelles<br>47 York Road, Brentford, Middlesex, TW8 0QP. |
| **Copyright** | Roger Lascelles |

All rights reserved. No Part of this publication may be reproduced, stored in a retrieval system or transmitted in any form by any means, electronic, mechanical, photocopying, recording or otherwise, without the written permission of the publisher and copyright owner, except brief extracts for the purpose of review.

# Distribution

| | | |
|---|---|---|
| **Africa:** | Enquiries invited | |
| **Americas:** | Canada — | International Travel Maps & Books, P.O. Box 2290, Vancouver B.C. |
| | U.S.A. — | Bradt Enterprises, 95 Harvey Street, Cambridge, MA. 02140 |
| **Asia:** | Hong Kong — | The Book Society, G.P.O. Box 7804, Hong Kong Tel: 5-241901 |
| | India — | English Book Store, New Delhi |
| **Australasia** | Australia — | Rex Map Centre, 413 Pacific Highway, Artarmon NSW 2064 |
| | New Zealand — | International Travel Guides, P.O. Box 4397, Christchurch 1 |
| **Europe:** | Belgium — | Brussels, Peuples et Continents |
| | GB/Ireland — | Available through all booksellers with a good foreign travel section. |
| | Italy — | Libreria dell'Automobile, Milano |
| | Netherlands — | Nilsson & Lamm BV, Weesp |
| | Denmark — | Copenhagen — Arnold Busck, G.E.C. Gad, Boghallen |
| | Finland — | Oslo - Arne Gimnes/J.G. Tanum |
| | Sweden — | Stockholm - Esselte/Akademi Bokhandel Fritzes/Hedengrens<br>Gothenburg - Gumperts/Esselte<br>Lund - Gleerupska |
| | Switzerland — | The Travel Bookshop, Seilergraben 11, 8001 Zurich<br>Librairie Artou, 8 rue de Rive, 1204 Geneve. |

# Contents

| Postal Districts | Shop No's |
|---|---|
| E1 | 1—6 |
| E4 | 7—9 |
| E6-11 | 10—16 |
| E13-18 | 17—23 |
| | |
| EC1 | 24—27 |
| EC2 | 28—38 |
| EC3 | 39—45 |
| EC4 | 46—58 |
| | |
| N1 | 100—113 |
| N3-7 | 114—130 |
| N8-15 | 131—143 |
| N16-22 | 144—156 |
| | |
| NW1 | 200—225 |
| NW2 | 226—228 |
| NW3 | 229—241 |
| NW4 | 242—246 |
| NW5-9 | 247—266 |
| NW11 | 267—273 |
| | |
| SE1 | 300—311 |
| SE3 | 312—315 |
| SE5-6 | 316—320 |
| SE8-18 | 321—346 |
| SE20-27 | 347—358 |

| Postal District | Shop No's |
|---|---|
| SW1 | 400—437 |
| SW3 | 438—451 |
| SW4-6 | 452—466 |
| SW7 | 467—481 |
| SW9-10 | 482—487 |
| SW11-16 | 488—508 |
| SW17-19 | 509—522 |
| | |
| W1 | 600—682 |
| W2 | 700—707 |
| W3 | 708—714 |
| W5 | 715—720 |
| W6 | 721—727 |
| W8-9 | 728—744 |
| W11-12 | 745—757 |
| W13-14 | 758—761 |
| | |
| WC1 | 800—855 |
| WC2 | 900—991 |

Subject Index
Shop Index

# E1

**1 TOWER HAMLETS ARTS PROJECT BOOKSHOP**
**178 Whitechapel, London E1 1BJ.**          **01-247-0216**

**Subjects:** General, Local history, Bi-lingual books for Bengali Community, Children's books.
**Hours:** Tue - Fri 10.00 - 6.00. Sat 10.00 - 5.00.
**Services** Savings cards. Bookstalls in local Colleges.

Great enthusiasm and initiative started this community bookshop in Tower Hamlets and continues to-day. Vivid colours attract the eye and apart from the general stock they specialise in the history of the East End. Their children's section is very important and they have a policy of not stocking sexist or racial books and reach schools and colleges with their bookstall system. Savings cards enable the children with little money to save for a chosen book. The bi-lingual section is a great asset to the Bengali Community, also specialist books for adult literary courses and help and advice for the local inhabitant is always on hand.


**2 BARKER & HOWARD LTD.**
**Barker House,**
**106 Watney Street, London E1 2QE.**          **01-790 5081/2**

**Subjects:** General, Maritime.
**Hours:** Mon - Fri 9.00 - 5.00. Sat 9.30 - 12.30.
**Services:** Credit cards, special orders.

A jewel in the mud, a clean airy shop in a rather run-down area. All the stock is clearly sectioned and they have a good range of paperbacks and children's books. At the rear is the shop's specialization, books to do with all things maritime.

### 3  DILLONS Q.M.C. BOOKSHOP
**Dillons University Bookshop Ltd.**
**Queen Mary College,**
**Mile End Road, London E1 4NS.**                    **01-980 2554**

**Subjects:** Science, technology.
**Hours:** Mon - Fri 9.00 - 5.00 (Wed 9.00 - 4.30)
**Services:** Credit cards, special orders.

The bookshop is within the college but open to the public. There is some paperback fiction but most of their stock is course orientated for the students. Science, computing and engineering books clearly marked out.


### 4  R. GOLUB & CO. LTD.
**27 Osborn Street, London E1 6TD.**                 **01-247 7430**

**Subjects:** Judaica, Hebraica
**Hours:** Mon - Thu 10.00 - 5.00. Fri & Sun 10.00 - 1.30. Closed Sat.
**Services:** Special Orders. Mail Order.

A very scruffy outward appearance might allow you to pass this shop without realising it was selling books. Inside are shelves of books in no particular order to interest the browser in this rag trade area of London. Known as "The Jewish Bookshop of the East End" it stocks books in both Hebrew and English and a very relaxed atmosphere on the part of the staff


### 5  THE LONDON YACHT CENTRE LTD.
**13 Artillery Lane, London E1 7LP.**                **01-247 0521**

**Subjects:** Sailing.
**Hours:** Mon - Fri 9.00 - 5.30 (Thu 9.00 - 7.00).
**Services:** Credit cards, special orders.

A small department at the Yacht Centre is allocated to books for 'the sailor'. Yachtsmen's charts, books on navigation and the practical side of sailing are stocked. Special orders taken.

## 6  FREEDOM BOOKSHOP
**84b Whitechapel High Street.**
**(Angel Alley), London E1 7QX**         01-247 9249

**Subjects:** Anarchist Politics.
**Hours:** Tue - Sat 10.00 - 6.00.
**Services:** Mail Order (Catalogue).Special Orders.

Freedom publishers have their offices here but the pupils are welcome to purchase books on anarchist politics on the second floor.

# E4

**7 RICHARD TUDOR**
   **135 Station Road, Chingford, London E4 6AG    01-524 5518**

   **Subjects:** General.
   **Hours:** Mon - Fri 9.30 - 5.00 (Thu 9.30 - 1.00) Sat 10.00 - 5.00.
   **Services:** Special orders, picture framing.

   A cheery atmosphere in this shop which sells a general line of hard and soft backed books. The other string to its bow is a small gallery of pictures integrated with the books, hence the picture framing service.


**8 N.S.S.NEWSAGENT (RETAIL) LTD.**
   **52-54 Station Road, London E4 7BE.    01-529 1289**

   **Subjects:** General, maps and guides.
   **Hours:** Mon - Sat 7.30 - 5.30. Sun 7.30 - 12.00.
   **Services:** Special orders.

   As the name suggests primarily a paper shop but with a range of popular non-fiction maps and guides quite well represented for the ambitious commuter.


**9 ARNOTS**
   **28 The Avenue, Highams Park, London E4 9LD.    01-527 6771**

   **Subjects:** General, Maps, Children's Books.
   **Hours:** Mon - Sat 9.00 - 5.30 (Thu 9.00 - 1.00).
   **Services:** Special orders, Credit Cards.

   Inevitably stationery, but towards the back of the shop up a few steps there is a general stock of books with children's books and a map and guide section quite strong.

# E6-11

**10 C. & J. FOSTER**
**79 Shopping Hall, Myrtle Road,**
**London, E6 1HY.** **01-552 2263**

**Subjects:** Second hand paperbacks and new children's books.
**Hours:** Mon - Sat 9.00 - 5.30. Thu 9.00 - 1.00.

Small market shop selling secondhand paperbacks with a section of children's books — new but reasonably priced.


**11 W.H. SMITH & SON LTD.**
**125 High Street North, London E6 1HZ.** **01-552 4875/6**

**Subjects:** General.
**Hours:** Mon - Sat 8.30 - 5.30.
**Services:** Special orders, Credit cards.

A long shop, shelving books under subject headings with a corner for children's books. There is a permanent table top display of remaindered and bargain books.


**12 ROUND ABOUT BOOKS**
**368 Mare Street, London E8 1HR.** **01-985 8148**

**Subjects:** General.
**Hours:** Mon - Sat 6.30 - 6.00.
**Services:** Special orders.

Firstly a functioning newsagent but with a general stock, mainly paperbacks. Bibles, dictionaries and guides have here and elsewhere a prominence suggesting a theological, lexicological earnestness not apparent in society at large.

## 13 CENTERPRISE BOOKSHOP
136-138 Kingsland High Street,
Hackney, London E8 2NS.     01-254 9632/5

**Subjects:** General, Feminist, Radical, Black Culture.
**Hours:** Tue - Sat 10.00 - 5.30 (Thu 10.30 - 2.00).
**Services:** Special orders.

This is a community bookshop with a coffee and snack bar attached. The emphasis is on multi-racial, non-sexist and working class books. The shop also stocks its own publications on local history as well as those of other small publishing houses.


## 14 T. DITCHFIELD LTD.
790-794 High Road, Leyton, London E10 6AE.     01-559 2821

**Subjects:** General.
**Hours:** Mon - Sat 9.15 - 5.30 (Thu 9.15 - 1.00).

'Gifts for all occasions' is how Ditchfield's describe their stock. Bicycles to porcelain but with a small stock of books of general appeal.


## 15 VANES OF WANSTEAD
27 Cambridge Park, Wanstead,
London E11 2PU.     01-989-4358

**Subjects:** General.
**Hours:** Mon - Sat 9.00 - 5.00 (Wed 9.00 - 1.00) closed for lunch Fri/Sat 12.30 - 1.30.
**Services:** Special orders.

The last shop from the station, it could be missed by a stranger to the area. Their range is general but children's books are well covered.


## 16 WILLEN LTD.
Howard House, Howard Road, London, E11.     01-556 7776

**Subjects:** Railways and guns.
**Hours:** Mon - Fri 9.15 - 5.15.
**Services:** Mail order. Special orders.

This is a distributor for their specialist subjects but the public are able to purchase books at these premises.

# E13-18

**17  PAPERBACKS CENTRE (Newpark Publications Ltd.)**
**389 Green Street, Upton Park,**
**London E13 9AR.**                                            **01-470 1388**

  **Subjects:**  General, Politics, History, Philosophy, Economics.
  **Hours:**     Mon - Sat 9.00 - 6.00.
  **Services:**  Special orders, college and school supply.

The shop, opposite Queens Market has a pleasing atmosphere with plenty of space, longer in fact than their Charlotte Street branch. Hardbacked books are also sold and the selection of books in their specialist subjects is good. Student needs are primary but there is a good children's section.


**18  PARENTS CENTRE ACTIVITIES (NEWHAM) LTD.**
**747 Barking Road,**
**Plaistow, London E13 9ER.**                                  **01-472 2000**

  **Subjects:**  General, Educational.
  **Hours:**     Mon - Fri 9.30 - 5.30 (Thu 9.30 - 6.00). Sat 10.00 - 5.00.
  **Services:**  Special orders, school and college supply, newsletter. Reading help scheme.

This centre is a charity open to individuals and groups living or working in Newham. It's aim is to seek out and publicise information on education, therefore their stock of educational books is their speciality. This includes reading schemes in schools, adult literary schemes and an excellent children's section, including an Under Five Resource room with a wide range of free literature available. There is a Reading Help Scheme backed by a mobile Education Shop which travels to Dockland sites. Reference books have their section and the Arts include East End Writings and Poetry. A most enterprising venture.

### 19 W.H. SMITH & SON LTD.
The Stratford Centre,
41-42 The Mall, London E15 1EX.     01-534 5955

**Subjects:** General, cookery.
**Hours:** Mon, Wed, Thu 9.00 - 5.30. Tue 9.30 - 5.30. Fri 9.00 - 6.00. Sat 8.30 - 5.30.
**Services:** Credit cards, special orders.

This branch of Smiths is located in the new shopping centre at Stratford. There is a general range of hard and paper-backed books with cookery as the longest section. Medical and technical books for students reflect the hospitals and colleges hereabouts.

### 20 THE WHOLE THING
53 West Ham Lane,
Stratford, London E15 4PH.     01-534 6539

**Subjects:** Student, Political, local and feminist books and childrens.
**Hours:** Mon, Tue, Wed, Fri 9.30 - 5.30. Sat 9.30 - 4.00. Closed Thu.
**Services:** Special orders.

This is a workers co-operative bookshop aided by the Greater London Arts Association with a wholefood department at the rear, and has informative books on how to set up a co-operative movement.

Multi-racial sections are well covered with third world, politics and local books their speciality.

### 21 FANFARE BOOKCENTRE
2 Chingford Road, Bell Corner, London E17 4PJ.     01-527 4296

**Subjects:** General, School text books, computing.
**Hours:** Mon - Fri 9.30 - 5.30. Sat 10.00 - 5.00.
**Services:** School supply, Revision aids, Computer software, Photocopying, Cassettes.

This bookshop runs a service to supply students at Waltham Forest College, Redbridge and Havening Technical College which gives an idea of the academic books available. A room is set aside for this section which includes a large range of books on computers together with software. The main shop is convenient for the general customer and a small room has been given to the children's section which is well planned at a sensible height with appropriate cassettes.

## 22 E. & R. ABBOT LTD.
**135 George Lane, South Woodford, E18 1AN.**  **01-989 6164**

**Subjects:** General.
**Hours:** Mon - Fri 9.00 - 5.30 (Thu & Sat 9.00 - 5.00).

A stationers with a well chosen selection of general books. Strong on sport and gardening.


## 23 APEX STATIONERY  01-989 6253
## APEX CHRISTIAN BOOKS  01-504 4280
**72 George Lane, London E18 1JJ.**

**Subjects:** General, Christianity.
**Hours:** Mon - Fri 9.15 - 5.15 (Thu 9.15 - 12.30). Sat 9.30 - 5.00.
**Services:** Special orders.

Principally a stationers and printers. They sell a range of paperbacks for adults and children, also maps and guides. Orders are taken for hardbacks. A small room at the back of the shop specializes in christian literature.

# EC1

**24 DENNY'S BOOKSELLERS LTD.**
**2 Carthusian Street, London EC1M 6ED.**         **01-253 5421**

**Subjects:** General, medical and nursing.
**Hours:** Mon - Fri 9.00 - 5.30.
**Services:** Mail order.

In a side street near St. Bartholomew's Hospital this rather modest looking shop belies its interior which is book crammed, its shelving overwhelming the assistant who is tucked away at the back. Mr. Maher who runs it says that there is no book in print he cannot obtain, and that because of the extensive ordering of books for libraries and institutes the public have a chance to see books which are not usually accessible to them. It is a good general shop and has a prominent medical section because of the proximity to 'Bart's'.


**25 W.H. SMITH & SON LTD.**         **01-242 0535**
**Holborn Circus, 124 Holborn, London EC1N 2TD.**
        Travel Department **01-242 9826**

**Subjects:** General, Travel.
**Hours:** Mon - Fri 8.00 - 5.30. Sat 9.00 - 4.00.
**Services:** Credit cards, special orders.

Opened only in 1980 this large branch is rather good for travel books because it has a travel department next door and because Hatton Garden is adjacent and the jewellers sparkle when it comes to travel. The book section is at the back of the ground floor, the rest of the shop sells magazines, toys, stationery and odds and ends.

## 26 GENESIS BOOKS
**East West Centre,**
**188 Old Street, London EC1V 9BP.**  **01-250 1868**

**Subjects:** Alternative medicine, spiritual development, astrology.
**Hours:** Mon - Fri 11.30 - 7.30, Sat 11.30 - 3.30.
**Services:** Mail order, catalogue, magazine subscriptions.

The East West Centre houses this shop specialising in books on alternative medicine and oblique ways to spiritual health, surprising in this hard-nosed area.

How you'd exult if I could put you back
Six hundred years, blot out cosmogony,
Geology, ethnology, what not------
And set you square with Genesis again.


## 27 MENCAP BOOKSHOP
**National/Royal Society for Mentally Handicapped Children and Adults,**
**117/123 Golden Lane, London EC1Y ORT.**  **01-253 9433**

**Subjects:** Mental handicap
**Hours:** Mon - Fri 9.00 - 5.30
**Services:** Lists, quarterly journal, mail order.

This is a bright and colourful shop selling gifts as well as books. Its books are for those helping with the care of the mentally handicapped children and adults and the books range through directories of residential accommodation, educational courses, sex education and language stimulation.

# EC2

### 28 BROWN & PERRING
**36 Tabernacle Street, London EC2A 4DT.**     **01-253 4517**

**Subjects:** Maritime.
**Hours:** Mon - Fri 9.00 - 5.15. Sat 9.00 - 12.00.
**Services:** Special orders, chart agents.

Not many books accessible to the public at this counter service shop. Expert advice is on hand for all who would go down to the sea. Brown and Perring are primarily chart agents.


### 29 JOHN MENZIES LTD.
**56 Old Broad Street, London EC2M 1RX.**     **01-588 1632**

**Subjects:** General Business.
**Hours:** Mon - Fri 8.30 - 5.30.
**Services:** Credit cards.

A large shop with two sets of doors to the ground floor where the general titles are kept, together with books on banking, insurance, accountancy and other business studies. On the first floor they keep paper backs and computer equipment.


### 30 CHAIN LIBRARIES LTD.
**151 Moorgate, London EC2M 6TX.**     **01-606 5061**

**Subjects:** General (Paperbacks only).
**Hours:** Mon - Fri 10.00 - 5.30.

This is a small shop selling paperback books, both fiction and non-fiction, in the general popular range. The one room at street level also sells a few cards.

## 31 OYEZ STATIONERY LTD.
### 105-107 Moorgate, London EC2M 6SL.        01-588 1478

**Subjects:** Law.
**Hours:** Mon - Fri 8.30 - 5.30.
**Services:** Credit cards.

Primarily a stationers serving the City, the shop does stock a small but comprehensive range of law books.

A spacious premises with ledgers, legal tape and other appurtenances of the trade well displayed.


## 32 W.H. SMITH & SON LTD.
### Liverpool Street Station, London EC2M 7QA.

**Subjects:** General.
**Hours:** Mon - Sat 7.00 am - 7.30 pm.
**Services:** Credit cards.

Quite a large stock of hard and paperback books with the usual general subjects well stocked.

This bookstall is reinforced at rush hours by a kiosk on the concourse which is open from 7.00 - 10.30 and 3.30 - 7.00 p.m.

On the east side, there is a bookstall opposite Platforms 11 & 12
**Subjects:** General.
**Hours:** Mon - Sat 7.00 am - 7.45 pm. Sun 8.30 am - 7.45 pm.
**Services:** Credit cards.

This eastern bookstall is reinforced at rush hours by a kiosk at Platform 18 (The entrance from Bishopsgate) 7.00 - 10.30 and 3.30 - 7.00 pm.


## 33 JOHN MENZIES LTD.
### 50 Cheapside, London EC2V 6AT.        01-248 5315

**Subjects:** General.
**Hours:** Mon - Fri 8.30 - 5.30.
**Services:** Credit cards.

This shop in the Menzies chain is one of the few to concentrate on books and not have stationery. The range of stock is general but at the popular end, with both hard and soft-backed books.

## 34 CITY BOOKSELLERS LTD.
**80 Cheapside, London EC2V 6EE.**  01-248 2768

**Subjects:** General.
**Hours:** Mon - Fri 8.30 - 5.30.

A yellow painted shop with large open doors which admit one to a range of popular hard and soft backed books generously displayed with outward facing covers. The shop sells toys, cards and wrapping paper.

## 35 MUSEUM OF LONDON BOOKSHOP  01-600 3699
**150 London Wall, London EC2Y 5HN.**  Ext 266 or 267

**Subjects:** Books on London.
**Hours:** Tue - Sun 10.00 - 5.30.
**Services:** Mail order, catalogue.

The London Museum is on the fringe of fortress-like Barbican. It sells books on London and its history as well as gifts and souvenirs.

## 36 W.H. SMITH & SON LTD.
**145-147 Cheapside, London EC2Y 6BJ.**  01-606 2301

**Subjects:** General, business studies, British travel.
**Hours:** Mon - Fri 8.30 - 5.30.
**Services:** Credit cards, special orders.

This branch has quite a large general book department in the basement. There is a good British Travel and camping guide section. The shop has the usual Smiths blend of magazines, books and stationery plus sweets.

## 37 BARBICAN CENTRE SHOP  01-638 4141
**The Barbican, London EC2Y 8DS.**  Ext. 322

**Subjects:** General.
**Hours:** Mon - Sat 11.00 - 9.30. Sun 12.00 - 9.00.
**Services:** Credit cards.

This is a small shop on level 4 of the Barbican Centre selling arts related books including a selection of Royal Shakespeare Company publications. The odd hours harmonise with concert, theatre and film goers.

## 38 THE BARBICAN BUSINESS BOOK CENTRE
**9 Moorfields, London EC2Y 9AE.**  01-628 7479

**Subjects:** Business, Banking.
**Hours:** Mon - Fri 9.00 - 6.00.
**Services:** Credit cards, institutional supply, mail order, catalogue.

A well ordered shop nestling at the base of one of the City's towering office blocks, it serves the business and banking community around. The various subjects covered are clearly marked and the books arranged alphabetically within subject.

# EC3

### 39 KELVIN HUGHES
**100 Leadenhall Street, London EC3A 3BP.**　　　　**01-623 3301**

**Subjects:** Maritime books and charts.
**Hours:** Mon - Fri 9.00 - 5.30.
**Services:** Credit cards, Admiralty Chart Agents, chart advisory service, mail order, special orders.

All books nautical are here, from dinghy sailing to marine insurance. Probably advisable to mug up here before becoming a Broker at Lloyds opposite.
'-----it tolls for thee'.


### 40 FEN BOOKS
**79 Fenchurch Street, London EC3M 4BT.**　　　　**01-488 0210**

**Subjects:** General, maps and guides, local history.
**Hours:** Mon - Fri 9.30 - 6.00.
**Services:** Credit cards, special orders.

Hurray! A new City bookshop, bright, modern and the books housed in attractive wooden shelving. They have a wide range of books and provide an efficient ordering service for any not in stock.


### 41 J.D. POTTER LTD.
**145 Minories, London EC3N 1NH.**　　　　**01-709 9076**

**Subjects:** Maritime books, Admiralty charts.
**Hours:** Mon - Fri 9.00 - 5.30.
**Services:** Mail order (lists sent world-wide), credit cards.

The City seems a rather unlikely location for this trading specialist bookseller in all things maritime. It is a well lit modern bookshop, established in 1830, with books, binnacles and compasses attractively displayed against a blue hessian backcloth. As well as books and charts they also sell all the instruments needed for yachtsmen and students of maritime subjects.

## 42  TOWER BOOKSHOP
**10 Tower Place, London EC3R 5BT.**                     **01-623 1081**

**Subjects:** General, tourist books.
**Hours:** Mon - Fri 9.30 - 6.00.
**Services:** Credit cards.

Books are shelved under subject headings but are selected for the needs of the tourists visiting the Tower of London so you can find the popular hardback under gardening and cooking with books on London also prominent. Souvenirs and cards take up a good deal of space so this is not the place for the serious bookworm.


## 43  NEW CITY BOOKSHOP
**7 Byward Street, London EC3R 5AS.**                 **01-626 3649/3346**

**Subjects:** General, remainders.
**Hours:** Mon - Fri 9.00 - 5.30.
**Services:** Special orders for any British book in print.

On the ground floor the hardbacks are arranged by subject with headings and there is a central table for the remaindered books. Downstairs is the paperback section, which is large and has sections for travel guides and Open University studies. Here also is a central table of hardbacked remainders.


## 44  CITY BOOKSELLERS LTD. (G.N. DAVIS)
**64 Leadenhall Market, London EC3V 1LT.**                **01-626 5811**

**Subjects:** General.
**Hours:** Mon - Fri 8.30 - 5.30.
**Services:** Special orders.

Though the shop is called City Booksellers the name of the owner, G.N. Davis, is over the door. It is in the old covered market where food is the main commodity. The ground floor sells cards, wrapping paper and china, but down a wide staircase are books, records and cassettes. Central tables are piled with popular glossy books and the shelves around the walls have hard and soft backed books in the general range and also a 'Teach Yourself' section. The owner finds that this part of the City there is a call for books on hobbies such as gardening and cookery.

## 45 J. ASH
**25 Royal Exchange, London EC3V 3LP.**  01-626 2665

**Subjects:** First editions, antiquarian, books, maps and prints on London.
**Hours:** Mon - Fri 10.00 - 5.30.
**Services:** Mail order, catalogues, valuations, credit cards.

This small shop is built into the outer arches of the Royal Exchange. The rare and antiquarian books are in a small room at street level and a spiral staircase leads up to a room where maps and prints are displayed. There is another small room in the basement where there are a few books. The window display of books is representative of the range with priced items such as a first edition of a Winston Churchill for £80.

# EC4

### 46 JEWISH CHRONICLE BOOKSHOP
**25 Furnival Street, London EC4A 1JT.**          01-405 9252

**Subjects:** Judaism.
**Hours:** Mon - Fri 9.30 - 5.00 (closed Fri afternoon).
**Services:** Lists, mail order, subscription to Jewish Chronicle.

This is the headquarters of the leading Jewish newspaper in the country and behind the reception area is a fairly small book section on all aspects of Judaism, including some books for the very young.


### 47 PROTESTANT TRUTH SOCIETY (INC)
**184 Fleet Street, London EC4A 2H5.**          01-405 4960

**Subjects:** Christian literature (mainly Protestant).
**Hours:** Mon - Fri 9.00 - 5.30.
**Services:** Mail order.

Well, both Protestantism and Fleet Street believe in the power of the word, so it should be a good address. The window displayed rather a lot of books about the Royal Family so there again you have a concordance of interest. As with most shops selling religious books there is an ample children's section and it also sells cards.


### 48 OYEZ STATIONERY LTD.
**191 Fleet Street, London EC4A 2JA.**          01-405 2847

**Subjects:** Legal books.
**Hours:** Mon - Fri 9.00 - 5.15 (Thu 9.00 - 5.15)
**Services:** Credit cards.

Legal forms and general stationery are more prominent here than the small book section but with the proximity of the Law Courts and British libel laws, trade should be brisk.

### 49 THE BOOKCASE
Roy Bloom Ltd.
26 Ludgate Hill, London EC4M 7DR.    01-236 5982

**Subjects:** General, remainders.
**Hours:** Mon - Fri 9.00 - 6.00 (Jun - Sep Sunday 12.00 - 4.00).
**Services:** Credit cards.

Another of those open brightly lit places with generous displays of bargains, which one trusts is carrying literature to the shopping man and woman.

### 50 CHRISTIAN LITERATURE CRUSADE
2 Cathedral Place,
London EC4M 7EY.    01-248 5528/6274

**Subjects:** Christianity, books for Sunday Schools, etc.
**Hours:** Tue - Fri 9.30 - 5.30. Sat 9.30 - 4.00.
**Services:** Mail order, 10% reduction for Church bookstalls.

The shop is in St. Paul's Cathedral Shopping Centre and is part of the Evangelist movement. There is a large open shop at ground floor level and down some stairs are the children's books, suitable as Sunday School prizes and that sort of thing, also records and cassettes.

### 51 JONES & EVANS BOOKSHOP LTD.
70 Queen Victoria Street,
London EC4N 4SR.    01-248 6516

**Subjects:** General, business and banking books.
**Hours:** Mon - Fri 9.30 - 5.15.
**Services:** Special orders, library and institutional supplies

A family business since 1816, the shop specialises in books on banking and finance and stocks the syllabus for the Institute of Bankers. Its one room at street level also stocks fiction, history, biographies, etc.

## 52　WITHERBY & CO. LTD.
### 147 Cannon Street, London EC4N 7BR.　　01-626 1912

**Subjects:** Shipping, marine insurance.
**Hours:** Mon - Fri 6.00 - 5.00.
**Services:** Mail order, special orders.

The long hours this shop keeps are because half of its business is as a newsagent and stationers. The books here are mainly on general and marine insurance, invisible but important activities hereabouts.

## 53　BIBLE SOCIETY BOOKSHOP
### 146 Queen Victoria Street, London EC4V 4BY.　　01-248 4751

**Subjects:** Bibles, Bible studies.
**Hours:** Mon - Fri 9.00 - 5.00.
**Services:** Special orders, catalogue, lists.

Quite a large shop with bibles of many shapes, sizes and languages. Gifts and Christian literature for children also sold.

## 54　SIMMONDS BOOKSHOP
### 16 Fleet Street, London EC4Y 1AX.　　01-353 3907

**Subjects:** General, academic, journalism.
**Hours:** Mon - Fri 9.00 - 5.30.
**Services:** Mail order, library supply.

This narrow (10' wide) shop has been run by Mr. & Mrs. Simmonds since 1945. The premises are ancient and its history pre-dates Henry VIII. The general books are at ground floor level and the academic ones, which cover the nearby King's College syllabus in the basement. It is a busy shop and not unexpectedly, journalism features strongly on the shelves.

## 55　BOOKS, ETC.
### 174 Fleet Street, London EC4Y 1HY.　　01-353 5939

**Subjects:** General.
**Hours:** Mon - Fri 9.00 - 6.30.
**Services:** Credit cards.

Small but well stocked, this shop has a good range of hard and paperback fiction and non-fiction. It has a strong emphasis on up-market paperbacks and classics. There is also a bargain basement which helps to attract a busy lunch time trade.

## 56 GEOGRAPHIA LIMITED
63 Fleet Street, London EC4Y 1PE.                01-353 2701/2

**Subjects:** Maps, atlases, guides, globes.
**Hours:** Mon - Fri 9.00 - 5.25.
**Services:** Mail order, Maps mounted.

For the peregrinating journalist this corner store with its well ordered displays is a first resort. Coverage extends from town plans of Britain to celestial globes. Their spectrum of coverage is broad and replenishment of stock frequent. They are old hands at the game and have steady sales in office wall maps as well as the more familiar folded and covered variety.

## 57 PICKERING & INGLIS LTD.
1 Creed Lane, London EC4Y 5BR.                01-248 2246

**Subjects:** Christianity, reference, B.B.C. publications.
**Hours:** Mon - Fri 8.30 - 5.00. Sat 9.30 - 12.00.
**Services:** Mail order.

The small entrance and window of this shop belie its extensive interior. Besides the many bibles and prayer books on sale there is also a more general section, strong on works of reference. Religious bookshops flourish like Wren churches in this part of town.

## 58 J. CLARKE-HALL LTD.
7 Bride Court (off Bride Lane),
London EC4Y 8DU.                                01-353 4116

**Subjects:** Antiquarian, secondhand, Johnsoniana, review copies.
**Hours:** Mon - Fri 10.30 - 6.30.
**Services:** Mail order, catalogues, library and institutional supply.

The shop is in a small arcade opposite St. Bride's Church and has a tiled front and windows protected by grills. There are many new looking books for sale which are in fact review copies which carry a 20% price reduction. The shop specialises in work by and about Samuel Johnson, the great exemplar in these parts, who lived nearby. There is a good selection of antiquarian and second hand books, and also some children's books. The same firm has a print shop at 22 Bride Lane.

# N1

**100  UPPER STREET BOOKSHOP**
   **182 Upper Street, London, N1 1RQ.**                    **01-359 3785**

   **Subjects:**  Art, Architecture. (Secondhand)
   **Hours:**     Tue - Sat 9.00 - 6.00.
   **Services:**  Book search service, postal service.

   Most of the books are priced between £5 and £30 but there is a selection of more valuable items. The stock is secondhand, both hard and paperbacked and all arranged in subject order. There is a section of books on Islington local history and architecture.


**101  SISTER WRITE**
   **190 Upper Street, London N1 1RQ.**                     **01-226 9782**

   **Subjects:**  Feminism, Lesbianism, Black Womens literature.
   **Hours:**     Tue - Fri 11.00 - 7.00. Sat 10.00 - 6.00.
   **Services:**  World wide mail order, Credit cards.

   This is a bookshop run on co-operative lines, by women and for women. Women in history, politics, literature and any other area where they are to be found is covered. Well they said Islington had been gentrified but here is a counterattack. Men are allowed to enter if they dare.


**102  G.W. WALFORD**
   **186 Upper Street, Islington, London N1 1RU.**          **01-226 5682**

   **Subjects:**  Fine and Rare Antiquarian books.
   **Hours:**     Mon - Fri 9.30 - 4.30.
   **Services:**  Mail order catalogues.


   A notice on the door makes it clear that browsers are not welcome but genuine collectors will be attended although mail order is the main way business is conducted. Illustrated, travel and natural history are among the subjects with sets of fine bindings and antiquarian books stocked in these rather sombre premises fronted by a window with an elegant piece of furniture and a book or two.

## 103 CANONBURY BOOKSHOP
**Islington Books Ltd.**
**268 Upper Street, London N1 2UQ.**          **01-226 3475**

**Subjects:** General, Childrens books, Art, Local history.
**Hours:** Mon - Sat 9.00 - 6.00.
**Services:** Credit cards, special orders, postal service.

As they own the Art Shop two doors away, Art and Artists are one of the favoured subjects, together with a good selection of general books on the ground floor. A section on the locality is of special interest with cards of Islington scenes.

Downstairs is their special Children's Department with rocking horses to keep children amused. Books line the walls with high quality book orientated toys to compliment them and plenty of room for mother and child to browse.

## 104 T. MILES & CO. LTD.
**323 Upper Street, London N1 2XQ.**          **01-226 3445**

**Subjects:** General, fishing, maps and guides.
**Hours:** Mon - Fri 9.00 - 5.30. Sat 9.00 - 1.00.
**Services:** Special Orders.

The shop has a good general range, but is strong on fishing, maps and guides. They are library suppliers and keep a large selection of text books. The majority of the stock is paperbacked.

## 105 THE OTHER BOOKSHOP
**328 Upper Street, London N1 2XQ.**          **01-226 0671**

**Subjects:** Socialism, feminism, 'gay' and generally radical literature.
**Hours:** Mon - Tue - Sat 10.00 - 6.00. Wed 12.00 - 7.00. Thu - Fri 11.00 - 7.00.
**Services:** Mail order, special order, credit cards, bookstall service and events notice board.

This radical bookshop is run by Labour party members and therefore stocks left wing books. They desribe their stock as "Red books, Black books, Peace books and story books". American, Soviet, Irish, African and Asian books are stocked together with gay feminist books, both old and new. Appropriate journals and posters available.

## 106 THE LIBRARY BOOKSHOP
**Shoreditch Library, Pitfield Street,**
**London, N1 6EX.**  01-729 4723

**Subjects:** General, Lithuania.
**Hours:** Mon - Thu 11.30 - 2.00, 3.00 - 6.30. Fri 11.00 - 2.00, 3.00 - 6.00.
**Services:** Special orders.

This is a small shop in the corner of Shoreditch library. Students needs are reflected in the general stock. Did you know that Lithuania was more extensive than Russia in the 14th century? Sic transit gloria mundi.


## 107 CND BOOKSHOP   01-250 4010
**22-24 Underwood Street, London N1 7JQ**   (Provisional)

**Subjects:** The Nuclear Debate.
**Hours:** Mon Closed, Tue - Fri 10.00 - 5.30, Sat 10.00 - 4.00.
**Services:** Catalogue, Book Club, Mail Order.

The bookshop moves to this address just after we go to press as part of a centralisation move by the organisation. A description will follow in our next edition.


## 108 CHAPTER ONE
**Pierrepoint Arcade, Pierrepoint Row,**
**(Camden Passage)—Islington, London N1 8EF**   01-359 1185

**Subjects:** A general range but all finely bound.
**Hours:** Wed & Sat 10.00 - 5.00.
**Services:** Credit cards.

A small shop in Cambden Passage selling attractively leather bound books on a variety of subjects such as history, antiques, gardening and fiction.

### 109 ANGEL BOOKSHOP
**102 Islington High Street, London N1 8EG.**         01-226 2904

**Subjects:** General, reference books on antiques.
**Hours:** Mon - Sat 9.30 - 6.00.
**Services:** Special orders, postal service world wide.

The speciality of this bookshop is a good antique reference section which must be welcomed by the many antique dealers in the area. General subjects are well stocked with an excellent paperback department at the rear of the shop. They have a strong children's section and cooking and wine are well represented.


### 110 W.H. SMITH
**Kings Cross Station, London N1 9AP.**         01-837 5580

**Subjects:** General.
**Hours:** Mon - Sat 7.00 - 8.45. Sun 9.00 - 8.45.
**Services:** Credit cards. Special orders.

Quite a large shop at Kings Cross with access from the street or the station. General subjects are covered in hardback and paperback with people working in the vicinity in mind as well as travellers.


### 111 MODEL RAILWAY (MFG) LTD.
**14 York Way, London N1 9AA.**         01-837 5551

**Subjects:** Rail and Road Transport.
**Hours:** Mon - Sat 9.30 - 5.30.
**Services:** Credit cards, mail order, name plates.

All the paraphernalia for the railway enthusiast in this shop close to King's Cross Station. One wall is filled with books on rail and road transport including American and Continental books. All aspects of the railways are covered with some in foreign languages.

## 112 HOUSMANS BOOKSHOP LTD.
**5 Caledonian Road,
King's Cross, London N1 9DX.**                    **01-837 4473/4**

**Subjects:** Pacifism, Anarchism, gay and feminist literature.
**Hours:** Mon - Fri 10.00 - 6.00. Sat 10.00 - 5.00.
**Services:** Special orders, mail order catalogue, distribution service to the book trade.

Near King's Cross Station this bookshop has a wide range of books orientated to their own specialist subjects. The basement is their pacifist, anarchist and anti-military department with a large range of left wing magazines and journals. The ground floor is more general in subject but very much in line with the left wing movement. Plenty of room upstairs and downstairs in which to browse.


## 113 UNIVERSITY BOOKS
**29 Upper Street, London N1 9HD.**               **01-226 9806**

**Subjects:** General remainders.
**Hours:** Mon - Sat 9.45 - 5.00. Thu 9.45 - 12.30.
**Services:** Mail order.

A small shop with quite a good range of 'bargain' books. The prestigious name is unexplained.

# N3-N7

### 114 MARTINS
**29-31 Ballards Lane, Finchley, N3 1XP.**          01-346 9303

**Subjects:** General.
**Hours:** Mon - Wed & Sat 8.30 - 6.00. Thu 8.30 - 7.00. Fri 8.30 - 8.00.
**Services:** Credit cards, special orders.

A stationers and booksellers with the usual range of general stock. Some headings are Hobbies — T.V. — Adventure — Horror. Maps and guides are sold.

### 115 FACULTY BOOKS
**98 Ballards Lane, N3 2DN.**          01-346 7761
         01-346 0145

**Subjects:** General, Education, Travel.
**Hours:** Mon - Sat 9.30 - 5.30.
**Services:** Special orders, school and library supply.

There is another branch of this shop at the Middlesex Polytechnic which ensures that it provides for student needs. The general section is better than average, with history and art especially well covered.

### 116 THE MUSLIM INFORMATION SERVICE
**233 Seven Sisters Road, N4 2DA.**          01-272 5170

**Subjects:** Islam, books in English and Arabic.
**Hours:** Mon - Fri 9.30 - 5.30. Sat 10.30 - 7.00.
**Services:** Mail order, catalogue, lists, lectures, cassettes.

A religious bookshop which also sells gifts. Situated in a spacious room. Everything is very accessible.

## 117 BOOKMARKS
### 265 Seven Sisters Road, N4 2DE.     01-802 8773/6145

**Subjects:** Left-wing literature, new and secondhand.
**Hours:** Mon - Sat 10.00 - 6.00. Wed 10.00 - 7.00.
**Services:** Mail order, political book club, tradue union book services.

A rather austere interior with two floors amply stocked with books. The shop is associated with the Socialist Workers Party and is unremittingly political. The secondhand department is upstairs together with 'kids' books. The staff are enthusiastically committed and proud of their large international section. A postscript for the politically nervous is that most left wing bookshops are not above punning their names and they keep gentlemens hours.

## 118 SUNPOWER BOOKS, CRAFTS
### 83 Blackstock Road, N4 2JW.     01-226 1799

**Subjects:** Ecology, alternative medicine and energy, feminism.
**Hours:** Mon - Sat 10.00 - 6.00
**Services:** Special orders.

The shop is run as workers co-operative and sells crafts and whole foods as well as books. Fiction is stocked as well, the specialist books. Perhaps more 'green' than 'red' but certainly more 'left' than 'right' is the coding here.

## 119 NEW BEACON BOOKSHOP
### 76 Stroud Green Road, N4 3EN.     01-272 4889

**Subjects:** Americana, Africana, Caribbean books.
**Hours:** Tue - Sat 10.30 - 6.00 (Monday closed).
**Services:** Catalogue, mail order, library supply, special orders.

Mainly concerned with non-fictional works on anthropology, politics, sociology and a strong Caribbean section. A good selection of books for children of Indian, African, West Indian etc. descent. Music and cook books relating to these countries are also sold.

## 120 NEW ERA BOOKS AND HANDICRAFTS
### 203 Seven Sisters Road, N4 3NG.     01-272 5894

**Subjects:** Marxist-Leninist, Chinese, Anti-Imperialist.
**Hours:** Mon - Sat 10.00 - 6.00. Thu 10.00 - 7.00.
**Services:** Mail order catalogue.

The Marxist classics and Mao, who is still in their pantheon, predominate. Sinophiles, post 1949, will find plenty to interest them here.

## 121 BARN BOOKS
### 1A Highbury Park, N5 1QJ.     01-354 0843

**Subjects:** General secondhand, Ireland.
**Hours:** Mon - Sat 10.30 - 2.00, 3.00 - 5.30 (closed Thu).
**Services:** Catalogue of secondhand Irish books.

A small secondhand bookshop with a general stock but specializing on books from and about Ireland. If one were to extract the Irish element from English literature it would be a much thinner affair.

## 122 BONAVENTURE
### 259 Archway Road, N6 5AX.     01-341 2345

**Subjects:** General, travel (second-hand)
**Hours:** Tue - Sat 10.30 - 6.00. Thu 10.30 - 1.00. Mon closed.
**Services:** Search service.

This small shop specializes in secondhand travel books, particularly on Latin America but it also has a range of general secondhand books. On Mondays the shop is closed because the owner is out hunting down choice items for his stock.

## 123 THE CHOLMELEY BOOKSHOP
### 228 Archway Road, London N6 5AZ.     01-340 3869

**Subjects:** Military, Aviation.
**Hours:** Mon - Sat 9.30 - 1.00. 2.00 - 5.30. (closed Thu).
**Services:** Special orders, credit cards.

The books are well ordered here with each specialist subject divided into new and secondhand stock. They have a large range of U.K. and overseas titles on aviation, naval and military matters. Some general titles are also stocked. The red striped awning outside the shop makes the enthusiasts' target easily identifiable.

### 124 AUSTEN—PARISH
**162 Archway Road, N6 5BB.**         **01-340 2575**

**Subjects:** Science, technology, reference, maps and guides.
**Hours:** Mon - Fri 9.00 - 5.30.
**Services:** Mail order, university and school supply.

The shop is geared for mail order supply to educational centres. It has a good selection of reference books but the stock is mainly academic in scope. Teaching English as a foreign language is well covered.

### 125 ARCHWAY DEVELOPMENT CENTRE BOOKSHOP
**173 Archway Road, N6 5Bl.**         **01-341 4403**

**Subjects:** Third World Development.
**Hours:** Mon - Fri 10.00 - 6.00 (telephone to confirm)
**Services:** Mail order, credit cards, catalogue for Oxfam. Educational materials, teaching packs for schools.

The shop is concerned with Third World affairs and in particular how they effect women in those parts. The bookshop is just one part of this Development Centre whose purpose is informative and educational.

### 126 HOWE & SON
**70/72 Highgate High Street, London N6 5HX.**     **01-340 3906**

**Subjects:** General.
**Hours:** Mon - Sat 5.00 (am) - 6.00. Sun 5.00 am - 1.00.

With these newsagent's opening hours insomniacs need no longer count sheep, they can get up and choose a book from the mainly paperbacked selection at the rear of this shop.

## 127 FISHER AND SPERR
**46 Highgate High Street, N6 5JB.**             **01-340 7244**

**Subjects:** General (antiquarian and secondhand)
**Hours:** Mon - Sat 10.00 - 5.30.
**Services:** Credit cards, 'Wants' list welcome.

This is an attractive seventeenth century, timber framed, bow-windowed, four storied cornucopia of secondhand and antiquarian books. There are 50,000 various titles which Mr. Sperr has lovingly assembled, as collecting is his hobby. The subject range is universal, but books about London has a special place in this splendid shop.

## 128 HIGHGATE BOOKSHOP
**9 Highgate High Street, London N6 5JS.**        **01-340 5625**

**Subjects:** General, Travel.
**Hours:** Mon - Sat 9.30 - 5.30.
**Services:** Special orders, credit cards.

This attractive white clapboard faced shop holds a prominent corner position in Highgate for its excellent general stock of paperbacks and hardbacks. No technical books available but the most popular sections namely children's and cookery are well stocked and easily accessible.

## 129 HOLLOWAY STATIONERS AND BOOKSELLERS
**357 Holloway Road, London N7 8HJ.**          **01-607 3972**

**Subjects:** General (all paperback)
**Hours:** Mon - Sat 9.00 - 6.00.
**Services:** Book exchange.

A stationers, but with a generous proportion given over to popular paperbacks including the 'Teach Yourself' series.

## 130  FANTASY CENTRE
**157 Holloway Road, London N7 8LX.**　　　　　　　**01-607 9433**

**Subjects:** Sci-Fi, Horror, Fantasy (New and secondhand)
**Hours:** Mon - Fri 10.00 - 6.00. Sat 10.00 - 5.00.
**Services:** Mail order, catalogue, wants list.

The shop covers its speciality well, selling both new and second hand books. At the rear is a section of first editions and collectors items including some 19th century detective fiction.

# N8-15

### 131 CROUCH END BOOKSHOP
### 60 Crouch End Hill, N8 8AG.  01-348 8966

**Subjects:** General, Travel.
**Hours:** Mon - Sat 9.00 - 6.00.
**Services:** Special orders, credit cards.

Located in an attractive corner situation, it has quite a good general range of hard and soft covered books, both new and second hand. The children's section features quite strongly.


### 132 BARGAIN BOOKSHOP
### 2 Concourse, Edmonton Green, N9 OTY.  01-807 7972

**Subjects:** General.
**Hours:** Mon & Thu 9.30 - 1.30. Tue & Wed 9.30 - 5.00. Fri 10.00 - 5.30. Sat 9.30 - 5.30.
**Services:** Special orders.

The shop is at the bus stop entrance to the shopping centre. Most of the stock is remainders with a few paperbacks on general subjects.


### 133 MUSWELL HILL BOOKSHOP
### (Fagins Bookshop Ltd.)
### 72 Fortis Green Road, Muswell Hill, N10 3HN.  01-444 7588

**Subjects:** General, Travel.
**Hours:** Mon - Fri 9.30 - 6.00. Sat 9.30 - 5.30.
**Services:** Special orders, postal service, credit cards.

An excellent general bookshop which omits only childrens books, there being that sort of shop opposite. All is well ordered and the place gives an impression of abundance. The Penguin section is generous and they stock Open University course books. Special orders are welcome.

## 134  W.H. SMITH & SON LTD.
117 Muswell Hill Broadway,
Muswell Hill, N10 3RS.                           01-883 1706

**Subjects:** General.
**Hours:** Mon - Sat 8.30 - 5.30.
**Services:** Credit cards, special orders.

Quite a small Smith's selling general titles. I am sure Muswell Hill would support something a little more ambitious. Several readers have been located thereabouts.


## 135  CHILDRENS BOOKSHOP
29 Fortis Green Road, N10 3RT.                   01-444 5500

**Subjects:** Childrens books.
**Hours:** Mon - Fri 9.15 - 5.45. Sat 9.15 - 1.15.
**Services:** Special orders, credit card, 'Post a Book'.

A bright and cheerful shop with discreet expertise on hand. Books to appeal to children from the beginning up to twelve or thirteen. There are no severe gradings of the stock by age group, which can of course embarass any of us under a hundred. Muswell Hill is lucky in its bookshops.


## 136  EDNA WHITESON LTD.
343 Bowes Road, N11 1AA.                         01-361 1105

**Subjects:**
**Hours:** General (secondhand and antiquarian)
Mon, Tue, Thu & Sat 10.00 - 5.00. Fri 10.00 - 5.30. Closed
**Services:** Wed.
Search service, mail order catalogue.

An interesting secondhand and antiquarian shop run by the owner. The sort of shop the metropolitan bibliophile likes to browse in and perhaps make a coup.

## 137 THE HISTORY BOOKSHOP
**2 The Broadway, Friern Barnet Road, N11 3DU.**     **01-368 8568**

**Subjects:** Militaria—Aviation—General—Nautical.
**Hours:** Wed—Sat 9.30 - 5.30.
**Services:** Catalogue for new & secondhand books — up dating lists. Special orders, mail order. Foreign books ordered.

A marvellous shop with a stock of between 60,000 and 70,000 secondhand books on general subjects and also a specialist section for new and secondhand militaria, collectors items and antiquarian books are also sold. The shop and cellar are crammed with books but there is expert advice on hand to guide the customer. They are closed Mondays and Tuesdays to enable them to deal with their large international postal service, the address may be peripheral but the journey would be very worthwhile for the enthusiast.

## 138 W.H. SMITH & SON LTD.
**766 High Road, N12 9QH.**     **01-445 2785**

**Subjects:** General.
**Hours:** Mon - Sat 9.00 - 5.30. Thu 9.30 - 5.30.
**Services:** Special orders, credit cards.

No nasty surprises for fans of smaller W.H.S's here, everything as it should be, with children's books getting a special mention.

## 139 W.H. SMITH & SON LTD.
**5 Alderman's Hill, N13 4YD.**     **01-886 4743**

**Subjects:** General.
**Hours:** Mon - Sat 8.30 - 5.30.
**Services:** Credit cards, special orders.

Because of a dearth of bookshops in the area at least one third of the space here is for bookselling. The books themselves are general and of popular interest.

### 140 OAKHILL COLLEGE BOOKROOM
Oak Hill College, Chase Side,
Southgate, N14 4PS.   01-449 0467/0041

**Subjects:** Theology.
**Hours:** Mon - Fri 9.00 - 5.00.
**Services:** Special orders.

The shop is just inside the entrance to this Anglican theological college. They stock, with their students very much in mind, commentaries, bibles, hymn books and a general range of hard and soft backed christian literature.


### 141 FAGINS BOOKS LTD.
62 Chase Side, Southgate, N14 5PA.   01-882 5690

**Subjects:** General — Education & Travel.
**Hours:** Mon - Fri 9.30 - 5.30. Sat 9.00 - 5.30.
**Services:** Credit cards — special orders.

A welcome rarity in these northern wastes, a good general bookshop. Much more than the latest best seller or T.V. serial book. All well selected and displayed. There is also a good range of college and school text books.


### 142 ARMS AND MILITARIA BOOKSHOP
34 High Street, Southgate, N14 6EE.   01-886 0334

**Subjects:** Militaria.
**Hours:** Mon, Wed & Sat 9.30 - 5.00. Fri 9.30 - 4.00. Closed Tue & Thu.
**Services:** Institute and library supply, search service.

A good specialist shop whose title explains itself. Within its field they have regimental histories, the development of weaponry and books on military uniforms. The staff is expert and the shop covers the field from the sixteenth century to the present.

## 143 OPERATION HEADSTART
### 25 West Green Road, London N15 5BX          01-802 2838

**Subjects:** Africana.
**Hours:** Mon - Sat 9.30 - 6.30.
**Services:** Special orders, school and library supply.

The shops's title is cryptic, but there's no confusion about the stock which is exclusively about the continent of Africa, and includes a section of African cookery. Gifts are also sold.

# N16-22

**144 THE HEBREW BOOK
AND GIFT CENTRE
18 Cazenove Road, N16 6BD**
            01-254 3963
            01-802 4567

**Subjects:** Rabbinical literature in Hebrew and English.
**Hours:** Mon - Thu 9.30 - 5.30. Fri & Sun 9.30 - 1.30.
**Services:** Mail order.

As well as the religious books there is quite a range of general. Books in Hebrew stocked. Hebrew is spoken in the shop, which also sells other items pertinent to the faith.


**145 BASHAREN TURKISH BOOKSHOP
123 Green Lanes, N16 9DA.**           01-226 3330

**Subjects:** Books relevant to the Turkish language in Turkish and English.
**Hours:** Mon - Sat 10.00 - 6.00.
**Services:** Credit cards and special orders. Mail order - (lists) - Library and school supply.

The owner of this bookshop claims that it is the only Turkish bookshop in the U.K. but it certainly serves the Turkish community which is established in this part of London plus offering Mail order and an ordering service for books in or about the Turkish language and Turkey. They have a good children's section which includes educational books in Turkish and English but all subjects have their place including religion and anything relevant to their countries origin.


**146 POPULAR BOOKS
373A High Road, Tottenham, N17 6QN.**

**Subjects:** General, secondhand, paperbacks.
**Hours:** Mon - Sat 10.00 - 6.30.
**Services:** Book exchange service.

Magazines and secondhand paperbacks joust for space here. I think the books just have it.

### 147 R.H. FAULKS & CO.
2 St. Loys Road, N17 6UA.　　　　　　　　01-808 3646

**Subjects:** General, Educational.
**Hours:** Mon - Sat 10.00 - 5.30.
**Services:** Special orders.

Stationery is the seller here but in a side room is a small quantity of general books and books on 'A', 'O' and C.S.E. exams and some on computers.

### 148 COMYNS BOOKS
61 Sterling Way, N18 2UE.　　　　　　　　01-807 3427

**Subjects:** General paperbacks.
**Hours:** Mon - Wed 9.30 - 6.00. Fri 9.30 - 6.30. Sat 9.00 - 6.00.
**Services:** Credit cards, a book exchange service.

This has been a bookshop for ninety years though the 'girlie' magazines were probably under the counter then. All the books are paperbacked and they can be exchanged as well as purchased.

### 149 W.H. SMITH & SON LTD.
104-110 Upper Fore Street,
Edmonton, N18 2XA　　　　　　　　　　　01-807 7637

**Subjects:** General.
**Hours:** Mon - Sat 9.00 - 6.00.
**Services:** Special orders, credit cards.

A general collection of books of popular appeal. No surprises here.

## 150 THE AVIATION BOOKSHOP
### 656 Holloway Road, London N19 3PD
### 01-272 3630

**Subjects:** Aviation — new and secondhand.
**Hours:** Mon - Sat 9.30 - 5.30.
**Services:** Credit cards, international mail order, special orders, catalogue.

'A unique shop in Europe' was how a passing German customer described this place. This is no catchpenny title, but exactly describes the shop's universal coverage of man and flight. The books are new and secondhand and the shop is bedecked with model aircraft and interesting bits of real aircraft which make it a fascinating place to browse around. The staff are, of course, expert, and besides the books on sale there are also related magazines and pin-up photos of your favourite aircraft.


## 151 WHETSTONE BOOKS
### 368 Oakleigh Road North, N20 0SP.
### 01-368 8338

**Subjects:** General (secondhand).
**Hours:** Tue, Wed, Fri 9.30 - 3.00. Sat 10.00 - 5.00.
**Services:** Search service.

One room filled with books on many things, all secondhand. The diligent searcher after an overlooked first imprint might have his senses alerted here.


## 152 MORGANS & CO. LTD.
### 1287 High Road, N20 9HS.
### 01-445 2692

**Subjects:** General.
**Hours:** Mon - Sat 9.00 - 5.00. Thu 9.00 - 1.00.

This is an emporium with books included, study aids are well represented.

## 153 BOOTS
**38-40 High Road, N22 6BX.**　　　　　　　　　　**01-888 8010**

**Subjects:** General.
**Hours:** Mon - Thu 9.00 - 5.30. Fri & Sat 9.00 - 6.00.
**Services:** Credit cards, special orders.

The books are found on the second floor of this branch of Boots. They are general, popular and hard and soft backed. Alas this chain of shops was once renowned more for books than soap. And does the lending library, solace of my maiden aunts, still operate.

## 154 W.H. SMITH & SON LTD.
**110 High Road, Wood Green, N22 6HE.**　　　　**01-889 0221**

**Subjects:** General.
**Hours:** Mon - Sat 9.00 - 6.00.
**Services:** Credit cards - Special orders.

One of the better W.H. Smiths for books, with the whole of the first floor selling them encumbered by stationery etc. They have a section for school books and tables of bargain books.

## 155 READING MATTERS
**10 Lymington Avenue, N22 6JA.**　　　　　　　**01-881 3187**

**Subjects:** Community politics, feminism, black studies, third world, C.N.D.
**Hours:** Tue - Sat 10.00 - 5.30.
**Services:** Special orders, credit cards, school and library supply (books classified as non-sexist, non-racial etc.)

This community bookshop, run as a charity, is situated behind Sainsbury's. If the shop's title is read as a statement all bookmen can but agree. The titles they stock offer radical alternatives across the spectrum from health to politics. Writing groups and a history workshop are run from here and they publish their own titles.

## 156 RUSHWORTH LITERATURE ENTERPRISES
### THE BAPTIST CHURCH,
**Westbury Avenue, N22 6SA.**  01-888 4551

**Subjects:** Religion, sacred music.
**Hours:** Mon - Sun 9.00 - 5.00 (Closed Sat)
**Services:** Mail order, catalogue.

This bookshop within the church is being redesigned and will be one room on the ground floor selling books and sheet music, while in the background church music will be played, which could be an overwhelming experience, could be an irritating one.

# NW1

**200 KIMON BOOKSHOP**
**87/88 Plender Street, London NW1 OJN.**          **01-387 8809**

**Subjects:** Greek books.
**Hours:** Mon - Sat 9.00 - 8.00.
**Services:** Special orders for Greek books.

Mainly a newsagents but with a small back room containing new Greek books and dictionaries. It serves the large Greek community in this area.


**201 ATHENE BOOKSELLERS**
**261 Eversholt Street, London NW1 1BA.**          **01-387 1958/3537**

**Subjects:** Secondhand, foreign languages.
**Hours:** Mon - Sat 9.00- 7.00.
**Services:** Discount for booksellers, credit cards, subscription to Greek magazines.

This is an omnivour amongst shops, nearly ¼-million books packed into a modest premises, with CHAOS a Greek conception, only just held at bay. The owner buys books at auctions and has a tremendous variety which attracts the trade as well as the public. There is some organisation by subject — some new and antiquarian amongst the second-hand — but it is quite a personal thing. There are sections for the browsers and collectors will take a little time here.

## 202 FRIENDS BOOK CENTRE
**Friends House, Euston Road,
London NW1 2BJ.**  01-387 3601 Ext. 23

**Subjects:** Quakerism.
**Hours:** Mon - Fri 9.30 - 5.30, Sat occasionally.
**Services:** Mail order, catalogue, special orders, magazine subscriptions, discount for bookshops.

Opposite Euston Station is a large stone building named Friends House and on the ground floor is the Quaker book centre. It is the only bookshop in the British Isles to specialise and stock such a large number of British and American Quaker publications but it is their aim to be an outlet for religious literature and fringe subjects, so as well as their very comprehensive Quaker section they stock books on ecology, biography, conservation, vegetarianism and other relevant subjects. Children's books and study packs also have their place with sections on classes for parents and teachers. Quaker books at reduced prices are available — some are on bookshelves in the entrance and the shop itself is roomy and well lit.

## 203 JOHN MENZIES PLC
**The Colonade, Euston Station, London NW1 2DU.** 01-387 5354
Concourse 01-387 4640

**Subjects:** General.
**Hours:** Tue - Sat 7.30 - 10.00. Mon 7.30 - 9.00. Sun 9.00 - 9.00.
**Services:** Credit cards.

Two bookstalls are prominent on Euston station both belonging to John Menzies but the one to the right as you enter has the larger stock of books mainly paperbacks for the traveller backed by a few glossy hardbacks.

## 204 ISLAMIC BOOK CENTRE
**120 Drummond Street, London NW1 2HL.**  01-388 0710

**Subjects:** Islam
**Hours:** Mon - Sat 10.00 - 6.00.
**Services:** Mail order, catalogue, special orders, educational supply.

A religious bookshop for the faithful or curious. The shop is not altogether tidy but a brisk mail order trade probably sustains the business. Books are in English, Arabic and other languages of the Moslem world.

## 205 W.H. SMITH & SON LTD.
St Pancras Station, NW1 2QL.     01-837 5703

**Subjects:** General.
**Hours:** Mon - Fri 7.00 am - 8.00 pm. Sun 9.00 - 6.00. Sat 8.00 - 7.00.
**Services:** Credit cards.

Mainly paperbacks are sold at this bookstall on St Pancras Station to accommodate the travellers.


## 206 CHARLES HIGHAM
Holy Trinity Church,
Marylebone Road, London NW1 4DU.     01-387 5282

**Subjects:** Antiquarian and secondhand theological books.
**Hours:** Mon - Fri 9.00 - 5.00.
**Services:** Credit cards, mail order.

The stock of 26,000 books are in wooden shelves either side of the aisle and near the altar are the antiquarian books in showcases and glassfronted shelves. All the books are arranged by subject and there is a comprehensive range with books in foreign languages included. In the basement are a further 10,000 titles which is the replacement stock.


## 207 S.P.C.K.
Holy Trinity Church,
Marylebone Road, London NW1 4DU.     01-387 5282

**Subjects:** Religious.
**Hours:** Mon - Fri 9.00 - 5.00.
**Services:** Mail order, credit cards, Church and school supply.

Holy Trinity Church lost its Parish in 1952 but now houses two bookshops. The S.P.C.K. carries new religious books across the whole range of Christianity though Church of England predominates. It is a spacious premises and clearly laid out. There is a good Second Hand and Antiquarian Dept.

## 208 THE BUSINESS BOOKSHOP
**Alan Armstrong & Associates Ltd.**
**72, Park Road, London NW1 4SH.**      **01-723 3902**

**Subjects:** Business studies
**Hours:** Mon - Fri 9.00 - 5.30.
**Services:** Mail order, catalogue, special orders, institutional supply.

The shop which has moved to handsome new premises just north west of Baker Street is the bookshop of London Business School. The style of the frontage is rather moorish and blends well with the nearby mosque — all this has something to do with business studies if you look into it. Besides a comprehensive stock in their specialization they keep H.M.S.O. publications and European Community titles.

## 209 METHODIST MISSIONARY SOCIETY BOOKSHOP
**25 Marylebone Road, London NW1 5JR.**      **01-935 2541**

**Subjects:** Religion.
**Hours:** Mon - Fri 9.00 - 5.00.
**Services:** Mail order, special orders for religious books.

The Society's shop is in a large premises opposite Madame Tussauds, at street level. The books are mainly evangelical Christianity with much emphasis on the Third World, hunger and underdevelopment.

## 210 ARCHIVE BOOKSTORES
**83 Bellk Street, London NW1 6BT.**      **01-402 8212**

**Subjects:** Antiquarian, secondhand, local history.
**Hours:** Mon - Sat 10.00 - 6.00.
**Services:** Mail orders, bindings restored, valuations, search service.

The speciality of this shop is the local history of St. Marylebone and they have links with the St. Marylebone Society, stocking many of their out of print booklets. The rest of their books are general and they have a section of secondhand sheet music.

### 211 P.J. CASSIDY
**Antiquarian Book Co.**
**95 Bell Street, London NW1 6TB.**  01-262 7661

**Subjects:** Secondhand, antiquarian.
**Hours:** Tue - Sat 10.30 - 5.30.

Mostly a secondhand shop with bargains on tables and in boxes outside, and inside a general range of books excluding technical ones. Out of print, antiquarian books and some prints are also sold.

### 212 A.A. MILES
**105 Bell Street, London NW1 6TL.**  01-723 8455

**Subjects:** Secondhand.
**Hours:** Mon - Sat 10.30 - 6.00.

Two rooms absolutely crammed with books, leaving a small space for Monty, the owner, who although chairbound, will guide the browser through his rather personal arrangement of the secondhand stock if required.

### 213 RUDOLF STEINER BOOKSHOP
**35 Park Road, London NW1 6XT.**  01-723 4400

**Subjects:** The works of Rudolf Steiner.
**Hours:** Mon - Fri 10.00 - 6.00, Sat 10.00 - 1.30 (in term time).
**Services:** Mail order catalogue.

Located in Rudolf Steiner house, it looks more like a chapel from the outside. Books by and associated with the author are carried and there is quite a good children's section.

### 214 THE FOLK SHOP
**Cecil Sharp House,**
**2 Regents Park Road, London NW1 7AY.**  01-485 2206

**Subjects:** Folk music, folk dance.
**Hours:** Mon - Sat 9.30 - 5.30, Sat evenings 6.30 - 9.30.
**Services:** Mail order, catalogue, library, own magazine.

This large building houses the English Folk Dance and Song Society and just inside the entrance is their bookshop. The books cover the expected range and include some on customs and folk lore; records are also sold.

### 215 EAST ASIA CO.
**103 Camden High Street, London NW1 7JN.**　　　**01-389 5783**

**Subjects:** Oriental (new and secondhand).
**Hours:** Mon - Sat 10.00 - 5.30.
**Services:** Mail order, catalogue, credit cards, subscriptions to magazines, translation service.

This bright yellow shop is next to Mornington Crescent Underground station. It stocks books in all the Far Eastern languages and books about that region from British and American publishers. Their range is comprehensive with a special section on Oriental Art for the collector. Downstairs are books in the Chinese and Japanese languages and books for those learning Oriental languages. They have new, secondhand and antiquarian books and also sell craft items and cards.

### 216 O.C.S. BOOKSHOP　　　01-485 3698
**67 Parkway, London NW1 7PP.**　　　**01-485 4201**

**Subjects:** Japanese.
**Hours:** Tue - Sun 10.00 - 6.00, Sat 9.00 - 6.00.
**Services:** Mail orders, special orders, newsletters in Japanese.

A bookshop for the Japanese with the majority of texts in that language, though some in English. The shop is a centre for expatriates and provides a newsletter for Japanese living in Europe.

### 217 REGENT BOOKSHOP
**73 Parkway, London NW1 7PP.**　　　**01-485 9822**

**Subjects:** General.
**Hours:** Mon - Sat 9.00 - 6.30, Sun 12.00 - 4.00 (flexible).
**Services:** Special orders.

Bright as a new pin, with good general stock and aiming to keep all Penguin and Pelican books. They are willing to order books not in stock for their customers. A point of light in a postal district rather thin on good general bookshops.

## 218 SKOLA
**27 Delancey Street, Regents Park,**      01-388 0632
**London NW1 7RX.**      01-387 0656

**Subjects:** English language teaching, Education.
**Hours:** Mon - Fri 1.00 - 3.00 plus other times during office hours.
**Services:** Mail order, school and college supply, English language library.

An office as well as a shop became most business is mail order but visitors to the shop are welcome especially between one o'clock and three, and at other times for serious customers. They specialise in educational books and have an excellent selection of dictionaries both English and Foreign. You will find here all the revision books for schools and for adult language causes running through all the stages of general education. A specialist library downstairs for E.L.T.


## 219 OFFSTAGE
**37 Chalk Farm Road,**
**Camden Town, London NW1 8JA.**

**Subjects:** New and secondhand books on Theatre and Cinema and Dance.
**Hours:** Tue - Sat 10.00 - 6.00. Sun 11.00 - 5.00.
**Services:** Credit cards, Mail order, Catalogue, Special orders.

A lovely old "pay desk" adds to the fascination of this unusual bookshop which concentrates on all aspects of the theatre and cinema. Plays, literary criticism, biographies are well represented with sections on dance and original costume design and memorabilia which adds great atmosphere backed by posters and cards to make this well worth a visit.


## 220 WALDEN BOOKS
**38 Harmond Street, London NW1 8DP.**      01-267 8146

**Subjects:** Secondhand.
**Hours:** Thu - Sun 10.30 - 6.30.
**Services:** Book finding services, special orders.

A little off the beaten track and with rather odd opening hours, this shop offers a useful bookfinding service, free. The books are arranged by subject and there is a fairly good paperback section. On the pavement they stack some bargain books.

**221 THE MUSTARD SEED**
**21 Kentish Town Road, NW1 8NH.**     **01-267 5646**

**Subjects:** Christian literature.
**Hours:** Mon - Sat 11.00 - 7.00.
**Services:** Mail order exhibitions.

A yellow painted front is in keeping with its title for this bookshop one minute from Camden Town tube station. They describe the books as positive Christianity, the majority of them being in paperback. A little gentle evangelism goes on here and a fellowship has grown around this shop.

**222 COMPENDIUM BOOKSHOP**
**234 Camden High Street,**     **01-267 1525**
**London NW1 8QS.**     **01-485 8944**

**Subjects:** General, politics, psychology, music, alternative technologies. Feminism and Gay Books. Travel.
**Hours:** Mon - Sat 10.00 - 6.00.
**Services:** Mail order, catalogues, journal subscription.

There is plenty of room to browse among the sections on psychology, alternative medicines, politics in this bookshop in Camden Town. It is quite a surprise to find two large floors with striped wood shelves holding a great variety of new books. They cover all the general subjects but specialise in many; art, music, drama, philosophy, politics, education, and psychology. There are also good selections under religion combined with the occult, health, healing, food and nutrition, organic gardening, alternative technologies, urban studies, feminist and gay books and their range is very much wider than the average bookshop. There is a noticeboard advertising events related to their specialist subjects.

## 223 PRIMROSE HILL BOOKS
**134 Regents Park Road, London NW1 8XL.**         **01-586 2022**

**Subjects:** General (new and secondhand), antiquarian.
**Hours:** Mon - Sat 10.00 - 6.00.
**Services:** Credit cards, magazine subscriptions.

This shop is recognised by its attractive royal blue exterior and awning. Inside the entrance is the new stock, hard and soft backed, covering a wide range of subjects. At the back on the ground floor level is the antiquarian section, with first editions, sets and illustrated books with emphasis on travel. Down a spiral staircase are the secondhand books burgeoning from shelves and flowing on to the carpet, these are not arranged by subject but include books on art, history, English and French literature and philosophy. A most interesting shop between high bourgeois Regents Park and throbbing Camden Town.

## 224 L.C.L. BENEDICT LTD.
**65 Camden Road, London NW1 9EU.**         **01-267 3247/3673**

**Subjects:** Educational, languages.
**Hours:** Mon - Fri 9.30 - 6.00.
**Services:** Mail order, special orders, audio material in over 100 languages.

These educational booksellers and language consultants have expert staff on hand to guide, I would think particularly the student, through their extensive range of titles in over 100 languages. The range of dictionaries in foreign languages is impressive and all this polyglot reading matter is backed up by a large range of cassettes.

## 225 WRITERS & READERS BOOKSHOP
144 Camden High Street,    01-267 0511
London NW1 ONE.    01-485 3883

**Subjects:** Radical but general bookshop, specialising in children's books.
**Hours:** Mon - Sat 10.00 - 6.00.
**Services:** Mail order, Catalogue, Special orders, Credit cards.

General subjects with a definite emphasis on children's books selected as non-sexist, non racist are well displayed in this bright inviting bookshop in Camden Town. Writers and Readers Publications are stocked as they own the shop so the full range of their beginners books are available. Although general subjects are covered the selection of titles is influenced by a radical approach.

# NW2

### 226 BOOK MART
**62 Walm Lane, London NW2 4RA.**            **01-459 6190**

**Subjects:** Secondhand, paperback, general.
**Hours:** Mon - Sat 10.30 - 6.00.
**Services:** Part Exchange.

Shelved in subject order there is a large choice of secondhand paperback books — a few hardbacks are available but that is not the general stock. There is certainly plenty of cheap reading available here.

### 227 W.H. SMITH & SON LTD.
**82 Walm Lane, London NW2 4RA.**            **01-459 0455**

**Subjects:** General.
**Hours:** Mon - Sat 8.30 - 6.00.
**Services:** Special orders, credit cards.

If you want to buy a book in these parts this is where you will probably go. It is easy to be unfair to W.H.S's for the obvious reasons of their uniformity, general downgrading of bookspace in favour of stationery, etc. but the stock they do sell seems to be what is wanted.

### 228 GABRIEL'S BOOKSHOP
**47 Walm Lane, London NW2 4QU.**            **01-451 2047**

**Subjects:** General, Spain, Educational books.
**Hours:** Mon - Sat 10.00 - 6.30.
**Services:** Educational supply - book exchange service - Spanish spoken.

The shop specializes in Spanish books for school and colleges and stocks a good supply of these, new. This interesting shop next to Willesden Green station is also packed with general secondhand fiction, with bargain trays outside the shop. At the rear of the shop non-fiction is kept, together with more valuable items of stock. An interesting place where 'finds' might be made.

# NW3

**229 THE FLASK BOOKSHOP**
**6 Flask Walk, London NW3 1HE.**                      **01-435 2693**

**Subjects:** Secondhand, modern first editions, art.
**Hours:** Tue - Wed - Fri - Sat 10.00 - 6.00.
**Services:** Special orders.

For the last fifty years this has been a bookshop but Joseph Connolly has owned it for the last seven. The only two new books in his shop are written by him on two of his specialist subjects; collecting first editions and P.G. Wodehouse. The premises in the quaint pedestrian part of Flask Walk are ideal for a secondhand bookshop with a black painted shop front, fairly spacious room with shelves of books on various subjects including his specialist sections of modern first editions and some review copies. At the back the owner sits with more shelves of books including a few antiquarian. Through the door, down very narrow stairs, is a rather musty basement which is devoted to art with a very good selection and plenty of room to browse.


**230 STANLEY SMITH & KEITH FAWKES**
**1/3 Flask Walk, London NW3 1HJ.**                  **01-435 0614**

**Subjects:** Antiquarian and secondhand.
**Hours:** Mon - Sat 10.00 - 6.00.
**Services:** Mail order, catalogue.

White painted brick with turquoise blue painted windows and door describe the shop front at One to Three Flask Walk. In one window antiquarian books are laid open, the other window has a representative stock of their secondhand and out of print books. Inside you are greeted by rows of shelves in corridors filled with secondhand books under general subjects. Up a few steps into what used to be the next door shop are more secondhand books and a narrow room of antiquarian books sectioned off. This is their specialist section, rare English and foreign books on art, illustration, history, literature and First Editions, children's books, science, medicine, mining and travel. They have an excellent section of music and books on music and are proud of their large out of print paperback section. An interesting shop, well organised considering the range and variety of books.

## 231 HAMPSTEAD VILLAGE BOOKSHOP
**17 Flask Walk, London NW3 1HJ.**          **01-435 4741**

**Subjects:** Modern literature, arts, social science.
**Hours:** Mon - Fri 10.00 - 6.00, Sat 10.00 - 6.30, Sun 12.00 - 6.30.
**Services:** Credit cards, special orders (computer aided).

It would be a pity to miss this bookshop on the corner at the end of the pedestrian part of Flask Walk as it is in contrast to the other two secondhand shops nearby. At street level is a large specially selected section of fiction by modern international writers — inclined to the literary — a large feminist selection, classics, poetry, mysticism and reference.

In the basement, is a large theatre section (plays), plus sections on politics, history, social sciences, philosophy and expanded sections on food and secondhand books.

It is a bright new modern shop with adjustable shelves, so that all sections can be neatly rearranged according to demand and both floors are attractively carpeted and well lit. All subjects have clear headings. A great deal of thought has gone into the stocking and design of this shop including a computer to help with customers' orders.

## 232 HIGH HILL BOOKSHOPS LTD.
**6/7 Hampstead High Street, London NW3 1PR.**    **01-435 2218**

**Subjects:** General, local history, children's books.
**Hours:** Mon - Sat 9.30 - 6.30.
**Services:** Special orders.

Three generous rooms at street level make up this very good general bookshop. Mr. Norrie has a fastidious public in NW3 and the shop reflects their intellectual concerns. The paperback and children's sections are perhaps the best and they are also strong on the local history in this enviable area on the hill.

### 233 KEN TROTMAN
**2-6 Hampstead High Street, London NW3 1QQ.**  01-794 3277

**Subjects:** Military history, military equipment.
**Hours:** Mon - Fri 9.00 - 5.30, Sat 10.00 - 5.00.
**Services:** Mail order, Book Finding service, credit cards, catalogues.

The shop is situated above the High Hill Bookshop and the entrance is found by turning into the side passage between Wells Supermarket and Dupree Cleaners. This is one of the leading suppliers of both new and antiquarian military books, covering the complete range of military history; firearms, armour, edged weapons, tanks and artillery, uniforms and badges.

### 234 BASILISK PRESS AND BOOKSHOP
**32 England's Lane, London NW3 1YB.**  01-722 2142

**Subjects:** Private Presses, limited editions.
**Hours:** Mon - Sat 9.30 - 5.30.
**Services:** Mail order, credit cards, catalogue (£3.50), lists unbound colour plates from books in stock.

Basilisk are primary publishers but they do sell their fine books from these premises. Private press books from all over the world are sold here as well as their own, which include items like Robinson Crusoe, illustrated by Edward Gordon Craig, limited etchings, bookplates, cards and hand-marbled papers. Very much a specialist collector's shop.

### 235 THE BELSIZE BOOKSHOP
**193 Haverstock Hill, London NW3 4QG.**  01-794 4006

**Subjects:** General.
**Hours:** Mon - Fri 9.30 - 6.30, Sat 9.30 - 5.30.
**Services:** Special orders, college supply.

Bright, modern and well-lit, the Belsize Bookshop tries to cover most subjects expected fo a general bookshop. There are many cases and stands stocking a new hardback and paperbacks. Themes popular in the district are well covered such as art and travel and there is a good selection of children's books. The shop looks well organised, subjects are clearly marked and it has an inviting atmosphere, as befits a shop in one of London's more attractive 'villages'.

### 236 VILLAGE BOOKSHOP
**46 Belsize Lane, London NW3 5AR.**         **01-794 3180**

**Subjects:** Antiquarian, Secondhand, Germany, travel.
**Hours:** Mon - Sat 11.00 - 5.30.
**Services:** Mail order.

Once the Rosslyn Hill Bookshop but now moved to Belsize Village. Every inch of this shop is crammed with books and their German section, with books in German and on Germany, is impressive. There were no new books here but the range of titles and prices was wide, a good collector's hunting ground.

### 237 FITZJOHNS BOOKS
**27a Northways Parade, College Crescent,**
**Swiss Cottage, London NW3 5DN.**         **01-722 9864**

**Subjects:** General, secondhand and antiquarian.
**Hours:** Mon - Sat 11.30 - 5.30. Sun 9.00 - 6.00.
**Services:** Books purchased.

An interesting, tight little secondhand bookshop with a good range of titles as well as some sheet music. Only a few minutes walk from Swiss Cottage tube, but note the address as it is easily missed in passing.

### 238 W.H. SMITH & SON LTD.
**9-10 Harben Parade, Finchley Road,**
**London, NW3 6JS.**         **01-722 4441**

**Subjects:** General.
**Hours:** Mon - Sat 9.00 - 6.00.
**Services:** Credit cards, special orders.

Books do outshine cellotape here, betraying what we hope isn't a dangerous enthusiasm, that is to the manager of course. Quite a well stocked shop with tables of bargain books dotted about.

**239 PHASE ONE BOOKS**
1 Midland Crescent,
Finchley Road, London NW3 6NP.                    01-435 4634

**Subjects:** General, foreign language section (all secondhand)
**Hours:** Mon - Sat 10.30 - 7.00.
**Services:** Special orders.

An interesting secondhand shop run by a knowledgeable owner. The stock is catholic in range and has a substantial foreign language section.

**240 REEDMORE BOOKS**
1 Midland Crescent,
Finchley Road, London NW3 6ND.                    01-435 4634

**Subjects:** Science fiction, horror (paperback and secondhand)
**Hours:** Mon - Sat 10.30 - 7.00.
**Services:** Special orders.

This small shop is in the precinct of the old Frognal and Finchley Road Station. Besides Sci-fi and horror, they have titles on romantic fiction and some theatrical books.

**241 UNICORN BOOKS**
The Antique Emporium, 12 Heath Street,
Hampstead, London NW3 6TE.                        01-202 6342

**Subjects:** 19th and 20th century Children's and Illustrated books.
**Hours:** Tue - Sat 10.30 - 5.00.
**Services:** Mail order (Catalogue). Wants list.

A small but specialised selection of children's books is available at this stall in this Antique Market, where Alice has her own section 'In Wonderland' and 'Through the Looking Glass' and the best of books for children beautifully illustrated makes this worth a visit.

# NW4

**242 ENGLISH CONTINENTAL BOOKMARKET**
**57A Brent Street, London NW4 2EA.**  01-202 9248

**Subjects:** American publications.
**Hours:** Mon - Fri 9.00 - 5.00.
**Services:** Mail order, special orders.

Hard to gauge the shop by its stock as very few books are displayed but their speciality is in obtaining American publications to special order.

**243 C AND L BOOKSELLERS**
**13 Sentinel Square, Brent Street, NW4 2FR.**  01-202 5301

**Subjects:** General.
**Hours:** Mon - Sat 9.00 - 5.30
**Services:** Credit cards, Special orders.

This is quite a good general bookshop located in the small pedestrian square near Tesco's the supermarket. All the books are located on the one floor, with a 'hobbies' and 'childrens' section prominent.

**244 BOOTS THE CHEMISTS**
**Bent Cross Shopping Centre, NW4 3FB.**  01-202 5256

**Subjects:** General.
**Hours:** Mon - Fri 10.00 - 8.00. Sat 9.00 - 6.00.
**Services:** Credit cards.

The book department of the branch is on the lower level and stocks popular fiction and books of a general appeal. The ambition of Brent Cross to be a peripheral Oxford Street doesn't augur too well for the book trade hereabouts.

## 245 W.H. SMITH & SONS LTD.
**Brent Cross Shopping Centre, NW4 3FB.**　　　　　**01-202 4226**

**Subjects:** General.
**Hours:** Mon - Fri 10.00 - 8.00. Sat 9.00 - 6.00.
**Services:** Special orders, credit cards.

This shop has its counterparts all around the outer fringe of London, well ordered and presented, spacious and rather dull. But W.H.S. do not move a huge percentage of literature sold in this undemanding country of ours.

## 246 FACULTY BOOKS
**Middlesex Polytechnic,**
**The Burroughs, London NW4 4BT.**　　　　　**01-202 3593**

**Subjects:** Business studies and course related books.
**Hours:** 10 - 4 (in term time). First three weeks in October open until 8.00 p.m. Mon - Thu.
**Services:** Special orders.

The shop is in the grounds of Middlesex Poly. but is open to the general public. Rather cramped but the service is swift as most students seem to know what they want. The stock is course related and non-fictional.

# NW5-9

**247 BELLMAN BOOKSHOP**
**155 Fortress Road, London NW5 2HR.**          **01-485 6698**

**Subjects:** Marxist & English Literature, Politics and History.
**Hours:** Mon - Sat 10.00 - 5.00.
**Services:** Mail order, Special orders, Subscriptions to The Worker.

Marxist literature appears to be the main theme but other subjects such as Health, Hobbies, History, general interest books on Britain and childrens books are available in a very roomy and sparcely furnished shop where browsers are welcome if not converted.

**248 OWL BOOKSHOP**
**211 Kentish Town Road, London NW5 2JU.**          **01-485 7793**

**Subjects:** General.
**Hours:** Mon - Sat 9.30 - 6.00.
**Services:** Special orders, school supply.

A very spacious and brightly lit modern bookshop in Kentish Town, well planned with clear subject headings of all general sections. A large plate glass window fronts the shop with a few books displayed on cubes, not obscuring the open plan shop which is well lit with a skylight at the back adding extra natural light. Books are shelved in subjects around the walls and there are occasional cases scattered around this large showroom. There is a Polytechnic college nearby so they stock a good selection in their educational sections and literature, history and philosophy are well covered. An unexpected location to find an above-average bookshop.

## 249 GAME ADVICE
**1 Holmes Road, London NW5 3AA.**               **01-485 2188**

**Subjects:** Games, cookery (secondhand) children's books.
**Hours:** Tue - Thu 10.00 - 2.00, 3.00 - 5.30, Fri 10.00 - 2.00, 3.00 - 7.00, Sat 10.00 - 5.30.
**Services:** Mail order.

Deceptively small outward appearance, Game Advice is just off the main Kentish Town shopping centre but inside are four floors of books, toys and games. Children's books are well stocked and every inch of the shop including the staircase is used for display. Besides new books and toys there is a good secondhand cookery book section.

## 250 ERIC & JOAN STEVENS BOOKSELLERS
**74 Fortune Green Road, London NW6 1DS.**      **01-435 7545**

**Subjects:** Secondhand poetry, feminism.
**Hours:** Sat 10.00 - 6.00 (other days by appointment).
**Services:** Mail order, search service, specialist catalogues (feminism, poetry etc.)

As life ebbs away from West End Lane into Fortune Green Road one comes upon this rather marvellous shop, but alas again, open only on Saturdays as a rule. It passes the test of the aficionado by smelling right to start with. Inside its two heavily stocked rooms are thousands of books, mostly secondhand, on literature, poetry, feminism and all manner of things. Eric and Joan Stevens also publish contemporary poets and writers. The shop window, which unless you are forewarned, is all you will see, is feestooned with announcements about poetry readings, women's group meetings and other local events.

### 251 WEST END GREEN BOOKSHOP
**339, West End Lane, London NW6 1RS.**　　　　　　**01-431 0881**

**Subjects:** General.
**Hours:** Mon - Fri 10.00 - 7.00. Sat 10.00 - 6.00.
**Services:** Credit Cards, Special Orders.

West Hampstead now boasts a well lit, attractive and much needed new shop at the corner of West End Lane and Mill Lane. A good selection of poetry, drama and the classics is found on the ground floor as well as fairly up-market art books. The upstairs gallery house non-fiction and an especially impressive childrens section. They also sell post cards and greeting cards. Classical background music adds to the shop's relaxed and welcoming atmosphere.

### 252 SWISS COTTAGE BOOKS
**4, Canfield Gardens, London NW6 3BS.**　　　　　　**01-625 4632**

**Subjects:** General, drama, psychology, travel.
**Hours:** Mon - Sat 9.30 - 6.00.
**Services:** Credit cards, institutional supply, special orders.

This firm has moved from its old premises rather nearer to the Finchley Road Tube Station and although they have less floor space, they have compensated for this by constructing a small gallery of red scaffolding (children banned!).

Their psychology, drama and travel departments are strong but they aim to uphold their reputation as a good general bookshop. Aspiring scholars will note that they stock books relevant to English A & O levels.

### 253  CHANGES BOOKSHOP
**242 Belsize Road, London NW6 4BT.**  **01-328 5161**

**Subjects:** Books on Personal & Social Transformation, Psychology and Psychotherapy.
**Hours:** Tue - Fri 10.00 - 6.00. Sat 10.00 - 5.00.
**Services:** Mail order (Lists), Mail order — Bookstalls for conferences and workshops. Tea and coffee free. Toys to keep children amused. Notice Board for adverts.

This most unusual bookshop two minutes walk away from Kilburn High Road Station specialises in books on Psychology and in "all the dynamic and classical areas of psychotherapy". This includes Jungian and Analytic psychologies, Hypnosis, Art, Music and Creative therapies as well as Holistic health and healing, Acupuncture, Spirituality, Eastern religions and Astrology. You are made welcome here and with tea or coffee given free browse around to find the answer to your problems.


### 254  W.H. SMITH
**118 Kilburn High Street Road, London NW6 4HY. 01-328 3111**

**Subjects:** General.
**Hours:** Mon - Sat 8.30 - 5.30.
**Services:** Credit cards, special orders.

A formula W.H.S., clean, large and tidy with no unpleasant surprises in calf, vellum or crushed morocco. Magazines, which some call books are amply displayed.

## 255 THE KILBURN BOOKSHOP
**8 Kilburn Bridge,**
**Kilburn High Road, London NW6 6HT.**     **01-328 7071**

**Subjects:** General, Ireland, feminism, travel.
**Hours:** Mon - Sat 9.30 - 6.00.
**Services:** Credit cards, special orders.

As Kilburn High Street is full of unimpressive shops it is a pleasant surprise to find an excellent general bookshop which endeavours to cover most subjects within reason and also stocks new hardback fiction. They have a good feminist section which they are expanding. They specialise in Irish books, fiction, history and folk lore and they try to cater for the British Black Community with books on West Indian culture. Politics with left wing bias are well covered and supported by a wide range of alternative magazines. They pride themselves on a fast ordering service and stock books on travel and guides, etc. A well lit modern shop with subjects clearly marked.

## 256 W.H. SMITH & SON LTD.
**29 Broadway Mill Hill, London NW7 3DA.**     **01-959 1316**

**Subjects:** General.
**Hours:** Mon - Sat 8.30 - 5.30.
**Services:** Special orders, credit cards.

The only shop in the immediate vicinity selling books, general, popular and selling well. The latest COI figures showing that 'writer' has overtaken 'antique dealer' as an occupation on passport entries which may explain why 'reader' should have such humble expectations.

## 257 LIONEL HALTER
**7 Hale Lane, Mill Lane, London NW7 3NU.**     **01-959 2936**

**Subjects:** Secondhand, General specialising in Boxing.
**Hours:** Mon - Fri 9.00 - 5.30. Sun 10.30 - 1.00.
**Services:** Credit cards, Search service.

From paperbacks to some Private Presses the books in the secondhand shop are accessible under subjects for the browser. Childrens books have their section although boxing is the specialist subject backed by the preforming arts and many general titles varying by the availability at the time.

## 258  GILBERTS (CONFECTIONERS) LTD.
26 Circus Road, London NW8 6PD.    01-722 8863

**Subjects:** General.
**Hours:** Mon - Sat 8.45 - 6.00, Sun 10.00 - 1.00.
**Services:** Special orders.

In a small parade of shops is Gilberts, which at first looks like a confectioners shop, which it is, but it also sells books, and one window displays nothing else. Toys, cards, stationery and chocolates take up the main shop floor but upon entering there are shelves either side of the door, one of hardbacks and the other of paperbacks. In this confined space devoted to books there is a good selection of fiction and sport, poetry, art, biographies, particularly travel, and even some religious books.

## 259  CHAPTER TRAVEL
012 St. John's Wood Terrace,    01-722 0722

London NW8 6PL.    01-586 5517/8

**Subjects:** Travel, Cookery, Wine, Maps and Guides.
**Hours:** Mon - Fri 10.00 - 6.00, Sat 10.00 - 4.00.
**Services:** Travel agents, Credit card, Book list, travel accessories. Theatre booking agents.

A marvellous shop for the traveller run by Edward and Sue Marquis, which not only spans the large range of books, maps and guides but backs this up with the travel agency and travel accessories department. The books on continental wines and cooking supplement the travel section to make this a most worthwhile visit for all would be travellers — or armchair dreamers. The italian section is particularly strong on guides and cook books. The necessary impedimenta sold include, travel plugs, warning triangles for motorists, travel irons and headlamp convertors.

## 260 STRATHMORE BOOKSHOP LTD.
145 Park Road,
St. John's Wood, London NW8 7HT.          01-722 6166

**Subjects:** General.
**Hours:** Mon - Fri 8.30 - 5.00.
**Services:** Credit cards, special orders, university and library supply.

Mauve painted, bow windowed, the Strathmore Bookshop is a small general bookshop but they have agents in Brussels and Paris so they are happy to order European, American and English books. Their hardbacks are mostly classic fiction with cookery being a popular section. They also stock paperbacks and there is a small selection of children's books.


## 261 PEREIRA
35 St. John's Wood,
High Street, London NW8 7NJ.          01-722 3815

**Subjects:** General.
**Hours:** Mon - Sat 7.30 - 6.30. Sun 8.30 - 1.30.

Primarily a newsagents but with a small stock of general books and quite a good childrens section.


## 262 ST. JOHNS WOOD NEWSAGENTS
134 St. John's Wood High Street, NW8 7SE.          01-722 8800

**Subjects:** General and books in Arabic.
**Hours:** Mon - Fri 7.30 - 7.30. Sat 8.00 - 6.30. Sun 9.00 - 3.00.
**Services:** Credit cards, special orders.

This is a busy local newsagent with quite a good stock of general books including some in arabic for the local community of visitors from the middle east.

### 263 BIBLIOPOLA
**Stands 841/844, Alfie's Antique Market,**
**13 Church Street, London NW8 8DT.**  **01-723 0429**

**Subjects:** Antiquarian, private presses, modern first editions, children's books.
**Hours:** Tue - Sat 10.00 - 5.30.
**Services:** Mail order, search service, lists.

These stalls are on the first floor of the market opposite the coffee bar with the cases arranged to make it seem more enclosed and shop-like. There is a good general range of antiquarian, secondhand and illustrated books.


### 264 BARBARA STONE
**Alfie's Antique Market,**
**13 Church Street, London NW8 8DT.**  **01-723 2829**

**Subjects:** Children's books (antiquarian and secondhand), art books.
**Hours:** Tue - Sat 10.00 - 5.00 (advisable to phone)
**Services:** Mail order, catalogue, books bought.

Though part of the antique market, Barbara Stone has an advantageous window to display on to the street. Old and rare children's books are her speciality but she also has some illustrated and art books, and her knowledge and enthusiasm is infectious.


### 265 KINGSBURY STATIONERS
**527 Kingsbury Road, London NW9 9EG.**  **01-204 7400**

**Subjects:** General, revision books for school exams.
**Hours:** Mon - Fri 6.00 - 6.00. Sat 6.00 - 5.30.

Popular fiction, mostly paperbacked, childrens books, hobbies, cookery and gardening are what this newsagent finds sell. He no longer does special orders because of what he says is non co-operation from publishers. That in reality means that postage plus 33% discount for single copy orders is not too attractive a deal if you are a publisher. Not to mention, though I'm sure not in this case, a rather leisurely settling of accounts.

## 266 AGENTROSE
**207 Edgware Road, London NW9 6LD.**  01-200 0178

**Subjects:** Popular, general.
**Hours:** Mon - Sat 8.00 - 6.00.
**Services:** Special orders for Penguin.

A stationers which has space for mainly paperback books of general appeal including Penguins but very much orientated to the light reader.

# NW11

**267 AISENTHAL**
**11 Ashbourne Parade,**
**Finchley Road, NW11 OAD.**  **01-445 0501**

**Subjects:** Hebraica — Jewish literature.
**Hours:** Mon - Thu 9.00 - 5.45. Fri. 9.00 - 1.00. Sun 9.30 - 1.15.
**Services:** Special orders, mail order, catalogue.

The spiritual and cultural needs of the large Jewish community around Golders Green are well served by this shop. Besides the texts in English and Hebrew it also sells religious requisites.


**268 W.H. SMITH**
**22 Temple Fortune Parade,**
**London NW11 OQS.**  **01-455 2273**

**Subjects:** General.
**Hours:** Mon - Sat 8.30 - 5.30.
**Services:** Special orders, credit cards.

A limited amount of bookspace at ground level, no other good, general bookshops nearby so we must infer that the trading community is adequately served by this branch of W.H.S. The thing about the special order facility is its privacy, a secret deal between the shop and an individual which doesn't in the end enhance the public, the various or glorious image of the book-selling trade. Successfully test as one may the ability of a shop to obtain for you what is for them a certain sale, one would like to see individual managers hazard their reputations with more of a 'show'.


**269 MARTIN THE NEWSAGENTS**
**26 Market Place, Hampstead**
**Garden Suburb, NW11 6JJ.**  **01-455 9720**

**Subjects:** General.
**Hours:** Mon - Sat 7.30 - 5.30. Sun 7.30 - 1.00 p.m.

The hours here tell their tale, that this is primarily a newsagents with a small section of paperbacks and childrens books.

### 270 JERUSALEM THE GOLDEN
146A Golders Green Road,  
London NW11 8HE.

01-455 4960  
01-458 7011

**Subjects:** Hebrew Books.  
**Hours:** Mon - Thu 9.30 - 6.00. Fri 9.30 - 4.00. Sun 10.00 - 2.00. Sat closed.  
**Services:** Credit cards, Special orders.

Gifts, Religious requisites and books fill two small rooms of this shop in Golders Green. The books are selected for adults and children in the Jewish community and have a good selection of bibles and dictionaries as part of their religious and educational sections.

### 271 LAVELLS
40 Golders Green Road, London NW11 8LL.   01-458 5691

**Subjects:** General.  
**Hours:** Mon - Fri 7.30 - 7.00. Sat 8.15 - 6.00. Sun 9.15 - 5.00.  
**Services:** Special orders, credit cards.

This is a large stationers with some books of general appeal. If you have a hobby, want a guide book of London or want to check whether the book is as good as the T.V. serial, there is no reason to go any further.

### 272 W.H. SMITH & SON LTD.
889 Finchley Road, Golders Green,  
London NW11 8RR.   01-455 0036

**Subjects:** General.  
**Hours:** Mon - Sat 8.30 - 5.30.  
**Services:** Special orders, credit cards.

The whole of the first floor of this shop sells books and it has a childrens corner, and tables with guides and dictionaries. With dentists to the north of them, doctors to the south and a screen of innumerable vets surrounding, Golders Green serves the reading habits of the professional classes hereabouts, and they don't seem to vary much from those of the quantity surveyors, auctioneers and structural engineers farther to the north in Muswell Hill.

## 273 MENORAH PRINT AND GIFT SHOP
**227 Golders Green Road, London NW11 9ES.**     **01-458 8289**

**Subjects:** Hebraica.
**Hours:** Mon - Thu 9.30 - 1.00 p.m. 2.00 - 6.00. Fri 9.00 - 1.00.
Sun 9.45 - 1.00
**Services:** Special orders.

A shop with a bright blue front selling books on Jewish themes as well as gifts and religious artifacts.

# SE1

### 300 LONDON CITY MISSION
**175, Tower Bridge Road, SE1 2AH.**  01-407 7585/7

**Subjects:** Christian literature.
**Hours:** Mon - Fri 9.30 - 5.00.
**Services:** Special orders, Bible Readings, Missionary supply.

Just south of Tower Bridge is a modern building housing the London City Mission and the reception area is made over to their bookshop with tables displaying their Christian literature. Downstairs there are more tables of books and a book room with their stock of bibles and other religious subjects — all open to the public and of particular interest to people attending their meetings and bible readings.

### 301 DENNYS BOOKSHOP
**62-64 Weston Street, London SE1 3QJ.**  01-378 7834

**Subjects:** General, specialising strongly in medical.
**Hours:** Mon - Fri 9.00 - 6.00. Occasional Sats.
**Services:** Credit cards, Special order, Mail order (List and Catalogues)

The general stock of books is expanding but locally they are recognised as a medical bookshop (hardly surprising as it is located opposite Guys hospital). Their medical section is extensive ranging from scientific to technical but they still have room for fiction, reference, including a good stock of dictionaries.

### 302 IMPERIAL WAR MUSEUM SHOP
**Lambeth Road, London, SE1 6HZ.**  01-735 8922

**Subjects:** Wars from 1914 onwards.
**Hours:** Mon - Sat 10.30 - 5.30. Sun 2.00 - 5.30.
**Services:** Mail order. Lists of own publications.

A spacious shop inside this war museum with new hardback and paperback books mainly on the two World Wars. The books are on tables or shelves under the publisher with the museum's own publications being one of their specialities.

### 303 THE COLLEGE BOOKSHOP
**London College of Printing, Elephant and Castle,**
**London SE1 6SB.**　　　　　　　　　　　　　　01-735 8570

**Subjects:** Printing and Graphic Design.
**Hours:** Mon - Fri 10.15 - 1.30, 2.30 - 5.30 (Term time only).
**Services:** Special orders.

Up stairs opposite the main entrance is the college bookshop which sells books on printing and graphic design over a counter — no browsing here but orders will be taken for books relative to these subjects if they are not in stock. The Proprietor Francis Mersden has an excellent knowledge of the book trade but is not always available.

### 304 W.H. SMITH & SON LTD.
**Elephant & Castle Shopping Centre,**
**London SE1 6SZ.**　　　　　　　　　　　　　　01-703 8525/6

**Subjects:** General.
**Hours:** Mon - Sat 8.45 - 5.30 (Tue 9.30 - 5.30)
**Services:** Credit cards, special orders.

It is a relief to see the familiar well lit, well organised W.H. Smith cheer up this dismal shopping centre at the Elephant and Castle. Books have most of the top floor to themselves except for the travel section. An escalator outside can take you to this level and general subjects are covered with the usual glossy present books available and a good educational section. This is the only bookshop in the centre so their ordering service must be welcome to the local population.

### 305 THE BOOKSHOP
**4, Kennington Road, London SE1 7BL.**　　　　01-261 1385

**Subjects:** General.
**Hours:** Mon - Fri 9.30 - 6.00 (Tue 9.30 - 5.30) Sat 11.00 - 4.00.
**Services:** Credit Cards.

A good, small general bookshop with predominantly paperbacks but the hard backed section is expanding. The reference section is quite good and there are tables with the eye catchers on them and a stand of Faber paperbacks.

### 306 I.S.O. PUBLICATIONS
**137, Westminster Bridge Road,**
**London SE1 7HR.**
01-262 9588
01-261 9179

**Subjects:** Militaria.
**Hours:** Mon - Fri 9.00 - 5.30. Sat 11.00 - 3.00.
**Services:** Mail order (catalogue), Credit cards, Special orders.

A small shop stuffed with books about things that go bump in the night (laser guided of course). Combat on land, sea and in the air all covered, mostly by hard backed books but some paperbacks and magazines.


### 307 CHURCH MISSIONARY SOCIETY
**157 Waterloo Road, London SE1 8UU.**
01-928 8681

**Subjects:** Christian missionary work.
**Hours:** Mon - Fri 9.15 - 1.15.
**Services:** Mail order, Missionary supply.

The shop within the Society's premises sells very much what is suggested that is Christian literature for these propogating the faith overseas. The books are backed up by cassettes and audio-visual aids. I don't suppose an elephant gun is any longer part of the kit.


### 308 FESTIVAL HALL MUSIC AND BOOKSHOP
**The Royal Festival Hall,**
**South Bank, London SE1 8XX.**
01-633 9323

**Subjects:** Music.
**Hours:** Mon - Sun 11.00 a.m. -10.30 p.m.
**Services:** Credit cards. mail order.

This bookshop is on level two just inside the Royal Festival Hall and specialises in books on music and also sheet music but have a small selection of books generally appealing to the Tourists including books on travel and on London. Another section is books relevant to the exhibitions which are run but 95% of the stock is music, about music or musicians and this is the place to buy the score of the concerts.

**309 W.H. SMITH**
**Main Line Bookstall**
**Waterloo Station, London SE1 9NQ.**  **01-261 1616**

**Subjects:** General.
**Hours:** Mon - Fri 7.00 - 9.30. Sat 7.00 - 9.00. Sun 9.00 - 8.00.
**Services:** Credit cards.

This is the larger bookstall in the centre of Waterloo Station and holds the usual general subjects including childrens books.


**310 W.H. SMITH**
**Loop Bookstall,**
**Waterloo Station, London SE1 9NQ.**  **01-928 8478**

**Subjects:** General.
**Hours:** Mon - Sat 7.00 - 8.00.
**Services:** Credit Cards.

On the Windsor line side of Waterloo Station is the shelter bookstall selling mainly paperbacks to accommodate the travellers.


**311 GREENWICH BOOK COMPANY**
**23, St. Thomas Street, London SE1 9RY.**  **01-403 1152**

**Subjects:** General.
**Hours:** Mon - Fri 9.00 - 5.30.
**Services:** Special orders, Credit cards.

In contrast to their other shop in smart Covent Garden this location is in a rather gloomy street opposite Guys Hospital. The shop itself has a green awning and large windows which make it bright and pleasant. The stock is mainly popular and paperbacked and their ordering service takes care of anything else.

# SE3

### 312 EUROCENTRE BOOKSHOP
21 Meadow Court Road,
Lee Green, London SE3 9EU.              01-318 5633

**Subjects:** English as a foreign language.
**Hours:** Mon - Fri 1.30 - 3.15, 4.00 - 4.30.

A small room at this centre serves as a bookshop, providing books for the students but open also to the public, to some of whom English may well be a foreign language.


### 313 BOOKS OF BLACKHEATH
11, Tranquil Vale,
Blackheath Village, London SE3 OBU.              01-852 8185

**Subjects:** General.
**Hours:** Mon - Fri 9.30 - 1.00, 1.30 - 5.30. Sat 9.30 - 5.00.
**Services:** Special orders.

A small bright shop making the most of limited space. At ground level they have their new stock, grouped by subject and upstairs are books at reduced prices.


### 314 JOHN MENZIES
20 Tranquil Vale,
Blackheath, London SE3 OBA.              01-852 0367

**Subjects:** General.
**Hours:** Mon - Sat 8.30 - 5.30.
**Services:** Credit cards.

John Menzies sell some books in their branch in Blackheath, mainly paperback including the Penguin classics but also a small selection of popular hardback "glossies".

## 315 THE BOOKSHOP, BLACKHEATH LTD.
74, Tranquil Vale, London SE3 0BW.   01-852 4786

**Subjects:** New paperbacks and general secondhand.
**Hours:** Mon - Sat 9.30 - 5.00 (Closed Thu).
**Services:** Books bought and scarce and out of print books traced.

None of the usual gloom, dust and disorder that most secondhand bookshops seem to have here. This is a very attractive shop with new paperbacks arranged by the exchange and the comprehensive stock of secondhand books ranged over the remaining area. Local history is well represented. I think that with limited space it is rather a clever comibination of subjects.

# SE5-6

### 316 THE PASSAGE BOOKSHOP
**5, Canning Cross, Grove Lane,
Camberwell, SE5 8BH.**                   **01-274 7606**

**Subjects:** General, medicine, dentistry.
**Hours:** Mon, Tue, Thu, Fri 10.00 - 6.00. Wed 10.00 - 2.00. Sat 10.00 - 5.00.
**Services** Credit cards, special orders, mailing service.

As well as being a general bookshop with a good childrens section it also answers the needs of the doctors and psychiatrists at nearby King's College Hospital. It is a little difficult to locate.


### 317 STONE TROUGH BOOKS
**59 Camberwell Grove, SE5 8JA.**             **01-708 0612**

**Subjects:** Secondhand and antiquarian.
**Hours:** Tue - Sat 10.00 - 1.00, 1.30 - 6.00.
**Services** Mail order (catalogue)

"Books people like to read" is the idea behind the stock of secondhand and antiquarian books with English literature one of the main subjects and Art and Travel sections among the favourites. George Ramsden obviously enjoys his days in his bookshop and hand picks his stock rather than buying job lots. He has two rooms on different levels for the customers to browse and Camberwell Grove has two bookshops opposite each other since Camberwell Bookshop has opened.

### 318 THE CAMBERWELL BOOKSHOP
28A, Camberwell Grove,
Camberwell, SE5 8RE.  01-701 1839

**Subjects:** Antiquarian, secondhand, fine bindings.
**Hours:** Tue - Sat 10.00 - 6.00. Sun & Mon by appointment.
**Services** Book bindings, wants list.

This shop has many fine sets of English authors in uniform bindings as well as a large antiquarian section. At the cheaper end of the market are secondhand hard and paperbacked books. The binding service and a large collection of prints make it a rather special shop.

### 319 HOLY CROSS CATHOLIC BOOKSHOP
4, Brownhill Road, Catford, SE6 2EJ.  01-461 0896

**Subjects:** Catholic literature.
**Hours:** Mon - Sat 10.30 - 5.30.
**Services** Special orders, mail order, catalogue.

Bibles, Missals, prayer and hymn books are stocked by this Catholic bookshop. Subjects include doctrine, sacraments, scripture, liturgy, lives of Saints, Church history and classics of the Catholic faith. Deuetorial aids, cassettes and statues are much in prominence with the rear room given to their book section.

### 320 W.H. SMITH & SON LTD.
23, Winslade Way, Catford, SE6 4JU.  01-690 1972

**Subjects:** General.
**Hours:** Mon - Sat 8.30 - 5.30 (Thu 9.30 - 5.30)
**Services** Credit cards, Special orders.

Situated in a shopping precinct this branch of WHS has the familiar character of so many branches with a general stock around the walls and best sellers on tables.

# SE8-18

### 321 DEPTFORD BOOK TRADERS AND LITERACY CENTRE, 55, Deptford High Street, SE8 4AA.     01-691 8339

| | |
|---|---|
| **Subjects:** | General, children's, non racist/sexist books. |
| **Hours:** | Tue, Wed, Fri & Sat 9.30 - 5.30, Thu 9.30 - 1.30. Closed Mon & Sun. |
| **Services** | Special orders, parents advisory service, story titling for children. |

A community literacy centre, non profit making and run by enthusiastic volunteers. On Saturday mornings and Tuesday afternoons there are story telling sessions for children, perhaps while mother does the shopping. Apart from selling a wide range of paperback books for adults and children they sell cards, book tokens, wrapping paper and educational games and puzzles.

### 322 SWANS
### 27-29 Deptford Market,
### Deptford, London SE8 4NR.     01-691 3705

| | |
|---|---|
| **Subjects:** | Secondhand, paperbacks. |
| **Hours:** | Tue - Wed - Fri - Sat 9.30 - 4.30. |
| **Services** | Exchange at half price. |

Plenty of paperbacks to choose from at this secondhand market shop although this has to be done over a large counter display but an exchange service is available to make many popular titles excusable at a reasonable price.

### 323 THE ARCADE BOOKSHOP
### 3, The Arcade, Eltham High Street, SE9 1BE     01-850 7803

| | |
|---|---|
| **Subjects:** | General, computer science, educational. |
| **Hours:** | Mon - Sat 9.00 - 5.30 (Thu 9.00 - 1.00). |
| **Services** | Special orders, school supply, book parties for Schools |

Being located in an arcade allows a large display of remaindered books outside on the pavement. The staff are brimming with enthusiasm and their idea of book parties at schools to lay the seed corn for future readers is a good one. The computer sector is a growth outwith so many micro computers being sold and they cover this field well.

### 324 W.H. SMITH & SON LTD.
**92-94, High Street, Eltham, SE9 1BW.**     **01-859 3019**

**Subjects:** General.
**Hours:** Mon - Sat 8.30 - 5.30.
**Services** Special orders, credit cards.

This is a small W.H.S. here in Eltham, Bob Hope's home town but you wont find much else that's Morocco bound. The childrens section is being developed as that's what seems to sell here.


### 325 ROY HAYES
**Chequers Parade, Passey Place, SE9 1DD.**     **01-850 4658**

**Subjects:** General.
**Hours:** Mon - Sat 9.00 - 5.30.
**Services:** Special Orders.

This bookshop is attractively situated in Chequers Parade, a pedestrian way. It covers the whole range of new and soft backed publication with no specialisation, but they will take special orders on request.


### 326 SPREADEAGLE BOOKSHOP
**8, Nevada Street, London SE10 8QQ.**     **01-692 1618**

**Subjects:** Secondhand with emphasis on childrens and London and Kent history.
**Hours:** Mon - Sat 10.00 - 5.30.

Opposite the Greenwich Theatre this shop sells Victorian, Country and domestic antiques and printed ephemera as well as secondhand books at the rear divided in subject order. Their other shop at 23 Nelson Road stocks their maritime books with period furniture. Both interesting shops with plenty of scope for the bargain hunters.

### 327 BOOK BOAT (P.O. BOX 347)
**Cutty Sark Gardens, Greenwich Church Street,
London SE10 9DB.**             01-853 4383

**Subjects:** Childrens Books.
**Hours:** Mon - Sun 10.00 - 5.00 (closed Thu)
**Services** Special orders.

This shop is in fact a boat moored near the Cutty Sark. It is imaginatively arranged and colourfully decorated and would be something of a treat for children taken there.

### 328 THE GREENWICH BOOKSHOP
**37, King William Walk, SE10 9HU.**        01-858 5789

**Subjects:** General, new and secondhand.
**Hours:** Mon - Sat 10.30 - 5.30. Sun 1.00 - 5.00.
**Services** Credit cards, special orders.

This corner shop in Greenwich is strong on local history and things nautical. There are many visitors to the museum and the Cutty Sark nearby who will find a visit here worthwhile. The general sections are good as are travel and reference.

### 329 ANTHONY J. SIMMONDS
**15, The Market, Greenwich, London SE10 9HZ.**    01-853 1727

**Subjects:** New and secondhand Naval Maritime books.
**Hours:** Tue - Sun 10.30 - 6.00.
**Services** Mail order, catalogue.

In prime position in the Fruit market this shop has naval maritime books both new and secondhand filed A-Z under Author.
  Browsers are welcome and in fact their hours accommodate the visitors to Greenwich on a Sunday making this a worth while trip for people interested in naval history.

### 330 MARCET BOOKS
**4A Nelson Road, Greenwich, London SE10 9JB.**    **01-853 5408**

**Subjects:** Antiquarian and Secondhand books.
**Hours:** Tue - Sun 10.00 - 6.00.
**Services** Mail order, Credit cards, Book binding.

An alleyway off the Fruit market is the location for this secondhand bookshop covering most general subjects but with strong sections on Art, Design and Architecture. Books are well displayed with room for browsers and the out of print and antiquarian sections have some very interesting titles.


### 331 ROGERS TURNER BOOKS LTD.
**22 Nelson Road, Greenwich, SE10 9JB.**    **01-853 5271**

**Subjects:** General, Antiquarian and scholarly secondhand books.
**Hours:** Sun - Sat 10.00 - 6.00 except Thu 10.00 - 2.00.
**Services** Credit cards, Search service, Mail order (catalogues)

You are welcome to browse among the shelves of books but a thorough mail order service is available although Greenwich being popular with tourists most shops cater for visitors and this one is open every day. Their stock includes many scholarly titles, history of science and some valuable antiquarian volumes.


### 332 OBSERVATION BOOKSHOP
**141, Trafalgar Square, Greenwich, SE10 9TX.**    **01-858 8411**

**Subjects:** Secondhand paperbacks.
**Hours:** 9.30 - 4.00 approx.
**Services** Paperbacks bought.

A small printing company has used some surplus space to sell secondhand paperback books on general subjects mainly fiction. Books are placed out on tables and can be seen easily for hopefully rapid turnover. The prices involved in this trade seem so low as to make one wonder whether trade it can be called.

### 333 SOMA BOOKS
**38 Kennington Lane, London SE11.**　　　　　　　　**01-735 2101**

**Subjects:** Africana, Caribbean and Indian books.
**Hours:** Mon - Sat 10.00 - 6.00 except Tue closed.
**Services:** Mail order, Special orders.

General subjects related to India, Africa and the Caribbean are stocked by Soma books whose retail outlet is at the Commonwealth Institute but there is a small shop at this address where you can see and purchase their stock although mail order is the main function at this address. Many titles are available in English as well as the Indian languages and children of their specialist countries are well catered for with learning sections.

### 334 DAYBREAK BOOKS
**68 Baring Road, Lee, SE12 OPS.**　　　　　　　　**01-857 1188**

**Subjects:** Christian literature.
**Hours:** Mon - Sat 9.00 - 1.00. 2.00 - 5.30.
**Services** Special orders, hospital visiting programme.

A bright shop on several levels selling and in some cases even giving Christian literature, tapes and cassettes. There is also quite a large stock of conventional cards on sale.

### 335 THE ARMY AND NAVY
**45, High Street, Lewisham, SE13 5JR.**　　　　　　　　**01-852 4321**

**Subjects:** General.
**Hours:** Mon - Thu 9.00 - 5.30. Fri & Sat 9.00 - 6.00.
**Services** Special orders, Credit cards.

This large department store which dominates the high street does find a place for a small book department selling the usual general range of hard and paper backed books. Childrens books and maps and guides are perhaps more prominent than other subjects.

**336 POPULAR BOOK CENTRE**
**284 Lewisham High Street, SE13 6JZ.**                     **01-690 5110**

**Subjects:** General, secondhand.
**Hours:** Mon - Sat 10.00 - 5.30.
**Services** Exchange with half price credit.

Mainly paperbacks, some well used as this shop offers an exchange service and has a wide selection of popular books from which to choose.


**337 W.H. SMITH & SON LTD.**
**The Lewisham Centre, 59, Riverdale, SE13 7EP.**         **01-318 1316**

**Subjects:** General.
**Hours:** Mon - Fri 9.00 - 5.30 (Thu 9.30 - 5.30) Sat 8.30 - 5.30.
**Services** Credit cards, special orders.

Books share the space in this one level shop with W.H.S's other usual stock but their space allowance is not ungenerous. The general stock is shelved and there are tables displaying T.V. titles, books about film stars and eye catching cooking books.


**338 GOLDSMITHS COLLEGE BOOKSHOP**
**Lewisham Way, New Cross, SE14 6NW.**                      **01-692 7171**

**Subjects:** Educational.
**Hours:** Mon - Fri 9.00 - 7.00.
**Services** Special orders.

A large room has been made into a shop at this college with confectionary and stationary to the fore but at the rear are shelves of books with the courses of the University the main theme Open University subjects are catered for and a few books of general interest, mainly fiction with popular demand in paperback, but obviously text books fill most of the shelves.

### 339 BOOKS PLUS
**23, Lewisham Way, SE14 6PP.**                       **01-691 2833**

**Subjects:** Feminism, Socialism.
**Hours:** Mon & Fri 10.00 - 5.00. Tue, Wed, Thu & Sat 11.00 - 6.00.
**Services** Special orders.

This shop is opposite Goldsmiths college and is used a lot by the students. As well as their large sections on feminism and socialism, history and other "serious" things are well covered. The books here are new and secondhand.


### 340 THE BOOKPLACE
**13, Peckham High Street, SE15 5EB.**                **01-701 1757**

**Subjects:** General, local community themes.
**Hours:** Mon - Sat 10.00 - 6.00 (closed Thu)
**Services** Special orders, mail order.

A non-profit making community bookshop trying to serve the needs of the locals with a little agit-prop thrown in I expect. Those teeming minorities like the young blacks, women and gays have their interests well reflected in the stock, which is a good one. They run schemes to encourage writing and literacy.


### 341 W. CANNINGS
**South London Stationers Ltd.**
**23-25, Peckham High Street, SE15 5EB.**           **01-703 7182**

**Subjects:** Art, Dictionaries.
**Hours:** Mon - Sat 9.00 - 5.00 (Thu 9.00 - 1.00).
**Services** Special orders.

This shop is mainly concerned with Artists materials and stationery but they have a small book section specialising in hard and paperback books on Art. They also stock a good range of dictionaries in several languages.

### 342 HOUNDSDITCH IN PECKHAM
**1-41, Rye Lane, Peckham, SE15 5ES.**     **01-639 4321**

**Subjects:** Popular paperbacks.
**Hours:** Mon - Thu 9.00 - 5.30. Fri & Sat 9.00 - 6.00.
**Services** Credit cards.

This large department store has paperback books downstairs with the stationery. Popular paperbacks are stocked, fiction, thrillers etc. and some children's books.

### 343 AFFORD BOOKS
**214 Walworth Road, London SE17 1JE.**     **01-703 3808/9**

**Subjects:** New, reprints and remainders.
**Hours:** Mon - Sat 9.00 - 5.30.

Bargain books in hardback and paperback line the walls with offers of special prices if three are purchased with plenty of room to consider your choice.

### 344 LABOUR PARTY BOOKSHOPS
**150, Walworth Road, SE17 1JT.**     **01-703 0833**

**Subjects:** Politics.
**Hours:** Mon - Fri 9.30 - 5.15.
**Services** Mail order, special orders.

The shop is a room inside the Labour Party H.Q. stocking books on politics (left of course), trades unions, feminism and a range of biographies and autobiographies of Labour worthies.

### 345 W.H. SMITH & SON LTD.
**68-72, Powis Street, SE18 6LQ.**     **01-854 7108**

**Subjects:** General.
**Hours:** Mon - Sat 8.30 - 5.30 (Tue 9.30 - 5.30).
**Services** Special orders, Credit cards.

Out of the larger W.H.S. branches where the books share the first floor with the travel section and there is plenty of room to walk around. Central tables with fast sellers and 'coffee-table' books abound.

## 346 MERCURY BOOKSHOP
**Thames Polytechnic, Wellington Street, SE18 6PF. 01-317 0646**

**Subjects:** General and educational.
**Hours:** Mon, Tue, Thu & Fri 8.45 - 5.30. Wed 8.45 - 5.00. Sat 9.00 - 5.00
**Services** Special orders.

Although attached to the Polytechnic this bookshop has its own wide frontage to Wellington Street and is therefore used by the public for general books. It also bases its stock on the demand by the students so educational books needed for the courses are covered and both the public and the students appear to be well catered for, not forgetting their children's section which is always popular.

# SE20-27

**347 FINLAY**
**131, High Street, Penge, SE20 7DS.**         01-778 8265

**Subjects:** General.
**Hours:** Mon - Sat 7.30 - 5.30.
**Services** Special orders.

The early opening hours denote the fact that this is a newsagents with stationery and confectionary but they do stock books of popular appeal plus study aids, Atlases, maps and guides and a small children's section.


**348 THE ART STATIONERS**
**31, Dulwich Village, SE21 7BN.**         01-693 5938

**Subjects:** Children's, reference.
**Hours:** Mon - Sat 9.00 - 5.30.
**Services** Special orders, credit cards.

Books find a place here in a shop which is dominated by large toys and art materials. A speciality of the shop is pictorial historical guides to the area.


**349 GALLERY BOOKSHOP**
**1d, Calton Avenue, Dulwich Village, SE21 7DE.**         01-693 2808

**Subjects:** General, children.
**Hours:** Mon - Sat 9.30 - 5.30.
**Services** Special orders, Tele-ordering system, credit cards.

An attractive blue and white fronted shop just around the corner from Dulwich Village. A large part of the business is handled by the tele ordering system but there is plenty to see here, especially the childrens section which has nearly half the available space accounted for by the many schools in the district. The cookery and wine sections are also worth a mention.

### 350 COMMISSARIAT, DULWICH COLLEGE,
College Road, Dulwich, SE21 7LD.          01-693 4565

**Subjects:** Books of interest to boys at the college including syllabus books.
**Hours:** Mon - Fri 9.00 - 12.00. 2.00 - 5.00.
**Services** Credit cards.

The books share a shop with the school outfitters. The stock is mainly paperbacked and of interest to boys of 10 years and upwards. The shop is within the college grounds but open to the general public.


### 351 M. & J. COLLINS
84, Park Hall Road, Dulwich, SE21 8BW.          01-670 0044

**Subjects:** General.
**Hours:** Mon - Sat 9.00 - 1.00. 2.00 - 5.30.
**Services** Special orders.

Mainly a stationers shop but with a small selection of books on a few general subjects, reference and dictionaries among them. 'The layout is changed quite often to make it more interesting for regular customers', (I wonder if it works that way).


### 352 DULWICH BOOKS
6, Croxted Road, Dulwich, SE21 8SW.          01-670 1920

**Subjects:** General, travel, D.I.Y., children's books.
**Hours:** Mon - Sat 9.30 - 5.30 (closed Wed)
**Services** Special orders, Credit cards.

This is a fairly new bookshop, well ordered and brightly lit. The section headings are clear and they have a corner with books on Women's rights and also a children's corner. The travel section is divided between the places to go and travellers who have been there. Certainly one of the better general bookshops in the South East.

### 353 SOUTH LONDON CHRISTIAN BOOKSHOP
**17, Lordship Lane, East Dulwich, SE22 8EW.**     **01-693 7969**

**Subjects:** Christian literature.
**Hours:** Mon - Sat 9.00 - 5.30 (closed Thu).
**Services** Special orders, mail order, catalogue.

Two shops knocked into one here give ample well lit space for the stock of bibles and other christian literature. Ministerial advice is available here and much of the profit goes towards overseas missionary work.


### 354 CHENER BOOKS
**14-16 Lordship Lane, East Dulwich, SE22 8HN.**     **01-229 0771**

**Subjects:** General, travel.
**Hours:** Mon - Sat 10.00 - 6.00.
**Services** Credit cards, special orders, mail order, University stockists.

There is a large front room for new books and a room at the back for secondhand stock. Space is a problem for this shop but their large stock is well organised and grouped by subject. Travel and biographical writings are strongly represented. As University stockists they are able to serve the local student population. They are Charter Booksellers.


### 355 W.H. SMITH & SON LTD.
**Forest Hill Station, Devonshire Road, SE22 3HD.**     **01-699 2789**

**Subjects:** General.
**Hours:** Mon - Sat 8.30 - 5.30.
**Services** Special orders, credit cards.

A first floor divided between records and books with a table of bargain books. Plenty of space.

### 356 AMBASSADOR CHRISTIAN BOOKSHOP
Portland Road South, London SE25 4PN.  01-656 0189

**Subjects:** Christian books.
**Hours:** Mon - Fri 9.00 - 5.30. Sat. 9.00 - 4.00.
**Services** Special orders, Church book stalls, Mail order, On monthly sale or return, Church supply.

Parking is provided for this bookshop in Portland Road, so look for the junction of Werndee Road as the shop is not numbered. It is bright and roomy with records and tapes available as a back-up for their well displayed stock of Christian books.

### 357 KIRKDALE BOOKSHOP
272, Kirkdale, Sydenham SE26 4RS.  01-778 4701

**Subjects:** General, performing arts, militaria, national history.
**Hours:** Mon - Sat 9.00 - 5.30 (closed Wednesday).
**Services** Special orders.

This shop, under the same ownership for 20 years is, once entered rather impressive. On the ground floor are the new titles and general stock and downstairs a good secondhand section and some remainders.

### 358 PLUS BOOKS
224, Norwood Road, SE27 9AW.  01-670 8707

**Subjects:** Paperbacks, new and secondhand.
**Hours:** Mon - Sat 9.30 - 6.00.
**Services** Book exchange.

A large selection of new and secondhand paperbacks to buy or exchange. Books rather like clothes, private things usually preferred new but it is good to see that there are bibliophilic transactions of which we know little.

# SW1

**400   BOOKS, ETC.**
**66/74 Victoria Street, London SW1A 5LB.**          **01-828 8849**

**Subjects:** General.
**Hours:**    Mon - Fri 9.00 - 7.00. Sat 10.00- 6.30.
**Services:** Credit cards, Special orders.

Quite a large shop handily placed for those travelling from nearby Victoria Station. It has a good range of both hardback and paperback, fiction and non-fiction, as well as cards and giftwrap. Recently refitted there is ample room to browse amongst the very busy lunchtime office trade this shop attracts, and the excellent selection of titles in all the general subjects.


**401   ARMY & NAVY STORES**
**P.O. Box 189,**                                         **01-834 1234**
**101 Victoria Street, London SW1E 6QX.**                 **Extn 463**

**Subjects:** General, travel, B.B.C. publications.
**Hours:**    Mon - Thu 9.00 - 5.30, Fri & Sat 9.00 - 6.00.
**Services:** Credit cards, mail order, special orders.

This well known department store has a large book section on its second floor which is excellent in its range and arrangement. The paper and hard backed sections are equally balanced and the titles are arranged by subject and displayed on shelves, tables and stands. There is an extensive children's section including a mini-paperback shelf. This department is better than most shops in London which sell books exclusively.


**402   N.E.D.O.**
**1 Steel House,**
**11 Tothill Street, London SW1H 9LJ.**          **01-222 0565/0676**

**Subjects:** Books on industry.
**Hours:**    Mon - Thu 9.30 - 5.15, Fri 9.30 - 4.30.
**Services:** Mail order catalogue.

The National Economic Development Office, which is a Government backed body, has a bookshop here which sells films and reports on industry.

### 403 COOK, HAMMOND & KELL LTD.
**(The London Map Centre)**                **01-222 4945 (general)**
**22 Caxton Street, London SW1H OQU. 01-222 2466 (O/S sales)**

**Subjects:** Maps, Guides.
**Hours:** Mon - Fri 9.00 - 5.00.
**Services:** Mail order, O.S. catalogues.

This is a two-level shop with over a million Ordnance sheets stored with military precision in the basement, and general maps and town plans at ground level. Though concentrating largely on London and Britain, a range of foreign maps and guides is carried, and most normal enquiries can be dealt with — from travellers to Spain on charter flights to those week-ending in Paris or taking an intercontinental journey. It never pays to be secretive when buying maps. By explaining why you want a certain map, the staff can quite often come up with a better one than you may have thought possible.


### 404 POPULAR BOOK CENTRE
**87 Rochester Row, London SW1P 1LJ.**          **01-834 3534**

**Subjects:** General, secondhand.
**Hours:** Mon - Sat 10.00 - 5.30.
**Services:** Exchange with half-price credit.

True to its title popular books are stocked with the choice to exchange at half price, so plenty of reading at a very low price.


### 405 CATHOLIC TRUTH SOCIETY
**25 Ashley Place, Westminster Cathedral Plaza,**
**London SW1P 1LT.**          **01-834 1363**

**Subjects:** Catholic Religion.
**Hours:** Mon - Fri 9.15 - 5.00. Sat 9.15 - 1.00.
**Services:** Special orders.

Children's and adult books relevant to the Catholic religion are sold here with cards, rosaries and other gifts available. Bibles and Prayer books have a special place but the general atmosphere is one to attract the visitors in the Cathedral Piazza.

### 406 WESTMINSTER CATHEDRAL BOOKSHOP
**The Piazza (42 Morpeth Terrace),**
**Victoria Street, London SW1P 1QW.** 01-828 5582

**Subjects:** Roman Catholic books.
**Hours:** Mon - Sat 9.30 - 5.00.
**Services:** Mail order.

Since the Piazza has been opened to Victoria Street this shop by the side entrance to the Cathedral, has become easy to locate. Inside it has a modern well lit layout. The books are of course, mainly about the Roman Catholic faith, with a small gesture towards oecumenism in a Jewish and Orthodox section. Records and cassettes are also stocked.


### 407 BONANZA BOOKS
**(Bonanza Stores Ltd.)**
**43 Strutton Ground, London SW1P 2HY** 01-222 0521

**Subjects:** Quality discount books.
**Hours:** Mon - Sat 9.00 - 6.00.
**Services:** Credit cards.

Ground floor split level premises, just off Victoria Street. Part of an expanding chain and the only such specialists in the SW postal districts.


### 408 CHURCH HOUSE BOOKSHOP
**Church House,**
**Great Smith Street, London, SW1P 3BN.** 01-222 9011

**Subjects:** Christian literature.
**Hours:** Mon - Fri 9.00 - 5.00.
**Services:** Credit cards, mail order catalogue.

A shop at street level with a small gallery. Predominately Church of England in emphasis but not exclusively so. There are a few general books and a small Tolkien/C.S. Lewis section.

### 409 WESTMINSTER ABBEY BOOKSHOP
**20 Deans Yard, London SW1P 3PA.**  **01-222 5565**

**Subjects:** General.
**Hours:** Mon - Sat 9.30 - 5.00.
**Services:** Special orders by mail.

This shop, set in the wall of Westminster Abbey, concentrates on things of interest for the visitor or tourist. It is quite spacious with half the room selling cards and souvenirs and the remainder stocking a general range of books including anything that has been written about the Abbey.

### 410 THE CHURCH LITERATURE ASSOCIATION
**Faith House,**
**7 Tufton Street, London SW1P 3QN.**  **01-222 6952**

**Subjects:** Theology, Church history.
**Hours:** Mon - Fri 9.30 - 5.00.
**Services:** Credit cards, mail order, lists.

A most unusual looking shop, it was designed by Lutyens to more resemble a church, with ornate ceilings, small balconies and a cross and it is a listed building. The books are well displayed in plenty of natural light and there is ample room to browse. As well as books they supply parishes with devotional articles, sheet music, etc.

### 411 UNITED SOCIETY FOR THE PROPAGATION OF THE GOSPEL
**15 Tufton Street, London SW1P 3QQ.**  **01-222 4222**

**Subjects:** Religion.
**Hours:** Mon - Fri 9.30 - 5.30.
**Services:** Mail order, discount for sister societies.

This is a shop for missionary societies and many of the books are about the 'Third World'. Apart from the religious books, which include their own publications, they sell children's study packages and posters.

### 412 MOTHERS UNION
Mary Sumner House,
24 Tufton Street, London SW1P 3RB.          01-222 5533

**Subjects:** Religious education, Mother's Union Publications.
**Hours:** Mon - Fri 9.30 - 5.00.
**Services:** Credit cards, special orders.

This is a corner shop with an attractive wood panelled interior. The books are grouped by subject with an emphasis on family and Christianity. The ambience is relaxed and friendly.

### 413 TATE GALLERY SHOP
Millbank, London SW1P 4RY.          01-834 5651

**Subjects:** Art.
**Hours:** Mon - Sat 10.00 - 5.30, Sun 2.00 - 5.30.
**Services:** Special orders, catalogue of Tate Gallery publications.

Quite a large shop selling art books and postcards, with the more expensive items in glass cases. The books reflect the gallery's interest in British and contemporary art.

### 414 BERGER & TIMS
7 Bressenden Place, London SW1P 5DE.          01-828 8322

**Subjects:** General, travel.
**Hours:** Mon - Fri 9.30 -5.30.
**Services:** Credit cards, special orders, University and library supply.

A spacious modern bookshop two minutes from Victoria Station. The range is comprehensive with children's, travel and reference books strongly featuring. The staff are friendly and helpful and it is a good shop in which to browse.

**415 THE LONDON VISITOR AND CONVENTION BUREAU**
**National Tourist Information Centre,**
**Forecourt - Victoria Station, SW1V 1JT.**　　　　　**01-730 3488**

Subjects: Guide books on London and Great Britain — maps.
Hours: Mon - Sat 9.00 - 6.00 (longer hours in Summer)
Services: Mail order (list). Credit cards.

This shop is now on a corner site at Victoria Station, a very strategic for one selling guide books to the capital and the country generally. Besides the more general guide there are books on walks, buildings, canals and bridges. If the vagaries of British Rail timetables have caught you out there is no better place to kill time than here.

**416 W.H. SMITH & SON LTD.**　　　　　Eastern Shop **01-828 0174**
**Victoria Station, London SW1V 1JT.**　Western shop **01-834 4277**

Subjects: Popular fiction, hobbies, travel.
Hours: Mon - Sat 6.30 - 10.00.
Services: Credit cards, special orders.

There are two WH Smiths at Victoria Station for the historic reason that two railway companies used the station until their amalgamation in 1923. Victoria East is By Platform 15 and has a good selection of Continental Maps and Guides, whereas Victoria West is on what might be called the 'Brighton Side' and is more the usual station mix of best sellers and magazines.

**417 W.H. SMITH & SON LTD.**
**36 Sloane Square, London SW1W 8AP.**　　　　**01-730 0351**

Subjects: General.
Hours: Mon - Fri 9.00 - 7.00. Sat 9.00 - 6.00.
Services: Credit cards, special orders.

One of the best WHS shops in London situated in the lucrative catchment area of Sloane Square station, at the east end of the Kings Road, and serving the Chelsea set.
　The books are on the ground floor, generously displayed and the shop has a high turnover of best sellers.

### 418  PETER JONES
**Sloane Square, London SW1W 8EC.**　　　　　　　　**01-730 3434**

**Subjects:** Children's books.
**Hours:** Mon - Fri 9.00 - 5.30, Wed 9.30 - 7.00, Sat 9.00 - 1.00.
**Services:** Credit cards.

On the third floor of this department store is a small adjunct to the toy department selling children's books.


### 419  THE WELL
**2 Eccleston Place, London SW1W 9NE.**　　　　　　**01-730 7303**

**Subjects:** Christian books.
**Hours:** Mon - Fri 8.00 - 6.00. Sat 8.00 - 2.00.
**Services:** Coffee bar, special orders.

Opposite Victoria Coach Station in Elizabeth Street is the Well Bookshoop at the side of a large coffee bar which must be a pleasing sight to travellers who are welcome and can browse among the Christian books and videos. Children's stories, bibles and prayer books are available as the shop is in association with St. Michael's Church, Chester Square.


### 420  H.R. STOKES
**58 Elizabeth Street, London SW1W 9PB.**　　　　　**01-703 7073**

**Subjects:** General.
**Hours:** Mon - Fri 8.30 - 6.00, Sat 8.30 - 1.00.
**Services:** Special orders, printing.

Primarily a stationers with printing facilities. There is a small book section, rather inaccessible, with a selection of coffee table books, maps, guides and children's books. In the two small windows clearly priced books are displayed.

### 421 BELGRAVIA BOOKS (BERRY & GOFF LTD)
43 Elizabeth Street, London SW1W 9PP.          01-730 5086

**Subjects:** General.
**Hours:** Mon - Fri 10.00 - 6.00, Sat 10.00 - 1.00.
**Services:** Credit cards, mail order, special orders.

A small attractive bookshop which makes the most of its limited space with a gallery to extend browsing facilities. Books are vaguely arranged by subject and the range is wide, excepting sport and horses, says the owner. An old fashioned swinging signboard outside marks and place.

### 422 J.A. ALLEN & CO. LTD.
(The Horseman's Bookshop),
1 Lower Grosvenor Place,          01-828 8855
Buckingham Palace Road, London SW1W OEL. 01-834 5606/7

**Subjects:** Horses.
**Hours:** Mon - Fri 9.00 - 5.30, Sat 9.00 - 1.00.
**Services:** Mail order, catalogue, credit cards, magazine subscriptions.

Appropriately located opposite the Royal Mews, this shop and publishing house stocks books on all aspects of the Equine World, racing them, breeding them and caring for them. Principally new stock but they will obtain out of print and antiquarian books for their customers. It aims to keep every book current in Britain, and the major foreign ones, on horses.

### 423 GIRL GUIDES ASSOCIATION
17-19 Buckingham Palace Road,
London SW1W OPT.          01-834 6242

**Subjects:** Guide and Brownie Books.
**Hours:** Mon - Fri 9.00 - 5.30, Sat 9.00 - 1.00.
**Services:** Mail order, catalogue.

A spacious, wood panelled premises opposite the Royal Mews. Most of the space is given over to equipment but the first section of the shop on entering is books. The Guide movement's own publications feature strongly as well as books on the outdoor life in general, wildlife and a children's section.

## 424 HARVEY NICHOLS & CO. LTD. (HATCHARDS)
Knightsbridge, London SW1X 7RT.　　　　　　01-235 5000

**Subjects:** General.
**Hours:** Mon - Sat 9.30 - 6.00 (Wed 9.30 - 7.00)
**Services:** Credit cards, mail order, catalogue.

This offshoot of the excellent Hatchards is on the fourth floor of Harvey Nichols and carries on a smaller scale much of the same quality books in the general range as the parent shop. The shelves and tables where the books are displayed have bright green backing and are arranged under clear subject headings.

## 425 HARRODS
Knightsbridge, London SW1X 7XL.　　　　　　01-730 1234

**Subjects:** General, children's books, secondhand, antiquarian (very
**Hours:** small).
**Services:** Mon - Fri 9.00 - 5.00 (Wed 9.00 - 7.00) Sat 9.00 - 6.00. Credit cards, mail order, lists, secondhand wants list, library.

There are three large book sections on the second floor, one for children's books, one general books and the third for paperbacks. The book department does not let down this store's paramount reputation, it is generous, attractively displayed and comprehensive in range. Pale green carpets, red and gold lettering announcing subjects and substantial wooden shelving to give a sumptuous atmosphere.

The paperbacks are displayed obliquely to enable the customer to examine the cover and spine. Another praise-worthy feature is the number of books in the major European languages. On the fourth floor are a few antiquarian books in the Fine Arts department and on the same floor a library and secondhand section.

The books in the secondhand department have been in the library for six months and are then sold at half price, and a customer may leave his name for when it comes available. Harrods absorbed the old Times Bookshop of Wigmore Street but the excellence of that missed shop has been maintained.

### 426 THE SPIRITUALIST ASSOCIATION OF GREAT BRITAIN
**33 Belgrave Square, London SW1X 8QL.**　　　　**01-235 3351**

**Subjects:** Spiritualism.
**Hours:**　　Mon - Fri 10.00 - 7.00, Sat 10.00 - 4.30, Sun 3.00 - 8.00.

This is a small shop in the foyer of the Association selling books, pamphlets and journals on their subject. They are rather precise about the psychic world and do not have books from the wilder shores of occult and magic.


### 427 TRUSLOVE & HANSON LTD.
**205 Sloane Street, London SW1X 9LG.**　　　　**01-235 2128/9**

**Subjects:** General, travel, gardening, children.
**Hours:**　　Mon, Tue, Thu, Fri 9.30 - 5.30, Wed 10.00 - 7.00, Sat 10.00 - 5.00.
**Services:** Credit cards, W.H. Smith tokens, mail order, catalogue, special orders.

An excellent bookshop in the W.H. Smith's group, which, sensitive to its literate location, is wide and comprehensive in its range. Books are shelved by subject with new publications arranged on central tables. Children's, travel, natural history, gardening and biographical books are on the ground floor and downstairs are art, literature, reference and paperbacked books. The shop is modern and spacious, with plenty of room to browse its shelves.


### 428 DESIGN CENTRE BOOKSHOP　　　　01-839 8000
**28 Haymarket, London SW1Y 4SU.**　　　　**Extn. 109 or 122**

**Subjects:** Design.
**Hours:**　　Mon, Tue 10.00 - 6.00, Wed - Sat 10.00 - 8.00. Sun 1.00 - 6.00.
**Services:** Mail order, lists, credit cards.

At the rear of the Design Centre, up some stairs, is the book section. Among the clearly marked sections are photography, design, history, architecture, crafts and environmental design. The stock is chiefly hardbacked. The whole shop is well worth a visit for the constantly changing ranges of interesting items exhibited.

### 429  WHITCOULLS NEW ZEALAND BOOKSHOP
6 Royale Opera Arcade, London SW1Y 4UY.     01-930 4587

**Subjects:** New Zealand publications, travel.
**Hours:** Mon - Fri 9.00 - 5.00. Sat 9.30 - 12.00.
**Services:** Mail order catalogue, Agent for New Zealand Government printers, window of small ads. mostly accommodation.

This shop is in the arcade between The Haymarket and Lower Regent Street. It is quite small inside but stocks many books from or about New Zealand. It has a good range of travel books not unsurprisingly, as Kiwis counter the peripheral with the peripatetic. Craft items, jewellery and postcards are also sold.

### 430  INSTITUTE OF CONTEMPORARY ARTS BOOKSHOP
The Nash House,
12 Carlton House Terrace, London SW1Y 5AH.     01-930 0493

**Subjects:** The Arts, general, feminism.
**Hours:** Tue - Sun 12.00 - 9.00.

The I.C.A. is at the Trafalgar Square end of the Mall. The shop is a small part of a complex of galleries, cinemas, theatres, etc. and is located to the side of the main entrance. There are books on photography, psychology, philosophy, politics, films and a good selection of modern fiction, also an unusual range of artists' postcards. It is a very British solution to 'the modern' to house it in Regency grandeur.

### 431  THE PLANNING BOOKSHOP
Town and Country Planning Association,
17 Carlton House Terrace, London SW1Y 5AS.     01-930 8903

**Subjects:** Environmental studies, transportation, energy, housing.
**Hours:** Mon - Fri 9.30 - 5.30.
**Services:** Catalogue, mail order, suppliers to institutions.

You enter this building from Carlton House Terrace which backs on to the Mall and walk up a grand staircase or take a lift to the first floor where the shop occupies one room. The Association is a voluntary body founded in 1899, whose aim is to revitalise Britain's regions and fight urban decay, and the books it stocks are towards this end.

### 432 PICKERING AND CHATTO
**Incorporating Dawsons of Pall Mall,**
**16/17 Pall Mall, London SW1Y 5NB.**         **01-930 2515**

**Subjects:** Antiquarian specialising in English Literature, Economics, Science, Medicine, Manuscripts and Autographs.
**Hours:** Mon - Fri 9.30 - 5.30.
**Services:** Mail order catalogue and lists. Library & Institutional supply.

One rings a bell to enter this deep carpeted shop in Pall Mall which has changed to Pickering & Chatto from the Brunswick Centre to incorporate Dawsons. The interior is as sumptuous as the address is prestigious with books impressively marshalled in old cabinets and cases. The stock is entirely antiquarian, the service expert and helpful, but it is really a place for the uniniated.

### 433 FARLOWS OF PALL MALL
**5b Pall Mall, SW1Y 5NP.**         **01-839 2423**

**Subjects:** Shooting and fishing.
**Hours:** Mon - Fri 9.00 - 5.00 (Thu 9.00 - 6.00). Sat 9.00 - 4.00.
**Services:** Credit cards, Special orders.

The shop at the Trafalgar Square end of Pall Mall is principally a tackle shop but they do have books on how to cook the victims who find themselves at the wrong end of their excellent equipment.

### 434 ST GEORGE'S GALLERY BOOKS LTD.
**8 Duke Street, St. James', London SW1Y 6BN.**     **01-930 0935**

**Subjects:** Art.
**Hours:** Mon - Fri 10.00 - 6.00, Sat 10.00 - 1.00.
**Services:** Mail order, catalogues from recent exhibitions.

Four rows of books in the window give a good representation of the stock inside, which covers the whole range of the pictorial and decorative arts. Despite appearances inside, with people working at desks, etc., it is a shop with a basement and upper floor crammed with books and monographs. In its field of specialisation it is most comprehensive.

### 435 CAVENDISH RARE BOOKS
**2-4 Princes Arcade,**
**Picadilly, London SW1Y 6DS.**  01-734 3840

**Subjects:** Antiquarian (Travel and exploration).
**Hours:** Mon - Fri 10.00 - 6.00, Sat 9.00 - 1.00.
**Services:** Mail order, catalogue, credit cards.

Barbara Grigor-Taylor runs this extremely approachable antiquarian bookshop in Princes Arcade, off Piccadilly. Maritime history, travel and exploration are the main themes here but there are also fine bindings and general literature. Often full of travellers and collectors, attracted by the expertise and personality of the owner.

### 436 SIMS, REED & FOGG LTD.  01-493 0952
**58 Jermyn Stret, London SW1Y 6LX.**  493 660

**Subjects:** Antiquarian, out of print books.
**Hours:** Mon - Fri 10.00 - 6.00.
**Services:** Mail order, catalogues.

An inviting shop selling rare and antiquarian books, specialising in the fine and applied arts. The books are arranged by subject but it would be best to locate something by asking the friendly assistant, as the sense of order seems personal. Twelve catalogues are produced yearly and mail order accounts for most of their business.

### 437 SPINK & SON LTD.
**5/7 King Street, London SW1Y 6QS.**  01-930 7888

**Subjects:** Coins and medals.
**Hours:** Mon - Fri 9.30 - 5.30.
**Services:** Mail order, special orders, catalogue.

Numismatists will probably know this third floor book room where new, secondhand and antiquarian books on coin and medal collection are sold. Much of Spink's business is mail order but browsers are welcomed.

# SW3

### 438 HERALDRY TODAY
**10 Beauchamp Place, London SW3 1NQ.**          01-584 1656

**Subjects:** Heraldry, genealogy, topography.
**Hours:** Mon, Tue, Wed 9.30 - 5.00.
**Services:** Mail order, catalogue, library and institution supply, search service.

Up and down a few stairs, through a courtyard, one finds the two rooms where the books are. Most of the trade is mail order, in one room are new books and in the other antiquarian and secondhand ones.


### 439 SIFTON, PRAED & CO. LTD.
**54 Beauchamp Place, London SW3 1NY.**          01-589 4325

**Subjects:** Antiquarian maps and prints.
**Hours:** Mon - Fri 9.45 - 5.45, Sat 10.30 - 4.00.
**Services:** Credit cards, special orders.

This shop is for collectors of rare maps and atlases as well as prints. There are a few modern books for sale on the collecting of these items.


### 440 STEPHANIE HOPPEN at the STUDIO
**17 Walton Street, London SW3 2HX.**          01-589 3678

**Subjects:** Food, wine, early travel, rare maps.
**Hours:** Tue - Sat 10.00 - 6.00.
**Services:** Mail order, catalogues.

A new, small and elegant shop in South Kensington, specialising in gastronomy, early voyages and rare maps. They produce an excellent catalogue and seem to be in the right area, with many fine restaurants, for the stimulation of their gourmet customers.

## 441 JOHN SANDOE (BOOKS) LTD.
**10 Blacklands Terrace, London SW3 2SP.**      **01-589 9473**

**Subjects:** General.
**Hours:** Mon - Sat 9.30 - 5.30.
**Services:** Mail order, catalogue at Christmas.

Mr. Sandoe, who has been running a shop here for 25 years, has certainly made the most of a little. This shop, on three levels, is overflowing with books in every corner. On the first floor are the paperbacks, well displayed and various, in the basement is a small room for children's books, and at ground level the general stock with new titles on window ledges and tables. Technical and academic books are not stocked, but the shop is a cornucopia of good things rather randomly arranged though helpful assistance is readily to hand.


## 442 NATIONAL ARMY MUSEUM BOOKSHOP
**Royal Hospital Road, London SW3 4HT.**      **01-730 0717**

**Subjects:** British and Indian Armies.
**Hours:** Mon - Sat 10.00 - 5.00. Sun 2.00 - 5.00.
**Services:** Book list, mail order.

A small room inside this Army Museum stocks books on the British and Indian armies with biographies, histories, campaigns and uniforms. They have a children's section and although not a large stock it must be very convenient for visitors interested in the battles of the past to be able to further their knowledge by buying books before they leave.


## 443 DON KELLY
**Antiquarius Stand T5,**
**135 Kings Road, London SW3 4PW.**      **01-352 8882**

**Subjects:** Reference books on the Antique trade.
**Hours:** Mon - Sat 10.00 - 6.00.

Mr. Kelly, who sells antiques in this market, stocks a selection of books on the trade as he finds that here there is quite a demand for them.

### 444 A.H. LESTER
Chenil Gallery,
183 Kings Road, London SW3 5EB.                    01-352 0703

**Subjects:** Orientalist specialising in works of David Roberts.
**Hours:** Mon - Sat 10.00 - 6.00.
**Services:** Credit cards.

A few specialist books relative to the works of David Roberts are stocked in this stall down steep steps just inside the side entrance of the Chenil Gallery, i.e. Travels in the Holy land.


### 445 IL LIBRO
Stall C 8/9 Chenil Gallery,
181/183 Kings Road, London SW3 5EB.               01-352 9041

**Subjects:** Antiquarian.
**Hours:** Mon - Sat 10.00 - 6.00.

Quite a large stall in the antique market specialising in ornithological and botanical books, also some antiquarian books in French.


### 446 JOANNA BOOTH
247 Kings Road, London SW3 5EL.                    01-352 8998

**Subjects:** French antiquarian books.
**Hours:** Mon - Sat 10.00 - 6.00.
**Services:** Mail order, catalogue.

An intriguing melange of things to buy here as well as old French books, there are carvings, textiles and old master drawings. Pleasantly informal and has more of the appearance of a private house than a shop.


### 447 SANFORD BOOKS WITH C. MOOR & R. CAMERON
The Chelsea Antique Market,
253 Kings Road, London SW3 5EL.                    01-352 5581

**Subjects:** Antiquarian, secondhand.
**Hours:** Mon - Sat 10.30 - 6.00.

A collector's corner covering five stands in the market on the south side of King's Road east of Old Church Street. They have out of print, antiquarian and secondhand books over a range of subjects — art, children's books, illustrated natural history as well as some modern first editions.

### 448 HARRINGTON BROS.
**The Chelsea Antique Market,**
**253 Kings Road, London SW3 5EL.**  **01-352 5689**

**Subjects:** Antiquarian (Travel and Maps)
**Hours:** Mon - Sat 10.00 - 6.00.
**Services:** Mail order, occasional lists.

The window of this small antique market is filled with antiquarian books and inside at street level is a small stall displaying an introductory stock. Anyone showing genuine interest will be taken up a narrow staircase to a large room, with many books, colour plates and bound sets, a reward for the curious.


### 449 SLANEY & MACKAY BOOKSELLERS
**263 Kings Road, Chelsea, London SW3 5EL.**  **01-352 7123**

**Subjects:** General.
**Hours:** Mon - Sat 10.00 - 7.00.
**Services:** Credit cards, Special orders, Mail order (Lists).

Two well designed floors with an excellent selection of books covering general subjects with a children's department well stocked and a great deal of thought given to their customers. At ground floor level are the new hardbacks whereas downstairs is devoted to paperbacks in well lit spacious surroundings. Customers looking for books from travel to general fiction can find many titles here in comfort with knowledgable advice at hand.


### 450 CHELSEA RARE BOOKS
**313 Kings Road, London SW3 5EP.**  **01-351 0950**

**Subjects:** First editions, rare books, secondhand.
**Hours:** Mon - Sat 10.00 - 6.00.
**Services:** Mail order, catalogue.

An interesting shop for the collector or browser. Most books openly displayed with the rarer items in cabinets. At ground level the emphasis is on 18th and 19th Century English literature with tables and chairs provided for customers to examine the books. Downstairs are prints, maps, water colours, and books on art and architecture.

## 451 PENGUIN BOOKSHOP
**157 Kings Road, London SW3 5TX.**  01-351 1915

**Subjects:** General.
**Hours:** Mon - Wed 10.00 - 7.00. Thu - Sat 10.00 - 8.00.
**Services:** Credit cards, Post-a-book.

A contemporary black fronted shop with the Penguin emblem in-evidence is welcome in the Kings Road. Two floors of books with the complete selection of Penguins also other selected publishers with a small section of new hardbacks.

# SW4-6

**452 TETRIC BOOKSHOP**
**116 Clapham High Street, London SW4 7UH.**      **01-622 5344**

**Subjects:** General.
**Hours:** Mon - Fri 10.00 - 6.00. Sat 9.30 - 5.00.
**Services:** Special orders, local events board.

A good small general bookshop very much in tune with its local community. Mostly paperbacks with the 'serious' contemporary concerns of politics, feminism and sociology well represented.


**453 ORBIS BOOKS (LONDON) LTD.**
**66 Kenway Road, London SW5 ORD.**      **01-370 2210**

**Subjects:** Polish Books, Slavonic studies.
**Hours:** Mon - Fri 9.30 - 5.30, Sat 9.30 - 4.30.
**Services:** Credit cards, mail order, catalogue, library and university supply.

Stocked mainly with Polish books but also those of other Eastern European countries. Maps and dictionaries are the most accessible items for English speakers.


**454 W.H. SMITH & SON**
**266 Earls Court Road, London SW5 9AS.**      **01-370 3201**

**Subjects:** General.
**Hours:** Mon - Fri 9.00 - 7.00, Sat 9.00 - 5.30.
**Services:** Credit cards, Special orders.

A large one-floored branch of Smith's with plenty of table display room for their hard backed and new titles. Educational books and maps and guides are well represented.

### 455 NATIONAL POETRY CENTRE BOOKSHOP
**21 Earls Court Square, London SW5 9DE.**  **01-373 7861/2**

**Subjects:** Poetry.
**Hours:** Mon - Fri 10.00 - 5.00 (event evenings from 7.00)
**Services:** Mail order, catalogue.

This is a large, ground floor room crammed with slim volumes of verse, mostly contemporary. There are section headings for criticism, biography and poetry in translation. The National Poetry Centre also publishes its own magazine.


### 456 RESPONSE COMMUNITY BOOKSHOP
**300 Old Brompton Road, London SW5 9JE.**  **01-370 4606**

**Subjects:** Earls Court life, alternative life styles, general.
**Hours:** Winter: Mon 12.00 - 7.00, Tue - Sun 10.00 - 7.00.
Summer: Mon 12.00 - 8.00, Tue - Sun 10.00 - 8.00 (Thu 10.00 - 7.00)
**Services:** Lists, mail order, special orders, coffee bar for browsers.

The shop was launched on the success of a local community paper called Response and its stock reflects the life of the area, one of the most cosmopolitan in London. At the front of the shop are the current titles and at the rear secondhand books and the coffee bar where tea and cakes made by pensioners can be bought. Rocket, the resident cat, is a proven bibliophile and not averse to a bit of rock cake.


### 457 N.S.S. NEWSAGENTS LTD.
**214 Earls Court Road, London SW5 9QB.**  **01-370 0552**

**Subjects:** Popular best sellers.
**Hours:** 5.00 am — Midnight.

Newsagents more than bookshop but with some best sellers, hard and soft backed, and books on cookery and gardening.

## 458 WEST LONDON BOOKS
### 15 Jerdan Place, London SW6 1BE.    01-385 8334

**Subjects:** Remainders, general subjects, including children's section.
**Hours:** Mon - Sat 10.30 - 5.30.
**Services:** Credit cards.

Remainders in hardback and paperback are under subjects with sections marked clearly — antiques, cookery etc. mainly at about half price except for the paperbacks which are about thirty pence or four for one pound so there are plenty of bargains here for adults and children.


## 459 TETRIC BOOKSHOP
### 309 New Kings Road, London SW6 4RS.    01-731 2494

**Subjects:** General.
**Hours:** Mon - Fri 10.00 - 2.00. 2.30 - 5.30. Sat 10.00 - 5.00.
**Services:** Special orders.

This branch of the Tetric Bookshop has a general mainly paperback stock including a children's section but only a small selection of travel books which it leaves to it's Chelsea branch further along in the King's Road. Otherwise it caters for the residents with fiction, cookery and other subjects expected in a local bookshop.


## 460 THE BOOK ADDICT
### 186 Wandsworth Bridge Road, London SW6 2UF.  01-736 5802

**Subjects:** Christian Books.
**Hours:** Mon - Sat 9.00 - 5.30 except Thu - 9.00 - 1.00.
**Services:** Special orders, General Library supply.

As with most Christian bookshops this one is bright and cheerful with records, tapes and cards backing their books on religious subjects. They have a section for children and a good assortment of bibles.

### 461 PAUL CROMPTON
**638 Fulham Road, London SW6 5KT.**            **01-736 2551**

**Subjects:** Martial Arts and Kung-Fu.
**Hours:** Mon - Sat 10.00 - 6.00.
**Services:** Mail order.

Customers have to be invited the other side of the counter to move among the shelves of books about the Martial Arts. Mainly new titles are shelved in this depressingly badly appointed shop but they have a very adequate stock from all aspects of survival to the expertese of these Arts — maybe their customers are so expert in Kung Fu a check has to be kept on the browsing and the amiable chap in charge appears to have his coat and hat on ready for a quick get-away

### 462 BOOKS OF ASIA
**717 Fulham Road,**           **Han Shan Tang 01-731 2447**
**London SW6 5UL.**           **John Randall 01-736 9424**

**Subjects:** Asia.
**Hours:** Mon - Fri 10.00 - 6.00. Sat 10.00 - 4.00 (Variable in August).
**Services:** International Mail order, catalogue, institutional supply.

It is necessary to ring the bell in order to enter this bookshop which houses two companies under the heading 'Books of Asia'. Han Shan Tang Ltd. specialises in China and Japan and John Randall, India, South East Asia and the Middle East. Upon entering you will be directed to the section of your particular interest and allowed to browse with the knowledge there is a back up to the books on show with a basement stock. Mail order is the main concern here and they claim to have one of the largest stocks of books on the Arts and cultures of their specialist areas. Scholarly books are listed in their catalogue but interested customers are very welcome to browse and see the books in person.

### 463 THE CONSTANT READER BOOKSHOP
627 Fulham Road, London SW6 5UQ.                01-731 0218

**Subjects:** General, oriental.
**Hours:** Mon - Sat 10.30 - 6.30.
**Services:** Books bought, mail order.

An excellent secondhand bookshop covering a wide range of subjects both hard and soft backed. They are strong on illustrated books, the arts, military history and especially books on travelling in the Orient.


### 464 WINDMILL WHOLEFOODS
486 Fulham Road, London SW6 6NH.                01-385 1570

**Subjects:** Whole food cookery, health, alternative medicine.
**Hours:** Mon - Fri 9.30 - 6.00. (Fri 9.30 - 7.00).
**Services:** Special orders.

Located down a small alley at the side of their restaurant this small shop specializes in what seems to be a growth area, the dietary regulation of our eating habits — Sams fertilizer — Sams meat. So if your pulse beats a little faster books can be bought on how to slow it — or cook it!


### 465 ROWLAND WARD OF KNIGHTSBRIDGE
1 Salisbury Pavement, Dawes Road,
London SW6 7HT.                                  01-385 0824

**Subjects:** New and antiquarian books on Africa and Natural History.
**Hours:** Mon - Sat 9.30 - 5.30
**Services:** Mail order (lists)

A bright gift and toy shop with a few childrens books on Africa and Natural History. At the moment viewing them is difficult but the owners hope to provide more room for this side of their business and have their large stock displayed. Nevertheless the public are welcome although possibly a telephone call would save time and certain books could be available from their extensive stock.

## 466 BENEDICTS BOOKSHOP
### 92 Lillie Road, London SW6 7SR.  01-424 6102

**Subjects:** Language Teaching specialists with general, new and secondhand department.
**Hours:** Mon - Fri 9.30 - 6.00. Sat 10.00 - 6.00.
**Services:** School and library supply. Mail order, Special orders.

This bookshop specialises in language teaching materials with books in English and Foreign languages with audio video tapes, cassettes, film, etc. to assist foreigners with English and the English with foreign languages. They are also enlarging their general stock to provide books in this area both new and secondhand but maintianing their large specialist stock as their main function.

# SW7

**467 IMPERIAL COLLEGE BOOKSHOP**
223 Sherfield Building,
Imperial College, London SW7 2AZ.          01-589 5218

**Subjects:** Engineering, science.
**Hours:** Mon - Fri 9.15 - 5.15.

Although this shop is open to the public it is rather difficult to find at the centre of Imperial College. As well as the usual course books the shop also stocks some light fiction, cards, stationery and students equipment. C.P. Snow's injunction about two cultures still seems relevant here.

**468 GEOLOGICAL MUSEUM BPOOKSHOP**
Exhibition Road, London SW7 2DE.          01-589 3444, Ext 298

**Subjects:** Geology, minerology, etc.
**Hours:** Mon - Sat 10.00 - 5.30, Sun 2.30 - 6.00.
**Services:** Mail order, catalogue.

The shop is just inside the entrance to the Museum and has books which relate to all things geological, and they also sell gifts, but no pet rocks — yet. The stock is kept behind a counter, all rather impersonal.

**469 LAMLEY & CO. LTD.**
I Exhibition Road, London SW7 2EH.          01-589 1276

**Subjects:** General, science, natural history, art.
**Hours:** Mon - Fri 9.00 - 5.30 (closed 11.15 - 12.15), Sat 9.30 - 1.00.
**Services:** Special orders.

This lofty green painted shop sells books and stationery. At ground floor the books are arranged by subject with a separate room for stationery. In the basement are paperbacks and children's books, all of them fiction. It has been a bookshop since 1875 though changing hands many times. The science section next to the front window is accounted for by the proximity of Imperial College.

### 470 OPPENHEIM & CO. LTD.
**7 Exhibition Road, London SW7 2HE.**      **01-584 5641**

**Subjects:** General, Art, Remainders & Transport.
**Hours:** Mon - Sat 8.30 - 6.30. Sun - Various.
**Services:** Credit cards, special orders, library supply.

Sunday opening hours at this bookshop a short walk from the Science Museum will be welcome especially as there is a specialist transport department upstairs. The ground floor is divided into a constantly changing stock of remainders and a comprehensive range of paperbacks whereas upstairs new and out of print books on motoring, aviation, ships, aircraft and modelling have a separate room.

### 471 F. PULTENEY & CO. (BOOKS) LTD.
**22 Thurloe Street, London SW7 2LT.**      **01-589 0522**

**Subjects:** General, remainders.
**Hours:** Mon - Fri 9.00 - 5.30, Sat 9.30 - 2.00.
**Services:** Library supply.

A one-roomed shop at street level with stalls lined and tables piled with books. The window displays their bargain books clearly priced. The paperback selection is perhaps the best feature of this shop.

### 472 THE MEDICI GALLERY
**26 Thurloe Street, London SW7 2LT.**      **01-589 1363**

**Subjects:** Art.
**Hours:** Mon - Fri 9.00 - 5.30, Sat 9.00 - 5.00.
**Services:** Exhibitions, framing.

A shop selling artists materials and small book section of art books and Medici publications.

### 473 VICTORIA & ALBERT MUSEUM BOOKSHOP
Cromwell Road, London SW7 2RL.   01-589 6371

**Subjects:** Arts, crafts, antiques.
**Hours:** Mon - Fri 10.00 - 5.30, Sat 10.00 - 5.15, Sun 2.30 - 5.15.
**Services:** Mail order.ALD5

One of the more spacious museum bookshops, with many sections all devoted to the study, preservation and restoration of beautiful artifacts.


### 474 JOHN MENZIES (HOLDINGS) LTD.
50/52 Old Brompton Road, London SW7 3DX.   01-589 3769

**Subjects:** General.
**Hours:** Mon - Fri 9.00 - 8.30, Sat 9.00 - 8.30. Sun 12.00 - 6.00.
**Services:** Credit cards.

A combination of stationery and books sold, which is the usual mix with Menzies. A quite generous paperback section, mostly fiction, arranged alphabetically by author and central tables with hardbacked remainders.


### 475 SCHOLABOOKS
7 Harrington Road,
South Kensington, London SW7 3ES.   01-589 5991

**Subjects:** French books, guides and maps.
**Hours:** Mon - Sat 8.15 - 6.15, Sat 9.00 - 6.00.
**Services:** Subscription to French magazines, countdown exchange service for French books, credit cards.

It has the appearance at the front of a small stationers, but through the narrow shop and up a few stairs is a room full of French books with a French speaking assistant to help. They have an excellent system of exchange so that there is always a wide range of secondhand books available. Guides and maps to France are prominent.

### 476 KENSINGTON BOOK SHOP
9 Harrington Road, London SW7 3ES.   01-589 9054

**Subjects:** Music.
**Hours:** Mon - Fri 9.00 - 5.45, Sat 9.00 - 2.00.
**Services:** Credit cards, mail order, concert information.

Musicians' biographies, sheet music, instruction books for musical instruments; musical instruments and accessories are all sold here. There is a notice board for concert information.

### 477 THE FRENCH BOOKSHOP
28 Bute Street, London SW7 3EX.   01-584 2840

**Subjects:** French books.
**Hours:** Mon - Fri 10.00 - 6.00, (8.30 - 6.00 in term time), Sat 10.00 - 5.00.
**Services:** Special orders.

A bright blue painted shop with striped blue and white awning, spacious and friendly inside. They carry a whole range of French books, mostly paperbacked. There are cartoons by Claire Bletcher and others on sale. The bilingual owner, an ex librarian, can offer specialist advice on her extensive range of books and takes pride in her children's section. Students from the Lycee nearby are well served. Maps and guides of France, especially Paris, are stocked here.

### 478 WATERSTONES
99 Old Brompton Road, London SW7 3LE.   01-581 8522

**Subjects:** General.
**Hours:** Mon - Fri 9.30 - 10.30 . Sat 9.30 - 7.00. Sun 12.00 - 7.00.
**Services:** Credit cards, special orders, world wide postal service.

Waterstones are a very good thing and they are spreading! The brain child of a wealthy man who loves books and bookshops, they are expensive and comprehensive in their stock. The maroon awning without and black shelves within make it pleasing to the eye and the extended hours will suit the bio-rhythms of most browsers and buyers, who are as sensitive as to the right moment for these activities as they would be about more personal activities.

### 479 S.T.A. TRAVEL
**74 Old Brompton Road, London SW7 3LQ.**     **01-581 4751**

**Subjects:** Travel guides.
**Hours:** Mon - Fri 9.00 - 5.30. Sat 10.00 - 4.00.
**Services:** Credit cards.

Primarily a travel agency catering for the student market they do sell guides to all the continents. There are lists of their books provided and they will produce any title one is interested in.


### 480 H. KARNAC (BOOKS) LTD.
**56/58 Gloucester Road, London SW7 4QY.**     **01-584 3303**

**Subjects:** General, psychoanalysis, psychotherapy.
**Hours:** Mon - Sat 9.00 - 6.00.
**Services:** Mail order, catalogue, subscriptions to journals, library and institution supply.

This is two shops in one. One shop stocks a large range of paperbacks arranged by subject and in the other one are the general hardbacked titles and downstairs are kept the vast range of books on psychology. Altogether well laid out and run.


### 481 BRITISH MUSEUM (NATURAL HISTORY)
**Cromwell Road, London SW7 5BD.**

**Subjects:** Natural History.
**Hours:** Mon - Sat 10.00 - 5.30, Sun 2.30 - 5.30.
**Services:** Mail order, catalogues.

This is perhaps most children's favourite museum and the shop just inside the main entrance has books on animals quick and dead — humming birds and dinosaurs. The recently cleaned museum building is certainly one of London's handsomest.

# SW9 & 10

**482 UJAMAA CENTRE**
**14 Brixton Road, London SW9 6BU.**  01-582 5590

**Subjects:** Alternative books.
**Hours:** Mon - Fri 11.00 - 6.00.
**Services:** Special orders. School library supply.

The Ujamaa Centre is a co-operative and aims to stimulate interest in development education. Books are concentrated on the Third World countries, racism and international women's issues and children's books with an emphasis upon mother tongue bilinal texts. There is also literature by African and Caribbean writers, and a health and cookery section.


**483 PAPERBACK CENTRE**
**10-12 Atlantic Road, Brixton, London SW9 8HY.** 01-274 8342

**Subjects:** General, educational.
**Hours:** Mon - Sat 7.30 - 5.30 (Wed 7.30 - 2.30).
**Services:** Special orders, mail order, institutional supply, supply for events and exhibitions.

A well lit plate glass fronted shop which is unusual in this area of Brixton stocking a very good general selection of books with African and Caribbean sections for the local black community. There is a children's corner and other subjects are well defined with strong politics and history sections. They also have a good educational section as they supply schools and colleges — a very good well stocked bookshop.


**484 SAHARA BOOKS**
**378 Coldharbour Lane, London SW9 8LF.**  01-274 6785

**Subjects:** African and Caribbean literature.
**Hours:** Mon - Sat 10.00 - 6.00 (closed Wed).
**Services:** Special orders, mail order.

A spacious corner shop selling mostly paperback books on subjects related to Africa and the Caribbean — history, poetry, art and music are among the popular subjects and of course children's books. It is a non-profit making organisation and focuses its stock on the interest of the local black community.

### 485 THE HOLLYWOOD ROAD BOOKSHOP
8 Hollywood Road, London SW10 9HY.                     01-352 4659

**Subjects:** Astrology, mysticism, alternative medicine.
**Hours:** Mon - Sat 11.00 - 7.00.
**Services:** Special orders, credit cards, book search for out of print titles.

If the specialities of the shop interest you it is well worth a visit and besides the new stock there is a second hand and antiquarian section. In the future they are hoping to have a secondhand travel section.


### 486 PAN BOOKSHOP
158 Fulham Road, London SW10 9PR.                      01-373 4997

**Subjects:** General.
**Hours:** Mon - Sat 10.00 - 10.30. Sun 2.30 - 6.30.
**Services:** Special orders for any book in print.

This is a fairly large modern shop which specialises in paperbacks. The interior of the shop is well lit with the stock clearly displayed under subject headings. There is a separate section for hardbacked books and quite a good range of guides and maps is sold.


### 487 WORDS ETCETERA
327 Fulham Road,                                        01-352 3186
London SW10 9QL.                         Peter Jolliffe 01-351 2143

**Subjects:** Modern first editions, illustrated books.
**Hours:** Mon - Fri 10.00 - 6.00.
**Services:** Mail order (catalogue).

A bell to ring before entering up stairs to two rooms fitted with shelves of books. Obviously more geared to Mail Order although personal visits are welcome. This company specialises in modern first editions and illustrated books. In fact two businesses of similar nature are housed here as Peter Tolliffe has a similar stock but there seemed very little indication of division except different phone numbers. A great number of books but you would need guidance to find your subject.

# SW11-16

**488 MARTIN**
66-68 St. Johns Road,
Clapham Junction, London SW11 1PT.    01-223 9415

**Subjects:** General.
**Hours:** Mon 7.30 - 5.30. Tue - Sat 7.30 - 6.00.
**Services:** Special orders, credit cards.

One corner of Martin's is made over to books in this branch with a paperback stand down the centre selling the usual popular titles. Atlases, maps and dictionaries are stocked with a smattering of titles in most subjects.


**489 BATTERSEA ARTS CENTRE BOOKSHOP**
Old Town Hall, 176 Lavender Hill, SW11 5TG.    01-223 6557

**Subjects:** The Arts, general.
**Hours:** Wed - Sun 11.30 - 9.30.
**Services:** Special orders, credit cards.

The old town hall is used as a theatre now and a large room is made over to the sale of books, principally on theatre but with the arts in general quite well represented.


**490 THE BOLINGBROKE BOOKSHOP**
147 Northcote Road, SW11 6QB.    01-223 9344

**Subjects:** General, travel, children.
**Hours:** Mon - Sat 9.30 - 5.30 (Wed 9.30 - 1.00) (Thu 9.30 - 8.00).
**Services:** Special orders, credit cards.

An attractive corner shop with a spiral staircase inside (not for public use). They classify their stock as 'middle of the road' and keep a good travel and children's section, also, which people find convenient, a new publications section. In an area of book stalls and bargain bookshops this deserves to prosper.

### 491 POPULAR BOOK CENTRE
143 Lavender Hill, SW11 5QJ.

**Subjects:** General, secondhand.
**Hours:** Mon - Sat 10.00 - 5.30.
**Services:** Exchange with half price credit.

Plenty of reading here, some well 'thumbed' as they operate an exchange service but many subjects are covered although fiction is probably to the forefront.

### 492 BALHAM FOOD AND BOOK CO-OP
92 Balham High Road,, SW12 9AA.          01-673 0946

**Subjects:** Community issues.
**Hours:** Mon - Fri 9.30 - 6.00 (closed Wed). Sat 9.30 - 5.30.
**Services:** Special orders.

The books are kept at the rear of the health food section and there is a café upstairs. Most of the books take a radical or alternative line on political, sexual and racial subjects but they feel they are geared to local community interests.

### 493 ADDISONS
137 Balham High Road, SW12 9AY.          01-675 1143

**Subjects:** General paperbacks and remainders.
**Hours:** Mon - Sat 8.30 - 6.00.
**Services:** Special orders.

Half bookshop half confectioners, the stock is popular paperback and some remaindered hardbacks. There is a small section of G.C.E. revision titles.

## 494 RAZZALL'S RIVERSIDE BOOKS
**36A Barnes High Street, Barnes, SW13 9LP.**     **01-878 7859**

**Subjects:** General, local history.
**Hours:** Mon - Sat 9.00 - 5.30.
**Services:** Special orders.

Barnes is one of those enclaves of middle class civilization which dot the south west of London and manage to concentrate some worthwhile shops together of which this is one. The literary pages of the Sunday papers and weekly magazines are probably the main stimulus for buying new titles and they are sure to be found here and if not the owner makes a twice weekly visit to London publishers to maintain stocks and meet demands. The aforesaid proprietor is a literary man himself, as are probably many of the locals, and so the standard of book selection is good.

## 495 GORDONS
**8-9 High Street, Barnes, SW13 9LW.**     **01-878 1181**

**Subjects:** General.
**Hours:** Mon - Sat 9.00 - 1.00, 2.00 - 5.30. (Wed 9.00 - 1.00).
**Services:** Credit cards.

The shop sells popular paperbacks, cooking and childrens books but these are rather a sideline to the selling of stationery and toys.

## 496 BARNES BOOKS
**60 Church Road, Barnes, London SW13 ODQ.**     **01-741 0786**

**Subjects:** General.
**Hours:** Mon - Sat 9.30 - 5.30.
**Services:** Special orders, Credit cards.

Good parking will make this a convenient place to stop at this general bookshop in Barnes. A central table with chairs is a civilised way to display some of their hardback titles but surrounding shelves hold a good selection of hard and paperbacks in general subjects with a strong childrens section. Gill Metcalfe, the owner is on hand with helpful advice.

**497 'CAMPION'**
**71 White Hart Lane, Barnes, SW13 OPP.**         **01-878 6688**

**Subjects:** General.
**Hours:** Mon - Sat 10.00 - 1.00, 2.00 - 6.00.
**Services:** Credit cards.

This is an upmarket gift shop with a small, well stocked book section of mostly hobbies and childrens books, rather on the expensive side.


**498 VANDELEUR**                                                    **01-393 7752**
**69 Sheen Lane, London SW14 8AD.**                  **01-878 6837**

**Subjects:** Antiquarian and secondhand general.
**Hours:** Mon - Sat 11.30 - 6.00 - but moveable, advisable to
**Services:** phone.
Mail order - catalogue, wants list.

A tiny shop selling books priced from 5p to £1000, particularly on travel, topography, mountaineering and big game hunting. The owner is a helpful guide to the stock but it is advisable to phone first as he is often out treasure hunting himself.


**499 AT THE SIGN OF THE DRAGON**
**131 Sheen Lane, London SW14 8AE.**                **01-876 3855**

**Subjects:** Science fiction, fantasy, childrens books.
**Hours:** Mon - Sat 10.00 - 6.00 (Wed 10.00 - 1.30). Open until 8.00 p.m. the third Friday of each month.
**Services:** Special orders, credit cards, mail order, catalogue.

Space and time travellers would do well to arrive here. The shop makes a speciality of those alternative modes of transport and imagination, which seem to have a hold on the contemporary reader, who perhaps despairs of the more mundane probabilities on offer.

### 500 RICHARD WORTH
**Putney Bridge Bookshop,**
**7-9 Lower Richmond Road, Putney, SW15 1JN.**  01-788 9006

**Subjects:** General, politics, feminism.
**Hours:** Mon 12.00 - 6.00. Tue - Sat 10.00 - 6.00.
**Services:** Special orders, credit cards.

The shop is just around the corner from Putney High Street facing the river. They have a good general range of new books with politics and sociology well represented. Down a spiral staircase is the other part of this shared shop selling new and secondhand "Womens Literature."


### 501 COBB AND WEBB BOOKSELLERS
**J. & S. Willison**
**21 Lacy Road, Putney, SW15 1NH.**  01-789 8840

**Subjects:** Antiquarian and general secondhand.
**Hours:** Mon - Sat 10.30 - 5.30. Monday to Friday closed 2.00 - 3.00 p.m.
**Services:** Books bought.

Literature, theatre, natural history and the performing arts are the main themes here, with a selection of first editions for collectors. The olfactory senses are gratified here with that special blend of leather and mustiness half remembered from our church going days.

## 502 W.H. SMITH & SONS
### 111 Putney High Street, SW15 1SS.                01-788 2573

**Subjects:** General.
**Hours:** Mon - Sat 8.30 - 5.30.
**Services:** Special orders, credit cards.

This is a large WHS, centrally situated in this remarkably busy High Street. The ground floor has the stationery items and magazines, but stretches back to a well stocked record and cassette department.

The first floor is a very large room — hall might be a better word — jam packed with books of every description both in the wall fixtures and on the central display tables.

This is clearly the bookshop for Putney and a first class WHS shop.

Putney High Street, as everybody knows, should be three times its present width and parking is a fearsome problem, but somehow trade seems to thrive in this community lying just west of its very handsome Thames crossing.


## 503 RICHARD LALLY LTD.
### 152 Upper Richmond Road, SW15 2SW.              01-788 9123

**Subjects:** General, secondhand and antiquarian.
**Hours:** Mon - Sat 10.00 - 5.00 (closed Thu).

Mainly an antique shop with a room to the rear holding the books, which were usually acquired when buying the antique furniture which is their main line.


## 504 W.H. SMITH & SON
### 180-182 Streatham High Road, SW16 1BH.          01-677 3031/2

**Subjects:** General.
**Hours:** Mon - Sat 8.30 - 5.30.
**Services:** Special orders, credit cards.

One of the larger Smiths stocking a good range of books, spaciously housed at first floor level.

## 505 WALTONS
**15-17 Streatham High Road, SW16 1DS.**  01-763 3334

**Subjects:** General.
**Hours:** Mon - Fri 7.00 - 6.00. Sat 8.00 - 6.00.
**Services:** Special orders.

This is a large stationers and confectioners with a small selection of hand and paperbacked books with atlases prominent amongst them.


## 506 MANNA CHRISTIAN CENTRE
**149 Streatham High Road, SW16 1PW.**  01-769 8588

**Subjects:** Christian literature.
**Hours:** Mon - Sat 9.30 - 5.30.
**Services:** Special orders.

This shop stocks a comprehensive range of christian literature; bibles, Sunday school books, devotional literature and a supporting range of tapes, records and cassettes. A bright and friendly shop where those in need can drop in for a chat or a little counselling.


## 507 VILLAGE BOOKS
**17 Shrubbery Road, Stretham, SW16 2AS.**  01-677 2667

**Subjects:** General, antiquarian, secondhand.
**Hours:** Mon - Sat 10.30 - 7.00.
**Services:** Special orders, mail order.

An interesting shop just off Streatham High Road dealing in books which the local W.H. Smith does not cover. Social science, the occult and the women's movement are prominant amongst their titles and at the rear of the shop the antiquarian and secondhand is being developed.


## 508 NATIONAL BOOK EXCHANGE
**193 Streatham High Road, SW16 6EG.**  01-677 3740

**Subjects:** General, secondhand paperbacks.
**Hours:** Mon - Sat 10.00 - 7.00.
**Services:** Book exchange.

Rather a grandiose title for a secondhand paperback shop but this is a service which apparently fulfills a need. Much of the exchanged stock is well fingered.

# SW17-19

**509 BEC BUSINESS BOOKS**
**15 Trinity Road, SW17 7SD.**                             **01-767 5356**

**Subjects:** Business studies, management, educational.
**Hours:** Mon - Fri 9.00 - 5.00.
**Services:** Special orders (including imported American business books). Mail order, institutional supply.

Counter service here but the staff are helpful. They have books on computing science, politics, management and medicine.


**510 BOOKSPREAD**
**58 Tooting Bec Road, SW17 8BE.**                    **01-767 6377/4551**

**Subjects:** Childrens books.
**Hours:** Mon - Fri 10.00 - 5.00 (Thu 10.00 - 9.00). Sat 10.00 - 3.00.
**Services:** Mail order, special orders, story telling, reading advisory service.

An orange painted front marks this from other houses in the road and though one has to ring a bell to enter don't be put off as this is a most comprehensive bookshop and centre for children up to the age of eighteen. The stock attempts to be non-racist and non-sexist and has books in many languages to help immigrant parents. There is a front room for children up to eight years and a back room for older ones, a benign discrimination I think, for all. Story telling goes on, visits from authors and much else to encourage the reading habit.


**511 SWANS BOOKSTALL**
**No. 5 Tooting Market,**
**Tooting High Street, Sw17 ORH.**                         **01-672 4980**

**Subjects:** General.
**Hours:** Mon - Fri 9.00 - 5.30 (closed Wed)
**Services:** Exchange of half priced paperbacks.

The setting of new and secondhand paperbacks as well as the book exchange side of things has been going on here for thirteen years which speaks of some success. Some rather garish comics are also sold.

### 512 MARTIN THE NEWSAGENT
**38-39 The Arndale Centre,
Wandsworth, SW18 4TE.**                          **01-874 5110**

**Subjects:** General.
**Hours:** Mon - Sat 8.30 - 5.30.
**Services:** Special orders, credit cards.

A newsagent but quite good on gardening, cooking and travel with, of course, popular hard and paperbacked books as their stock in trade.


### 513 PLUS BOOKS
**19 Abbey Parade, Merton High Street, SW19 1DG. 01-542 1665**

**Subjects:** New and secondhand paperbacks.
**Hours:** Mon - Sat 9.00 - 6.00.
**Services:** Book exchange.

A large stock of new and secondhand books to buy or exchange from. I wonder if P.L.R. takes into account the exchange side of the business — authors be on your guard!


### 514 NATIONAL SCHIZOPHRENIA FELLOWSHIP BOOKSHOP
**5 Victoria Crescent, Wimbledon, SW19 1LG.**
**Subjects:** General.
**Hours:** Mon - Sat 10.00 - 4.00.

No one should be in two minds about going in here. It is a charity, with all stock donated by the public and money taken supporting the cause. The staff work on a voluntary basis. Because of the way the stock is procured it could be quite a good place for 'finds'. Everything is clearly headed and the variety is surprising.

## 515 THE LITTLE BOOKSHOP
### 39b The Broadway, Wimbledon, SW19 1QD.  01-543 1031

**Subjects:** General.
**Hours:** Mon - Sat 9.30 - 6.00.
**Services:** Special orders.

It is a small shop but the available space has been imaginatively adapted to hold a generally literary stock, with poetry and drama to the fore, but general books and a good childrens section are also available. Sout West London seems much happier ground for the bibliophile than its compass opposite.

## 516 TAKE 5 BOOKSHOP
### 5 Prince of Wales Terrace,
### Wimbledon, SW19 3RN.  01-947 4850

**Subjects:** General, secondhand.
**Hours:** Mon, Tue, Thu, Fri 9.30 - 5.30, Wed 9.00 - 3.00, Sat 9.00 - 4.00.

Under the threat of re-development opposite Wimbledon station this bookshop has an interesting stock of secondhand and paperback books in good order, so you can browse through the subject of your choice.

## 517 ELYS LTD.
### 16 St. George's Road, Wimbledon, SW19 4DP.  01-946 9191

**Subjects:** General.
**Hours:** Mon - Fri 9.00 - 5.30, Sat 9.00 - 6.00.

Elys is a department store and books have part of the ground floor to display themselves. Mostly popular stuff with current T.V. titles prominently displayed on tables. Atlases, guides and dictionaries well represented.

### 518 HILL BOOKSHOP
**87 High Street, Wimbledon, SW19 5BY.**         **01-946 0198**

**Subjects:** General, reference, children.
**Hours:** Mon - Sat 9.30 - 5.30 (Wed 9.30 - 1.00).
**Services:** Special orders.

Located in attractive Wimbledon Village this two roomed shop keeps a good general stock in the front, the rear is given over entirely to childrens books.

### 519 CHILDREN'S BOOKSHOP
**66 High Street, Wimbledon Village, SW19 5EE.**    **01-947 2038**

**Subjects:** Childrens Books up to 16 years old.
**Hours:** Mon - Sat 9.00 - 5.30.
**Services:** Credit cards, Special orders, School supply, Mail order.

Catering for children and parents bringing up children, this bright red fronted bookshop in Wimbledon Village is a joy to visit with its cheery atmosphere. Shelves of both paper and hardback books backed by tapes are arranged in age with a rear room devoted to the 'under fives' with many cloth books, reading schemes and scattered toys to keep the toddlers amused. Helpful and interested assistance is at hand making this shop well worth a trip to visit.

### 520 W.H. SMITH & SON
**Wimbledon Station, SW19 7NL.**         **01-946 6143**

**Subjects:** General.
**Hours:** Mon - Fri 6.00 - 5.45. 7.00 - 5.00.
**Services:** Special orders, credit cards.

This is quite a good little station bookshop although the opening hours are obviously meant to suit a lower animal, the newspaper reader. Quite spacious and easy to look around.

### 521 FIELDERS
**54 Wimbledon Hill Road, Wimbledon, SW19 7PA. 01-946 5044**

**Subjects:** General, educational, guides and maps.
**Hours:** Mon - Sat 9.00 - 5.30.
**Services:** Special orders, credit cards, educational supply.

One enters apparently a stationers but a glance onwards reveals a huge well supplied general bookshop. The paperback sectionm is excellent and is well supported by a comprehensive range of hard backed titles. The travel and map section is one of the more prominent ones but the whole is what one would ask of a good local bookshop.

### 522 WIMBLEDON EVANGELICAL BOOK CENTRE
**2 Queens Road, SW19 8LN.**                     **01-947 2982**

**Subjects:** Christian literature.
**Hours:** Mon - Sat 10.00 - 5.00 (Wed 10.00 - 1.00).
**Services:** Special orders, church supply.

Situated at the back of the town hall this religious bookshop keeps up a standard which it shares with other such shops of being a light, bright and spacious place with a cheerful atmosphere. The stock is as one would expect with quite a good children's section.

# W1

### 600 DEBENHAMS
**334-348, Oxford Street, London, W1A 1EF.**

01-580 3000
(ex 357)

**Subjects:** General.
**Hours:** 9.30 - 6.00 (Thu 9.30 - 7.30).
**Services:** Credit cards, Special orders.

The book department is on the lower ground floor and has a perhaps better than average selection of popular titles and often a table of books at half-price.

### 601 JOHN LEWIS & CO.
**278-306 Oxford Street, London W1A 1EX.**    01-629 7711

**Subjects:** Children's books.
**Hours:** Mon - Fri 9.00 - 5.30 (Thu 9.30 - 8.00), Sat 9.00 - 1.00.
**Services:** John Lewis cards.

The children's books make a pleasant extension to the toy department on the fourth floor. Imaginatively displayed and easy for youngsters to see. The sections are headed 'First Reading', 'Classics', etc.

### 602 THE PENGUIN BOOKSHOP
**Fenwick of Bond Street,
63, New Bond Street, London, W1A 3BS.**    01-629 9161

**Subjects:** General.
**Hours:** Mon - Sat 9.30 - 5.30 except Thurs 9.30 - 7.30.
**Services:** Special Orders. (Post a book). Credit cards.

A large corner in the basement of Fenwick's is made into an attractive Penguin bookshop which tries to stock everything in print in Penguin. Other publishers are also represented with some hardback new titles. Trolleys hold books on clearly marked subjects centrally and the walls are shelved with a good general stock making this the only bookshop of current titles in Bond Street.

### 603 CHARLOTTE ROBINSON
**35 Great Pulteney, Soho, London W1E 9AA.**     **01-437 3683**

**Subjects:** Modern first editions, illustrated and childrens, specialities the Great War and Henry Williamson.
**Hours:** Mon - Sat 11.00 - 6.00.
**Services:** Mail Order (catalogues)

Three booksellers contribute to the excellent stock of this bookshop in the heart of Soho. Mainly literature as the majority of stock is modern first editions with childrens and illustrated books prominent. Literature of the Great War is a speciality and books by Henry Williamson are the favourite of Clearwater. Obviously a collectors bookshop with a welcoming atmosphere.


### 604 THE SCRIPTURE UNION BOOKSHOP
**5 Wigmore Street, London W1H 0AD.**     **01-486 2561**

**Subjects:** Christian literature, records.
**Hours:** Mon, Tue, Fri, Sat 9.00 - 5.30, Wed 9.30 - 5.30, Thu 9.00 - 7.00.
**Services:** Special mail orders, book tokens.

This double-fronted stone faced shop is just around the corner from Cavendish Square. Inside it is quite large, brightly lit and plenty of room for browsing. The books are arranged under specialist headings. Doctrine, Christian life, etc. There is an impressive cabinet display of bibles and prayer books.


### 605 PADDINGTON & FRIENDS
**22 Crawford Place, London W1H 1JE.**     **01-262 1866**

**Subjects:** Paddington Books, Thursday Books, Ola the Polga — Childrens Books.
**Hours:** Mon - Sat 10.00 - 5.00. Closed 1st & 2nd Sats in month.
**Services:** Mail order, Book tokens, catalogue.

This is a pretty, white painted shop just off the Edgware Road near the junction with Marylebone Road. It is one floor at street level and sells all the Paddington Bear Merchandise which includes a small selection of books. A fascinating shop for children, brightly lit with Paddington Bear toys, games and bed linen attractively displayed. It is associated with Action Research which is a charity for crippled children.

### 606 FOYLES EDUCATIONAL LTD.                01-262 4699
37 Upper Berkeley Street, London W1H 8AS.    01-262 5310

**Subjects:** The whole educational spectrum
**Hours:** Mon - Fri 9.00 - 5.30.
**Services:** Mail order, catalogue, special orders.

Not connected with Foyles of Charing Cross Road, this shop works closely with Dillons of Malet Street. A most excellent and comprehensive shop located on two floors (ground and basement). Caters for the educational needs of schools, libraries, the Open University, etc: it has more textbooks for junior and secondary schools than any other shop in the country. There is a Central London English language showroom with cassettes and listening facilities. The whole range of Penguin paperbacks is carried.


### 607 SELFRIDGES (BOOK DEPARTMENT)
400 Oxford Street, London W1M 1AB.        01-629 1234

**Subjects:** General, best sellers, travel.
**Hours:** Mon - Sat 9.00 - 5.30, Thu 9.00 - 7.00.
**Services:** Mail order, credit cards, book tokens.

A generous part of this huge department store is given over to books. It is a well designed, open plan section and easy to browse in. The emphasis is on the current best seller list, though they are not negligible in cookery and travel books. At the time of going to press it was on the first floor.


### 608 THE EARLY MUSIC SHOP
47 Chiltern Street, London W1M 1HN.        01-935 1242

**Subjects:** Music.
**Hours:**
**Services:** Mail order, Special orders, Credit cards.

Brian Jordan music books have space in the basement for a selection of sheet music and books about instruments and musicians. Their main business is mail order outside London but some books can be seen here.

**609 CHRISTOPHER FOSS**
120 Baker Street, London W1M 1LD.                 01-935 9364

**Subjects:** General, feminist literature, psychiatry, philosophy, photography, travel, maps.
**Hours:** Mon - Fri 9.00 - 6.00, Sat 10.00 - 5.00.
**Services:** Credit cards, book tokens, special orders.

The shop has two large glass windows: on the ground floor stationery is sold and downstairs books. The book department seems rather cramped but is a mine of good things, with 'women's press,' and modern fiction and poetry strongly represented.

**610 THE DAVID & CHARLES BOOKSHOP**
36 Chiltern Street, London W1M 1PH.                 01-486 6959

**Subjects:** General and specialising in Railways and Transport.
**Hours:** Mon - Fri 9.30 - 5.30. Sat 10.00 - 1.00.
**Services:** Credit cards, Special orders, Mail order (Lists for Railways)

On the ground floor are the books in general subjects with several rooms making browsing interesting. Downstairs the basement is devoted to their specialist railway and transport section but consists of a good stock of books on these subjects all new and carefully arranged.

**611 WHOLEFOOD BOOKS**
24, Paddington Street, W1M 4DR.                 01-935 3924

**Subjects:** Nutrition, health, ecology, whole food cookery, natural childbirth, orthomolecular medicine.
**Hours:** Mon 8.45 - 6.00. Tue - Fri 8.45 - 1.00.
**Services:** Mail order.

Since its move the Wholefood Shop has improved it's book section at the rear. The subjects are the same but more attractively displayed with green the prominant colour — perhaps representing the countryside — and books for the Health fanatic with orthomolecular medicine and natural childbirth among the subjects.

## 612 THE CHIMES MUSIC SHOP
65 Marylebone High Street, London W1M 3AH.   01-935 1587

**Subjects:** Music, sheet music.
**Hours:** Mon - Fri 9.00 - 5.30, Sat 9.00 - 2.00.
**Services:** Mail order, record tokens, discount for students.

It is no accident that the Royal Academy of Music and Trinity College are only a trumpet blast away. The paraphernalia of the trade is on display in the window. The shop is rather narrow inside with shelves of sheet music and standard reference books.

## 613 B.B.C. PUBLICATIONS
35 Marylebone High Street, London W1M 4AA.
01-407 6961
01-580 5577

**Subjects:** B.B.C. Publications.
**Hours:** Mon - Fri 9.30 - 5.30, Sat occasional.
**Services:** Mail order, catalogue.

A small shop selling the Corporation's books: there is also a bookstall in the foyer of the B.B.C., Portland Place.

## 614 READS OF MARYLEBONE HIGH STREET
83 Marylebone High Street,
London W1M 4AL.   01-935 9303

**Subjects:** General secondhand, specialising in Art and Literature.
**Hours:** Mon - Fri 9.00 - 6.00. Sat 9.00 - 5.00. Sun 12.00 - 6.00.
**Services:** Credit cards, Mail order.

This shop was purpose built in the middle of the 19th century and is one of the most attractive bookshops with plenty of room and a gallery which adds to its fascination. Reads now fill its shelves with books on most subjects, art and literature being their strongest sections.

### 615 CLAUDE GILL BOOKS
**10-12 James Street, London W1M 5HN.** Ex-directory

**Subjects:** General.
**Hours:** Mon - Sat 9.30 - 6.00 except Thu 9.30 - 8.00.

This shop has two entrances, one leading into the fascinations of St Christophers Place. Claude Gill have spent time and money to up-date their shops making them bright and modern. This one is on two floors with plenty of room for their general section. They specialise in popular titles but do not neglect cookery, history and art.

### 616 E. JOSEPH
**1 Vere Street, London, W1M 9HQ.** 01-493 8353/4/5

**Subjects:** Antiquarian including English Literature. Illustrated and Fine Bindings.
**Hours:** Mon - Fri 9.30 - 5.30 or by appointment.
**Services:** Mail Order (Catalogue). Credit cards.

A far cry from the Charing Cross Road premises with the disadvantage of a lift but advantage of splendid rooms lined with books and antique tables and chairs to make viewing a pleasure. English literature is the strong subject but sets, private presses and illustrated books are all here with natural history and travel favourites among the excellent stock of fine books.

### 617 R.I.B.A. BOOKSHOP
**66 Portland Place, London W1N 4AD.** 01-580 5533

**Subjects:** Architecture.
**Hours:** Mon - Fri 9.30 - 5.30.
**Services:** Subscriptions to architectural magazines.

Located on the premises of the Royal Institute of British Architects is this carpeted shop which stocks all R.I.B.I. publications. Well displayed and clearly sectioned. Contemporary in appearance.

### 618 KIMPTONS MEDICAL BOOKSHOP
205 Great Portland Street, London W1N 6LR.  01-580 6381

**Subjects:** Medical.
**Hours:** Mon - Fri 9.00 - 5.30, Sat 9.30 - 5.00.
**Services:** Mail order, catalogue, credit cards, book tokens.

The arrangement inside is rather library like but the stock of medical books is well laid out and marked. A shop for the profession.


### 619 A.R. MOWBRAY & CO. LTD.  01-580 2812
28 Margaret Street, London W1N 7LB.  01-580 8614

**Subjects:** General, theology, reference, travel and second-hand theology.
**Hours:** Mon - Fri 9.00 - 5.30 (Thu 9.00 - 6.00) Closed Sat.
**Services:** Credit cards, mail order.

This shop is situated north east of Oxford Circus, it has three floors of books and is one of the half dozen or so really good general bookshops in Central London. The display of books on the ground floor will delight the browser as they are arranged in three-sided compartments by subject, providing areas of privacy. The ample paperback department is downstairs and they have added a computer section to their general subjects. Christian literature is well represented and they have a second-hand theology department in the gallery.


### 620 THE BOOK CENTRE
(THE FAMILY PLANNING ASSOCIATION)  01-636 7866
27-35 Mortimer Street, London W1N 7RS.  (Ext 45)

**Subjects:** Sex education, Birth Control, childcare, general medical.
**Hours:** Mon - Fri 10.00 - 5.00 (flexible), Sat closed.
**Services:** Mail order, book list issued, reduction on postage for bulk orders.

A small showroom at this shop with Family Planning Association books displayed. There is a receptionist at a desk to help with queries as a visit here probably entails extra bibliophilic preoccupations.

**621 R.D. FRANKS LTD.**
**Kent House, Market Place,**
**(Great Titchfield Street), London W1N 8EJ.**    **01-636 1244/5/6**

**Subjects:** Books about the clothing trade and Pattern Books.
**Hours:** Mon - Fri 9.00 - 5.00.
**Services:** Mail order catalogue, magazine subscriptions, credit cards.

A small corner shop just behind Oxford Circus and near to the fashion houses. Besides their small specialised book section they sell the tools of the trade.


**622 D.H. EVANS**
**318 Oxford Street, London W1N 9DA.**    **01-629 8800**

**Subjects:** General.
**Hours:** Mon - Sat 9.00 - 5.30 (Thu 9.30 - 7.00).
**Services:** Credit cards.

This general book department is on the third floor of the store. They mainly stock popular hard and soft backed books with some maps and guides.


**623 BONANZA BOOKS**
**(Bonanza Stores Ltd)**
**28-30 Oxford Street, London W1N 9FL.**

**Subjects:** Remainders
**Hours:** Mon - Sat 9.00 - 9.00.
**Services:** Credit Cards.

This is a new branch of an expanding chain (10 in the country) which opened mid-November 1981. With 5,000 square feet at street level, the owners claim it is perhaps the largest remainder shop in the British Isles. A stone's throw from St. Giles' circus the long trading hours should fit well with the habits of the district.

### 624 PILOT SOFTWARE LTD.
**32 Rathbone Place, London W1P 1AD.**　　　　01-636 2666

**Subjects:** Business and Home Computers.
**Hours:** Mon - Sat 9.30 - 6.00.
**Services:** Special orders.

A wide selection of books on subjects ranging from how to buy your first computer to advanced language applications. Books are mainly softback with emphasis on business computers.

### 625 BUNCH BOOKS LTD.
**14 Rathbone Place, London W1P 1DE.**　　　　01-580 6104

**Subjects:** Hi-Fi, Bruce Lee.
**Hours:** Mon - Fri 10.00 - 6.00.
**Services:** Mail Order.

Bunch Books have recently opened a showroom in the building where they have their publishing business. It is very bright and modern. Their own publications, both hard and soft backed, are mainly about hi-fi equipment and they also specialise in Bruce Lee — the Kung-Fu King. Take that!

### 626 THE BOOKEND
**50 Goodge Street, London W1P 1FB.**　　　　01-580 5132

**Subjects:** Remainders (general)
**Hours:** Mon - Fri 9.00 - 6.00, Sat 10.30 - 5.00.

A corner shop with striped awnings and tables of books on the pavement. The display of books in the window clearly marked and displaying their reduced prices, come from the upper-coffee-table end of the market.

### 627 PAPERBACKS CENTRE (NEW PARK PUBLICATIONS)
**28 Charlotte Street, London W1P 1HJ.**　　　　01-636 3532

**Subjects:** General, political (Socialist)
**Hours:** Mon - Thu 9.00 - 6.00, Fri 9.00 - 7.30, Sat 9.00 - 5.00.
**Services:** Special orders, book tokens.

A small shop with two rooms. Its strength is socialist literature in paperback but there are also a few shelves of hard back best sellers.

## 628 POLLOCK'S TOY MUSEUM
**1 Scala Street, London W1P 1LT.**           **01-636 3452**

**Subjects:** Books on dolls and toys. Theatres in book form.
**Hours:** Mon - Sat 10.00 - 5.00.
**Services:** Mail order, Museum, Toy theatre performances.

The museum shop is at street level and can be entered without paying to visit the Toy Museum and what a wonderful trip into the past with old fashioned toys and books (all new) about toys and dolls and specially selected children's books. Cut out books to make theatres including the characters with plays and Pollocks publications make this a most unusual and fascinating shop — a far cry from the computers of to-day.


## 629 MUSIC BOOK CENTRE
**78 Newman Street, London W1P 3LA.**       **01-636 7777**

**Subjects:** Music.
**Hours:** Mon - Fri 9.30 - 5.30.
**Services:** Credit cards, Mail order, Catalogue.

Song books and books relevant to the music industry are stocked here with emphasis on popular music. You can walk in to see the stock although mail order is the larger side of the business.


## 630 BOOK CLUB ASSOCIATES
**87 Newman Street, London W1P 3LE.**     **01-637 0341 Ext 236**

**Subjects:** General.
**Hours:** Mon - Fri 10.00 - 6.00, Sat 10.00 - 4.00.
**Services:** Facility to join club and purchase at reduced prices, credit card.

A large well lit carpeted showroom with well displayed books. One has to be a member of the association to purchase but one can sign up on the spot. There is an introductory offer of books at £1 each and a commitment to buy four more in the year at a reduced rate.

### 631 KIMPTONS MEDICAL BOOKSHOP
**49 Newman Street, London W1P 4BB.**     01-580 4250

**Subjects:** Medical.
**Hours:** Mon - Fri 9.30 - 5.30, Sat 9.30 - 1.30.
**Services:** Mail order, catalogue, credit cards.

The one small room has the books arranged by subject with headings on the shelves. There is also a section on popular medicine for those not in the profession. The Middlesex Hospital opposite will cure most of your discovered maladies.

### 632 STAR BOOKS INTERNATIONAL
**112 Whitfield Street, London W1P 5RU.**     01-388 9832

**Subjects:** Asian languages from India, Bangladesh and Pakistan.
**Hours:** Mon - Sat 9.00 - 7.30.
**Services:** Mail order (catalogue), Credit cards.

At first sight this appears to be a video shop but through a second door books are shelved in the main languages, and in English, of the Asian countries. General subjects are available in the five main languages and they have teaching books and children's learning series, backed by cassettes and videos.

### 633 FRENCH'S THEATRE BOOKSHOP
**52, Fitzroy Street, W1P 6JR.**     01-387 9373

**Subjects:** Theatre.
**Hours:** Mon - Fri 9.30 - 5.30.
**Services:** Special orders (catalogue), credit cards, sound effects (catalogue) play licencing.

Pre-eminent among theatre bookshops Samuel French's has been established for 150 years but has moved to a corner site just behind Warren Street tube station and will be missed in the Covent Garden area. Their new premises are modern, lacking the heavy wood of the old Southampton Street premises but they still have their excellent range of British and American theatre books, covering subjects from acting to direction, criticism to design and plays from all leading publishers in acting and reading editions.

### 634 PAPERCHASE
**216 Tottenham Court Road, London W1P 9AF.**  01-580 8496

**Subjects:** Art.
**Hours:** Mon - Sat 10.00 - 6.00 Thu 10.00 - 7.00.
**Services:** Mail order if in stock, credit cards.

This quite large shop in Tottenham Court Road sells paper artifacts from napkins to cut outs and decorations. The small book section is upstairs, most of the books are about artists and their styles and they also have colouring books.


### 635 BOOKS ETC.
**222, Tottenham Court Road, W1P 9AF.**  01-636 3270

**Subjects:** General, computing science.
**Hours:** Mon - Fri 9.00 - 6.30 (Thu 9.00 - 7.00) Sat 9.30 - 6.00.
**Services:** Special orders, credit cards.

Among so many shops specialising in radios, television sets, computers — Books Etc. has opened a branch of their general bookstore's but have a section specialising in computers with software available for the enthusiast. Otherwise they have a very good paperback fiction selection and other general subjects are covered with thought to give a good all round variety in both hard and paper back.


### 636 LION MICRO COMPUTORS
**Lion House, 227, Tottenham Court Road,**
**London, W1P OHX.**  01-580 7383

**Subjects:** Computors, micro technology.
**Hours:** Mon - Fri 9.00 - 6.00.

This comnputor company has a small book section dealing with the subject itself and the broad aspects of micro technology. There is plenty of expertise on hand.

### 637 CLAUDE GILL BOOKS
**19-23 Oxford Street, London W1R 1RF.**

**Subjects:** General.
**Hours:** Mon - Sat 9.30 - 8.00.
**Services:** Book tokens.

Enormous immitation books form the frontage of the Claude Gill shop in Oxford Street and inside its shelves and tables are attractively marked making this an inviting shop to enter. Its stock covers most fields except perhaps the technical and books arranged by subjects have a very ample stock of titles in both paperback and hardback with maps and guides near the entrance.

### 638 ATHENA
**119-121 Oxford Street, London W1R 1TF.**     **01-734 3383**

**Subjects:** General.
**Hours:** Mon - Fri 9.30 - 8.00; Sat 10.00 - 8.00.
**Services:** Credit cards.

A new parade of quality shops on the east side of Oxford Circus includes a large branch of Athena with a spacious book department downstairs.

The stock is described as upmarket but popular titles are well displayed with new titles in hardback. Gardening, Cookery, Music and a large fiction section have plenty of space and there is a selection of bargain books.

### 639 ANDREW EDMONDS
**44 Lexington Street, London W1R 3LH.**     **01-437 8594**

**Subjects:** Illustrated, antiquarian and rare books.
**Hours:** Mon - Fri 10.00 - 6.00.

Mainly a print shop but Andrew Edmonds does stock some rare books, art being one of the main subjects although illustrated books are the speciality.

### 640 BERNARD QUARITCH
5/8 Lower John Street,
Golden Square, London W1R 4AU.                    01-734 2983

**Subjects:** Antiquarian, rare books, manuscripts.
**Hours:** Mon - Fri 9.30 - 5.30 (closed 1.00 - 2.00).
**Services:** Mail order, 10 catalogues a year, valuation advice to collectors, auction services.

A rather awesome place, a minute's walk from Piccadilly Circus, with barred windows, security door and bags left with receptionist. The books are handsomely displayed against a green felt background with gold striplighting. There are nine specialist sections. Early printed books and M/S, Natural History, English Literature, Science, Medicine and Technology, Travel, Philosophy and Human Sciences, The Arts, and Private Presses. A pedigree amongst the Antiquarians: anyone who has attended the London auction houses will have seen Quaritch's at the forefront in bidding for the fine and rare books. Founded by Bernard Quaritch from Gottingen in 1847 and patronised by nineteenth Century celebrities, it was he who first published the Rubaiyat of Omar Khayyam.


### 641 SHOROUK INTERNATIONAL                    01-637 2743-4
316-318 Regent Street, W1R 5AB.                    01-580 9819

**Subjects:** Middle East.
**Hours:** Mon - Fri 9.30 - 6.00.
**Services:** Special orders, mail order (catalogue), credit cards, institutional supply.

This shop is in the part of Regent Street north of Oxford Circus and is a large premises extending over two floors. The books here are in English and Arabic, both for visitors and indigenes and cover all aspects of the heartland of the arabic world.


### 642 BOOKENDS
172, Regent Street, London, W1R 5DF.                01-734 5886/7

**Subjects:** General, Remainders.
**Hours:** Mon - Sat 10.00 - 6.00 except Thu 10.00 - 8.00.
**Services:** Special orders.

Bookends hope to make this a permanent bookshop and have two floors of reduced remainder books in subject sections. They do stock a small selection of new paperback titles.

### 643 LIBRAIRIE HACHETTE
**4 Regent Place, London W1R 5FD.**  01-734 5259

**Subjects:** Books on and from France, French language books.
**Hours:** Mon - Fri 9.30 - 6.00, Sat 9.30 - 1.00.
**Services:** Special orders for any book on the French market, library supply, subscriptions to French and international magazines.

Situated East of Regent Street this is the mecca for francophiles and francophones. Very good on the educational side with things like classic French texts for university study. They have a small travel section where national maps of France and town plans can be found. From time to time a French publishing house has an exhibition here on a given theme, and the shop will obligingly obtain foreign publications for the customer.


### 644 THE LONDON BOOKMARKET
**122 Regent Street, London W1R 5FE.**  01-439 8490

**Subjects:** Bargain books, general.
**Hours:** Mon - Sat 9.30 - 10.30. Sun 10.00 - 9.00.

New hardback books in general subjects at bargain prices here. Glossy covered remainders ideal for presents or to treat yourself when you would normally pay the full price.


### 645 WATERSTONES
**88 Regent Street, London W1R 5PA.**  01-734 0713/4

**Subjects:** General.
**Hours:** Mon - Fri 10.00 am - 10.00 pm. Sat 10.00 - 7.00 Sun 12.00 - 7.00.
**Services:** Special orders, Credit cards, Mail order, International mailing personal accounts.

This is a large two level (Ground and basement) deep rectangular shop towards Piccadilly Circus from Aquascutum. On the ground floor there is travel, fiction, biography, art and literature. Below decks is history, politics, economics, cookery and gardening — and also a classical record/tapes department. There is a central staircase leading from one level to the other.

This is the first occasion in modern times when a bookshop opening at such hours has been launched in Regent Street and it will be extremely interesting to see how the venture succeeds.

**646 TOKAMINE (JAPANESE PUBLICATION CENTRE)**
**5 Warwick Street, London W1R 5RA.**　　　　　　**01-439 8035**

**Subjects:** All things Japanese.
**Hours:** Mon - Sun 10.00 - 6.00.
**Services:** Special orders, mail order, magazine subscriptions, book lists.

A long narrow shop with a Japanese food store to the rear and books to the fore. Both these sections are on a self-service basis with a shared cash desk. Japanese music, games, posters etc. are also on sale.


**647 LIBERTY & CO. (BOOK DEPARTMENT).**
**210-220 Regent Street, London W1R 6AH.01-734 1234 Ext 336**

**Subjects:** General, cookery, children's books, travel.
**Hours:** Mon-Sat 9.30-6.00 Thu 9.30-7.00
**Services:** Special orders, mail order, credit cards, book tokens, the occasional book signing.

There is quite a small book department in this large exclusive store of world repute. The easiest access to the books is from the Great Marlborough Street entrance. Cookery is their long suit. The building is in the Tudor style, half timbered, with the coats of arms of Henry VIII's wives carved from the timbers of two men-of-war, H.M.S. Impregnable and H.M.S Hindustan.


**648 THE PENGUIN BOOKSHOP AT LIBERTY'S**
**Regent Street, London, W1R 6AH.**　　　　**01-734 1234 Ext 109**

**Subjects:** General Paperback.
**Hours:** Mon - Sat 9.30 - 6.00. Thu 9.30 - 7.00.
**Services:** Special orders, Credit cards.

At the rear of Liberty's ground floor is the Penguin bookshop which specialises in paperbacks. A large percentage of their titles is fiction but other subjects are well represented and clearly defined and although the majority of stock is from Penguin other publishers have their place especially in reference, travel, guides etc.

### 649 HAMLEY'S OF REGENT STREET LTD.
**200/202 Regent Street, London W1R 6BT.**     **01-734 3161**

**Subjects:** Children's books.
**Hours:** Mon - Sat 9.00 - 5.30.
**Services:** Mail order, book tokens, credit cards.

The book section of the world renowned toy shop is on a rather small scale and located at one end of the first floor. The younger child is rather better catered for, though the age range goes up to seventeen.


### 650 BOOTS THE CHEMISTS
**182 Regent Street, London W1R 6HY.**     **01-734 4934/7**

**Subjects:** General (paperbacks only).
**Hours:** Mon - Sat 9.00 - 5.30. Thurs 9.00 - 6.30.
**Services:** Credit cards, Boots own credit card, book tokens.

This is a small book department on the first floor chemists store. Very much geared to topical books mentioned on t.v. or radio.


### 651 BOOSEY & HAWKES LTD.
**295 Regent Street, London W1R 8JH.**     **01-580 2060**

**Subjects:** Music; with emphasis on instrument playing.
**Hours:** Mon - Sat 9.00 - 5.00.
**Services:** Mail order, special orders, credit cards.

One passes through a long carpeted showroom of musical instruments to get to the book section at the rear of the shop. The emphasis of the books displayed is on performing the art and there is a wide selection of sheet music.

### 652 WISDOM PUBLICATIONS
**23 Dering Street (2nd Floor),
London W1R 9AA.**                                   **01-499 0925**

**Subjects:** Buddhism, including manuscripts and teachings not available elsewhere.
**Hours:** Mon - Fri 9.00 - 6.00 also many evenings and weekends.
**Services:** Mail order (catalogue), Credit cards.

Wisdom's own publications can be seen here in an office atmosphere together with other publishers titles on Buddhism. As they are classed as a charity it is run on a semi-voluntary basis and their aim is to help perpetuate the Mahayana tradition of Buddhism by presenting it in English in its various forms, theory and practice, biography, history, art and literature for children. They are situated in a small street opposite D.H. Evans off Oxford Street and is worth making a lift journey to the second floor to receive courteous and enthusiastic advice on their extensive stock.


### 653 SCHOTT & CO. LTD.
**48 Great Marlborough Street, London W1V 1DB. 01-437 1246/8**

**Subjects:** Music, sheet music.
**Hours:** Mon - Fri 9.00 - 5.00.
**Services:** Credit cards.

Most of the stock is sheet music with a small book section on musical studies and the theory of music.


### 654 QUARTET BOOKSHOP
**45/46 Poland Street, London W1V 3DF.**              **01-437 1019**

**Subjects:** General, Own Publication, Women's Press.
**Hours:** Mon - Fri 10.00 - 6.00.
**Services:** Special orders, credit cards.

A small brightly lit shop in a street which runs south from Oxford Street. Quartet Books, who are publishers, own the shop and feature their own books which are primarily 'Women's Press, but they also have books on cooking, wine, photography and new novels.

### 655 THE POLAND STREET BOOK CENTRE
9 Poland Street, London W1V 3DG.  01-439 3658

**Subjects:** Environment studies.
**Hours:** Mon - Fri 9.30 - 5.00.
**Services:** Special requests by post.

This bookshop acts as a retail agency for the environmental pressure groups which are located in the building above.


### 656 THE CRAFTSMEN POTTERS SHOP
William Blake House, Marshall Street,
London W1V 1FD.  01-437 7605

**Subjects:** Books on pottery and ceramics.
**Hours:** Mon - Fri 10.00 - 5.30. Sat 10.30 - 5.00.
**Services:** Credit cards, Special orders.

A fine selection of hand made pottery takes up the majority of space in this unusual shop but they have a small section of books on all aspects of pottery for both the professional and the amateur. History of ceramics, techniques, health are among the aspects covered with plenty of space to browse.


### 657 PETERS MUSIC SHOP
119-125 Wardour Street, London W1V 4DN.  01-437 1456

**Subjects:** Music.
**Hours:** Mon - Fri 9.30 - 5.30.
**Services:** Mail order, catalogue.

Not just Peters publications but all music publishers titles are stocked making this an excellent shop for anyone wanting books connected with the music world. Biographies and Histories have their sections with printed music taking up the majority of space but a corner is reserved for books published by the Oxford University Press.


### 658 RAM BOOKS
10-11 Moor Street, W1V 5LJ.  01-437 6362

**Subjects:** General, mainly paperback.
**Hours:** Mon - Sat 9.30 - 8.30.

This shop is changing its image in Soho to provide a general stock of books including guides and maps.

### 659 ATHENA BOOKSHOP
Trocadero Centre, Coventry Street,
London W1V 7FE.　　　　　　　　　　　　　　　01-734 5061

**Subjects:** General.
**Hours:** Mon - Sun 10.00 a.m. - 11.00 p.m.
**Services:** Credit cards.

Athena have street frontage at this new centre near Piccadilly Circus and have two floors of books with subjects chosen to serve the general London public and tourists who will find their long opening hours convenient being open before and after the theatres and restaurants. Traditional Athena stock is backed by hard and paperback books, with air-conditioning for our hot summers!

### 660 GLC LONDON TOURIST & INFORMATION CENTRE
25 Shaftesbury Avenue,　　　　　01-437 1304 ex Bookshop
London W1V 7HA.　　　　　Tourist Information 01-437 1384

**Subjects:** Current and Historical information on London.
**Hours:** Mon - Sun 10.00 - 8.00.
**Services:** Books, Maps, Guides and Special orders.
　　　　　　Theatre bookings for GLC South Bank Concert Halls.

At the rear of these premises just off Piccadilly Circus is this bookshop specialising in maps, guides and general information on London including some hardback books both historical and current with London as their main theme.

### 661 THE VINTAGE MAGAZINE SHOP
39-41 Brewer Street, London W1V 7HF.　　　　01-439 8525

**Subjects:** Cinema and Theatre. Mainly secondhand. Magazines and childrens annuals.
**Hours:** Mon - Fri 10.30 - 7.00. Sun 2.00 - 7.00.
**Services:** Credit cards.

Two floors of this large shop are filled with magazines and books about movies and the theatre taking a step back into the past with Picture Post, old Radio Times and bound volumes of magazines including The Strand. The books are mainly situated in the basement and it is an interesting trip amongst the memorabilia.

## 662 THE ATOZ BOOK CENTRE
**3 Macclesfield Street, London W1V 7LB.**   **01-734 4142**

**Subjects:** Martial arts.
**Hours:** Mon - Sat 10.00 - 6.00.
**Services:** Mail order, catalogue at 30p.

This small shop on Shaftesbury Avenue has all the books a fighting monk may require from Kendo to Kung-Fu. Samurais will have to look elsewhere.


## 663 AUTOMOBILE ASSOCIATION
**Fanum House, 5, New Coventry Street, W1V 8HT.**   **01-839 4355**

**Subjects:** Motoring, guides, maps.
**Hours:** Mon - Fri 9.00 - 5.00. Sat 9.00 - 12.30.
**Services:** Credit cards.

This is the H.Q. of the A.A. and here besides all sorts of gadgets for the car one can purchase a good range of guides, atlases and maps, also some titles of general interest on the countryside and places of interest.

## 664 HATCHARDS
### 187 Piccadilly, London W1V 9DA.               01-439 9921

**Subjects:** General
**Hours:** Mon - Fri 9.00 - 5.30, Sat 9.00 - 1.00.
**Services:** Mail Order, Catalogue, Credit Cards, will obtain any British Book in Print. Section of large print books for the visually handicapped.

This shop has only one other possible rival in London to match its comprehensiveness and the expertise of its staff.

It was started in 1797 by John Hatchard with a capital of £5 and is now a Collins subsidiary with a £3m a year turnover. There are over 350,000 titles in stock, which will surprise those who judge it only by its small attractive exterior. It is a prestigious shop, with four Royal Warrants, many signing sessions by famous authors, and it gives an 'author of the year' party for about 200 luminaries of the writing and publishing world. There are four levels to the shop.

In the basement are the paperbacks with the fiction arranged alphabetically by authors around the walls, and there are tables with new titles and other specialities scattered throughout.

As they have acquired the shop next door Hatchards have been able to expand many of their sections particularly the travel and paperback department which now have very much more room enabling it to be approached directly from street level. Also at street level is current hardback fiction, biographies etc. at the front of the shop and at the back they keep the non-fictional titles — travel, history, religion, reference and so on.

On the first floor they have sport, gardening (huge!) art and other sections which are perhaps grouped for their illustrative or photographic suitability. The second floor has a wonderful children's section. One for classical literature and literary studies, and at the front an antiquarian and first editions department, with some of their treasures on display in cabinets.

### 665 CLAUDE GILL BOOKS
213 Piccadilly, London W1V 9LD.                          **Ex Directory**

**Subjects:** General, travel, children's books.
**Hours:** Mon - Sat 9.30 - 8.00, Sun 11.00 - 7.00.

Strategically situated near Piccadilly Circus this generously proportioned bookshop concentrates on popular lines over quite a large range of subjects, suited to the various interests of a passing trade. At ground floor level, these general books are found and downstairs in the basement the stock is divided between children's and bargain books: here they also sell cards and posters.

### 666 ROYAL ACADEMY OF ARTS BOOKSHOP
Burlington House,
Picadilly, London W1V ODS.                              **01-734 9052**

**Subjects:** Art.
**Hours:** Mon - Sun 10.00 - 5.30.
**Services:** Mail order for exhibition catalogues.

The shop which sells artists' materials as well as books and catalogues, is at the top of the grand staircase. They have a large range of quality reproductions from current exhibitions or from their permanent collection, as well as more general books on art.

### 667 WORLD OF BOOKS (PICCADILLY RARE BOOKS LTD.)
30 Sackville Street, London, W1X 1DB.            **01-437 2135**
                                                                **01-734 6608**

**Subjects:** Secondhand books with emphasis on travel, cookery, biography.
**Hours:** Mon - Sunday (all week) 10.00 - 6.00.
**Services:** Credit cards, mail order, catalogues on travel and cookery, search service.

This is a huge secondhand bookshop, perhaps the largest in London. The books are located under their subject headings, spread over a ground floor and basement. Downstairs you will find Victoriana, detective and more general fiction. The shop is bare boarded and has a little of the warehouse about it but will reward the diligent and the enthusiastic browser with finds.

### 668 NIGEL GREENWOOD LTD. BOOKS
**4 New Burlington Street, London W1X 1FE.**

**Subjects:** Books and catalogues on the Contemporary Arts.
**Hours:** Mon - Fri 10.00 - 6.00.
**Services:** Mail order (catalogue).

Nigel Greenwood will be opening at this new address in the middle of June where his very extensive stock of books and catalogues can be seen. Photography, Architecture and Design, Music, film and video art make up their speciality sections on the Contemporary Arts.


### 669 HENRY SOTHERAN
**2,3,4 & 5 Sackville Street, London W1X 2DP.**     01-734 1150

**Subjects:** Antiquarian, fine bindings, bibliography, ornithology.
**Hours:** Mon - Fri 9.00 - 5.30.
**Services:** Library supply, book binding, journal subscriptions, credit cards, export department, book restoration.

The oaklined interior has the proper air of gravitas with its glass topped cabinets and shelves of leather bound books. Sotherans have a claim to be the oldest antiquarian booksellers in London where they opened in 1815. They were the purchasers of Charles Dicken's library (he was a customer) and part of Sir Winston Churchill's. The ornithological section is fine — from Audubon to pocket guides. Bibliophiles will know it and the passer by will be surprised at its catholicity. In one corner of the showroom is a fascimile of the original shop front, which is now their new books sections.


### 670 CHAS. J. SAWYER
**No. 1 Grafton Street, London W1X 3LB.**     01-493 3810

**Subjects:** Antiquarian, fine bindings, private presses, Churchilliana, Africana.
**Hours:** Mon - Fri 9.00 - 5.30, Sat 9.00 - 11.30.
**Services:** Illustrated catalogue, mail order, credit cards.

An elegant show room and gallery at the top of Hay Hill, more for the collector than the casual passer by. One is shown around treasure houses like this.

### 671 MARLBOROUGH RARE BOOKS
**35 Old Bond Street, London W1X 4PT.**     **01-493 6993**

**Subjects:** Antiquarian, rare books, art, architecture, illustrated books before 1850.
**Hours:** Mon - Fri 9.30 - 6.00.
**Services:** Mail order, catalogue, advice on book collecting, valuation.

Up many flights of stairs or by lift, Marlborough Rare Books is rather inaccessible. Very much for collectors and not casual browsers. Visitors are welcome but advised to phone first for an appointment. They specialise in the arts but also have photography, topography and natural history books.

### 672 MAGGS BROS. LTD.
**50 Berkeley Square, London W1X 6EL.**     **01-499 2007**
    **01-499 2051**

**Subjects:** Antiquarian, early English literature, manuscripts, travel.
**Hours:** Mon - Fri 9.30 - 5.00.
**Services:** Book restoration, mail order, catalogues by subject (£10 to have the range posted), university and library supply.

A family concern since 1850 these elegant premises on the west side of Berkeley Square are of world repute to all collectors. To call these deep carpeted rooms on two levels a shop doesn't quite catch the atmosphere of bibliophilic earnestness which you find. Photographs of the generations of Maggs line the staircase connecting the two levels, sanctifying the serious pursuit of the arcane and valuable and a little unnerving to the passing browser.

### 673 READERS DIGEST
**22 Berkeley Square, London W1X 6HB**  **01-629 8144**

**Subjects:** Readers Digest publications plus other publishers books on travel, reference and languages etc. including Time Life and Childrens books.
**Hours:** Mon - Fri 9.00 - 5.30.
**Services:** Mail Order (Catalogue), Special orders.

Although the Readers Digest books are displayed here they have also a very good selection of unusual series maybe difficult to find elsewhere i.e. Time Life publications, a popular series of Library of Nations, also the 'Which' titles and an excellent travel and guide section. English language teaching series and dictionaries have their own corner with an imaginative children's selection and gardening/cookery and keep fit and health all well displayed.

### 674 AUSTRALIANA
**Stand A30, Gray's Antique Market,**  **01-629 2813**
**Davies Mews, London W1Y 1AE.**  **0491-35077 (Home)**

**Subjects:** Australiana.
**Hours:** Wed 10.30 - 6.00 or by appointment.

A very small stall in the basement of Gray's Antique Market, crammed with books, maps and prints on their special subject.

### 675 CAISSA BOOKS
**Gray's Antique Market, Stand A.18/19,**  **01-629 3644**
**1/7 Davies Mews, London W1Y 1AR.**  **01-399 6591 (evenings)**

**Subjects:** Secondhand and antiquarian books on Chess and Australiana.
**Hours:** Mon - Fri 10.30 - 6.00.
**Services:** Mail order, special orders, catalogues of chess books.

One of the larger stalls in the antique market run by Mike and Kaye Sheehan. Within the limited space of the market they display only a small part of their stock, which also includes prints and old chess sets. An unusual feature of the market is an underground stream running through it, the old River Bourne, I think.

### 676 THE BOOK GALLERY
**Grays Antique Market,**
**Davies Mews, London W1Y 1LB.**                 **01-408 1239**

**Subjects:** Secondhand specialising in Golf, Transport, Juvenile and Illustrated books.
**Hours:** Mon - Fri 10.00 - 6.00.

Look for the indoor stream in Grays Antique Market and you will find the small stall with books on Golf, Motoring/transport and some juvenile and illustrated books.


### 677 M. & R. GLENDALE
**121 Grays Antiques Market - 58 Davies Street,**
**London W1Y 1LB.**                               **01-629 2851**

**Subjects:** Victoriana, illustrated, children's books.
**Hours:** Mon - Fri 10.00 - 6.00.
**Services:** Mail order, catalogue.

This 'shop' is in fact one of 300 stalls in Grays Antique Market, one of the largest indoor markets in the country. Glendales is located in a corner downstairs and has a good collection of illustrated Victoriana. They also specialise in old Valentine and Christmas cards. Opposite the Oxford Street entrance to Bond Street Station there is a pedestrian thoroughfare which leads through to Davies Street.


### 678 JOHN O'CALLAGHAN
**Grays Antique Market**
**Davies Mews, London W1Y 1LB.**

**Subjects:** General, secondhand.
**Hours:** Mon - Fri 10.00 - 6.00.

A small stall not displaying its number or owners name but a fair selection of secondhand books mostly on antiques, jewellery or art. It can be found opposite the Book Gallery in the basement of Grays Antique Market.

### 679 BERNARD J. SHAPERO
**Stand 125, Grays Antique Market,**
**58, Davies Street, London W1Y 1LB.**             **01-493 0876**

**Subjects:** Travel, natural history, Baedeker guides.
**Hours:** Mon - Fri 10.00 - 6.00.
**Services:** Mail order, Book search.

Bernard Shapero has a large space in the basement of the antique market to display his collection of antiquarian illustrated and travel books including the Baedeker guides. Plenty of expertise here with an extremely interesting stock.


### 680 G. HEYWOOD HILL LTD.
**10 Curzon Street, London W1Y 7FJ.**             **01-629 0647**

**Subjects:** English literature, historical, antiquarian, fine bindings, children's books, general.
**Hours:** Mon - Fri 9.00 - 5.30, Sat 9.00 - 12.30.
**Services:** Bookbinding, world wide mail order service.

An attractive bow windowed 18th century front sets the right tone for this rather prestigious shop. Founded only in 1936, it is already rich in association, often being mentioned in the diaries of Waughs, Mitfords, etc. Nancy Mitford ran the shop for three years from 1942. Inside the shop the shelves and tables groan with good, rare and beautiful things destined, one likes to imagine, for private libraries in country houses, where the spirit of letters may still flourish. Down some marginally perilous stairs there is a good show of children's books. The service here is knowledgeable and attentive.


### 681 TURF NEWSPAPERS LTD.
**56 Curzon Street, London W1Y 7PF.**             **01-499 4391**

**Subjects:** Horse racing, hunting, horse breeding, biographies associated with the turf.
**Hours:** Mon - Fri 9.00 - 5.00, Sat 9.00 - 12.00.
**Services:** Mail order, lists, subscriptions to U.K. and foreign newspapers and magazines.

This small showroom in Mayfair provides for the racing fraternity which has always been found in this area. All books equine are generously displayed, and when Arkle's autobiography comes they'll be sure to have it.

## 682 CHAPPELL OF BOND STREET
**50 New Bond Street, London W1Y 9HA.**       **01-491 2777**

**Subjects:** Music.
**Hours:** Mon - Fri 9.30 - 6.00. Sat 9.30 - 5.00.
**Services:** Credit cards, Mail order.

Among the pianos and other instruments Chappells stock books and sheet music and have a very efficient postal service for UK and overseas customers. Vocal scores of shows can be obtained here and as they own the copyright of the majority it makes it easy for the customer. A vast range of music is covered and is catologised under instrument.

# W2

**700 JOHN MENZIES**
**Paddington Concourse,**
**Paddington Station, London W2 1HB.**          **01-723 3153**

**Subjects:** General.
**Hours:** Mon - Sun 7.00 - 10.00.
**Services:** Credit cards.

Quite a large shop on Paddington Station with general stock under subjects both paperback and hardback with a strong section on railways. Glossy gift books and childrens are available, with a table of remainders.


**701 HOSAINS**
**25 Connaught Street, London W2 2AY.**          **01-262 7900**

**Subjects:** Antiquarian and Secondhand books on the Middle East, North Africa, India, Tibet and Central Asia.
**Hours:** Tue - Fri 10.30 - 5.30. Sat 10.30 - 1.00.
**Services:** Mail Order (Catalogue). Credit cards. Search service.

Almost all the books are in English relating to their specialist regions with an excellent stock well displayed and accessable for their customers although mail order is a strong side of the business. Only books on their particular countries and Continents are stocked backed by manuscripts and miniatures related to those areas, but general subjects from religion, history to travel and art, with literature and illustrated books the largest section.

### 702 MODERN BOOK CO.
**19/21 Praed Street, London W2 1NP.**　　　　　　　**01-402 9176**

**Subjects:** Electronics, photography, engineering, general, travel, medical.
**Hours:** Mon - Fri 9.00 - 5.30, Sat 9.00 - 1.00.
**Services:** Library supply, mail order, microfiche available to check any book published in U.K. or U.S.A.

An impressive, large, brightly lit shop at the Edgware Road end of Praed Street with an extensive window display. Inside the sections are well marked and though the shop emphasises its technical books there are good sections on law, accountancy, economics and a good general section. The principal bookshop in this postal district and for some way beyond it.

### 703 BAYSWATER BOOKS
**27, Craven Terrace, W2 3EL.**　　　　　　　**01-402 7398**

**Subjects:** Antiquarian and general secondhand.
**Hours:** Mon - Sun 11.00 - 6.00 (erratic)
**Services:** Book search.

This shop is in the process of settling down and hopes to specialize in poetry. At the moment its stock is general with no particular emphasis. Its long opening hours are an attraction and a snare and it is probably advisable to check by telephone if you are coming any distance, to see that they are open. A good place for bookland to colonize as shops are thin on the ground in W2.

### 704 THE LONDON TOY AND MODEL MUSEUM
**23 Craven Hill, London W2 3EN.**　　　　　　　**01-262 7905/9450**

**Subjects:** Toys, models and childrens books.
**Hours:** Tue - Sat 10.00 - 5.30. Sun 11.00 - 5.00.
**Services:** Credit cards. Mail order (catalogue). Special orders.

Books on the toys and models are in the entrance of this museum so you can purchase or browse without paying the entrance fee. They have a wider selection of books in their catalogue than are on show but a visit is well worth while to this unusual museum for parents as well as children.

## 705 DAR AL DAWA BOOKSHOP
**32 Hereford Grove, Westbourne Grove,
Bayswater, W2 4AJ.**     **01-221 6256**

**Subjects:** Islamic, Arabic.
**Hours:** Mon - Sat 9.00 - 7.00.
**Services:** Special orders, Exhibition/University supply. Mail order. Magazine subscriptions.

Books in English and Arabic are stocked including books for children. They have a strong language section with reference titles mainly in English and Arabic. History and affairs of the Middle East can be obtained here in hardback and paperback with knowledgable help at hand.

## 706 KELTIC
**25 Chepstow Corner, Chepstow Place,
London W2 4TT.**     **01-229 8560/8456**

**Subjects:** English Language Teaching.
**Hours:** Mon - Fri 10.00 - 5.30, Thu 10.00 - 8.00, Sat 10.00 - 1.00.
**Services:** Mail order, lists, supply to language schools, seminars and talks.

With ground floor offices, one descends to the spacious, well lit, light coloured, basement showroom to get down to the business of selecting books. There are chairs for browsers and the whole presents a pleasing atmosphere.

## 707 AL SAQ'I BOOKS
**26 Westbourne Grove, London W2 5RH.**     **01-229 8543**

**Subjects:** New, secondhand and out of print books on the Arabian Peninsular and all other areas of the Moslem World.
**Hours:** Mon - Sat 11.00 - 7.00.
**Services:** Catalogue, mail order, credit cards.

A large stock of books in Arabic, which is probably the second language in the Bayswater Road, hinterland. The Manager and part-owner, Mr. Gaspar, who speaks Arabic, French and English will knowledgeably guide you around his stock which ranges in price from 20p to £100.

# W3-4

**708 ACTON BOOK CENTRE**
**144, Churchfield Road, Acton, London W3 6BS.**     **01-992 6029**

**Subjects:** Academic — all open university courses.
**Hours:** Mon - Sat 9.00 - 6.00 (Wed 9.00 - 2.00)
**Services:** Special orders — educational supply.

Unusual in the fact that this shop stocks Open University books for all courses, which number over fifty. An excellent stock of academic books as they run bookshops as various colleges hereabouts, also Penguin guides, and dictionaries in English and other languages. Knowledgable service as you would expect.

**709 EVANGEL HOUSE**
**50, Churchfield Road, Acton, London W3 6DL.**     **01-992 7123**

**Subjects:** Christian literature.
**Hours:** Tue - Thu 9.30 - 5.30, Fri 9.30 - 7.30, Sat 9.30 - 4.45.
**Services:** Teaching aids for Sunday schools, spiritual advice, coffee and snacks provided.

I expected a Church but this is a house with a Church upstairs where one could get advice and spiritual guidance. The entrance is a small shop with Christian books, cards, Sunday School aids and one table for coffee, cakes and snacks. Hymn books, Gospel Song books and missionary books are stocked. Devotional readings take place in a welcoming atmosphere. Satan will have a hard time in this suburb.

**710 JAY VEE NEWSAGENT**
**142, Horn Lane, London W3 6PG.**     **01-992 4413**

**Subjects:** General.
**Hours:** Mon - Fri 6.00 - 7.30. Sat 6.00 - 7.00.

A newsagent/tobacconist with a smattering of popular fiction, dictionaries and children's books.

### 711 BRANSDON NEWSAGENTS LTD.
### 118-120 High Street, Acton, London W3 6QX.   01-992 1746

**Subjects:** General, educational.
**Hours:** Mon - Sat 8.30 - 5.30.
**Services:** Special orders, credit cards.

This large newsagents has recently changed hands and I am told they intend to increase the book section by opening a second floor and devoting it entirely to books. They will be general in subject with an emphasis on educational books.

### 712 W.A. FOSTER
### 134, Chiswick High Road, London W4 1PU.   01-995 2768

**Subjects:** General, secondhand and antiquarian.
**Hours:** Mon - Sat 10.00 - 6.00 (Thu 10.00 - 1.30).

A good spread of books here with the bargains in boxes outside and the general stock ordered by subject together with some antiquarian books on the inside.

### 713 CONNOISSEUR CARBOOKS
### 32 Devonshire Road, Chiswick,
### London W4 2HD.   01-994 6783

**Subjects:** New books on cars, commercial vehicles and motor cycles.
**Hours:** Mon - Fri 9.00 - 5.30. Sat 10.00 - 4.00.
**Services:** Mail order (catalogue). Credit cards. Special orders.

An amazing selection of books about cars from their history to restoration, modelling, racing and rallying. All except repair manuals can be found here. There is a large space devoted to the various makes in alphabetical order and trucks and motor cycles have not been forgotten. There are book bargains and a small secondhand section and they produce an excellent catalogue which in itself must produce fascination for anyone remotely interested in cars.

## 714 W.H. SMITH
**370, Chiswick High Road, London W4 5TA.**  01-995 9427

**Subjects:** General.
**Hours:** Mon - Sat 8.30 - 5.30.
**Services:** Special orders, credit cards.

A medium sized Smith's which covers the range of general books adequately and probably well used as bookshops are thin on the ground in these parts.

# W5

**715 W.H. SMITH**
**21-23 The Broadway, Ealing, London W5 2NH.**      **01-567 1471**

**Subjects:** General.
**Hours:** Mon - Sat 9.00 - 6.00.
**Services:** Special orders, credit cards.

A very attractive spiral staircase leading to a basement of books in this large branch of W.H. Smith. They have an extensive stock, well laid out and more imaginatively displayed than many other branches. Paper and hard back in most subjects with tables of books well displayed and brightly presented.

**716 BENTALLS (EALING) LTD.**
**1-8, The Broadway, Ealing W5 2NJ.**      **01-567 3040**

**Subjects:** General.
**Hours:** Mon - Sat 9.30 - 5.30 (Thu 9.30 - 6.00).
**Services:** Credit cards, special orders.

Quite a small book section in this department store, mostly paperbacks with some hardbacked titles suitable as gifts.

**717 EALING BOOKS**
**5, Central Building,**
**The Broadway, London W5 2NT.**      **01 579 3727**

**Subjects:** General.
**Hours:** Mon - Sat 9.30 - 5.30 (Thu 9.30 - 6.00)
**Services:** Credit cards, special orders, library supply.

This is a good general bookshop opposite Ealing Broadway station. The books are clearly sectioned and the text book stock is increased at the appropriate times of the academic year.

### 718 SEAL BOOKS
2, Coningsby Road, London W5 4HR.   01-567 7198

**Subjects:** General, secondhand and antiquarian.
**Hours:** Wed - Sat 10.00 - 5.30 (closed August)
**Services:** Mail order, occasional catalogue.

An attractive black and white corner bookshop. There are three well ordered rooms brimming with books on English Literature, Poetry, History and an African section. The enthusiastic proprietor has been here since 1970.

### 719 CLAUDE GILL
64, Ealing Broadway Centre,
The Broadway, London W5 5JY.   Ex-Directory

**Subjects.** General.
**Hours:** Mon - Sat 9.30 - 6.00.
**Services:**

Still in the process of being built this Ealing Broadway Centre promises to be exceptional with unusual and imaginative architecture. Claude Gill have a prime site on this spectacular square and have two floors of books. General in subject but comprehensively covered, the design of the shop is itself worth seeing, with awnings over tables of books appearing like stalls — a very attractive idea.

### 720 HUDSONS BOOKSHOP
Ealing College of Higher Education,
St. Mary's Road, Ealing, London W5 5RF.   01-579 4111
Ext. 3255

**Subjects:** Management, catering, business studies, law, economics.
**Hours:** Mon - Fri 8.45 - 4.45.
**Services:** Credit cards, special orders.

An on campus shop open to the public but dealing mainly in textbooks for the students, though there is quite a good English literature section.

# W6

### 721 SKY BOOKS
**119, Shepherd's Bush Road, London W6 7LP.**　　　**01-603 5620**

**Subjects:** General secondhand paperbacks.
**Hours:**　　Mon - Fri 10.30 - 6.30.　Sat 10.00 - 5.00.
**Services:** Exchange service.

Popular fiction, sci-fi and other general subjects are sold or exchanged secondhand here. Old magazines are also sold.

### 722 RIVERSIDE STUDIOS BOOKSHOP
**Crisp Road, Hammersmith, London W6 9RL.**　　　**01-741 2251**

**Subjects:** General, art books
**Hours:**　　Tue - Sat 12.00 - 8.00 p.m.
**Services:** Special orders, book signings.

The shop is part of the arts complex, an altogether welcome addition to rather a down at heel area. Customers have to climb a wooden tower at the centre of the shop to examine the stock, which is fun. The written and performing arts are adequately covered and signed copies can be bought here. The centre also has a gallery, restaurant and bar to hand.

### 723 AUTOMOBILE ASSOCIATION
**24, King Street, Hammersmith, London W6 0OW.　01-381 3083**

**Subjects:** Motoring, guides and maps.
**Hours:**　　Mon - Sat 9.00 - 5.00.
**Services:** Travel agents and insurance.

Bright new offices in King Street opposite Marks and Spencer. Not primarily a bookshop though they do have a small hardbacked selection of guides, atlases and holiday route planners. Some of their own publications such as the Book of the Countryside are excellent and not just appendages to the motoring side of things.

### 724 W.H. SMITH
**Kings Mall, Kings Street**
**Hammersmith, London W6 OPZ.** 01-748 2218

**Subjects:** General.
**Hours:** Sat 9.00 - 6.00.
**Services:** Credit cards, Special orders.

W.H. Smith have one large floor in this shopping mall with the majority of space given to their general book department enabling their customers to meander amongst the displays of hard and paperback titles. To one side they have a selection of dictionaries, travel guides, reference books and students notes, while the centre tables hold the glossy new titles and of course they have the ever popular children's and gardening/cooking section.

### 725 HAMMICKS BOOKSHOPS LTD.
**Unit 9, Kings Mall,**
**Hammersmith, London W6 OPZ.** 01-741 2467

**Subjects:** General and childrens.
**Hours:** Mon - Sat 9.00 - 5.30.
**Services:** Credit cards, Special orders.

In a bright new corner in King's Mall in Hammersmith, Hammicks have opened their bookshop with easy access to shelves of most general subjects in hardback and paperback mixed under subject headings. There are a maps and guides and a childrens section with well selected titles, and of course gardening and cookery have their place.

### 726 MARTIN THE NEWSAGENT
**39-40 Kings Mall, King Street, London W6 OQB.** 01-748 2426

**Subjects:** Popular Fiction, Crime Thrillers, Childrens.
**Hours:** Mon - Sat 8.00 - 6.00.
**Services:** Credit cards.

This shop at the entrance to the Kings Mall shopping centre is firstly a stationers but they do have a small selection of popular hard and soft backed books on about six island stands.

## 727 KSIEGARNIA S.P.K.
P.C.A. Publications Ltd.,
238 King Street, London W6 ORF.     01-748 5522

**Subjects:** Poland.
**Hours:** Mon - Fri 10.00 - 6.00. Sat 10.00 - 2.00.
**Services:** Special orders, international mail order, educational and library supply.

The entrance to the shop is to the left of the Polish Social and Cultural Association. It has a comprehensive stock of books on Poland in Polish and English covering the literature, history and politics of that country.

# W8-9

**728 ACADEMY BOOKSHOP
LONDON ART BOOKSHOP LTD.
7/8 Holland Street, London W8 4NA.**    01-937 6996

**Subjects:** Books on fine and applied arts, architecture.
**Hours:**    Mon - Sat 9.30 - 6.00.
**Services:** Mail order, catalogue, credit cards.

This company operates three shops in this narrow street off Kensington Church Street. No.7 specialises in art, design and photography, next door are remaindered books and across on the north side of the road at No.8 is the shop specialising in architecture.

**729 THE PETERSFIELD BOOKSHOP
Stand 63 Antique Hypermarket,
26/40 Kensington High Street, London W8 4PF.**    01-937 8426

**Subjects:** Antiquarian, secondhand.
**Hours:**    Mon - Sat 10.00 - 5.45.
**Services:** Credit cards, picture framing, special orders.

The London arm of the Petersfield Bookshop has its niche in the Hypermarket and sells as above mentioned, also has some prints.

**730 NOTTING HILL BOOKS LTD.
132 Palace Gardens Terrace, London W8 4RT.**    01-727 5988

**Subjects:** Reduced price books (Remainders, some review copies, good second hand)
**Hours:**    Mon - Sat 10.00 - 6.00 (Thu 10.00 - 1.00)

This shop is part way along the one-way system from Notting Hill Gate to Kensington Church Street and is to be recognised by the blue awning and the tables, with second hand paperbacks, on the pavement.

It is a long narrow shop, well laid out, and its bargains are rather superior with an inclination towards art, literary criticism and history.

## 731 BARKERS OF KENSINGTON
### 63 Kensington High Street, London W8 5SE.     01-937 5432

**Subjects:** General.
**Hours:** Mon - Wed 9.00 - 5.30, Thu 9.00 - 6.30, Fri - Sat 9.00 - 6.00
**Services:** Credit cards, Special orders.

Not for this store the concessionary shelf of cookery books in a corner, but a really good, comprehensive book department run with enthusiasm. The department is strategically situated on the ground floor. It is spacious and easy to walk about and its sections are well ordered and helpful. Travel, children's books, works of reference and the classics are well represented. Authors often choose this department for personal signings which is a recommendation.


## 732 ST PAUL BOOK CENTRE
### 199 Kensington High Street, London W8 6BA.     01-937 9591

**Subjects:** Religious books.
**Hours:** Tue - Sat 9.30 - 5.30.
**Services:** Mail Order, catalogue, church and school supplies.

This shop is run by the Daughters of St. Paul and has a wide range of Christian literature, mainly Roman Catholic. These premises have been recently possessed after the move from Notting Hill Gate and retain the same bright and cheerful atmosphere. Books are on the ground floor and audio visual material on the first floor.


## 733 THE BOOKSMITH
### 201 Kensington High Street, London W8 6BA.     01-937 5002

**Subjects:** Paperbacks, remainders, feminism.
**Hours:** Mon - Sat 9.30 - 6.00.
**Services:** Mailing lists, credit cards.

A large brightly lit shop with good remaindered hardbacks and quite a good range of paperbacks at their normal published price, also a section of remaindered paperbacks with an offer of 4 for £1. The feminists and Virago Press well represented.

### 734 TRAILFINDERS
**46 Earls Court Road, London W8 6EJ.**     **01-937 3979**

**Subjects:** Travel.
**Hours:** Mon - Sat 10.00 - 6.00.
**Services:** Subscriptions to travel magazines, credit cards.

Primarily a travel agency for the budget long haul traveller, they have a small comprehensive book and map section with an emphasis on S.E. Asia. Certainly a good place for overlanders who require literature about places between London and Australasia.


### 735 SOMA BOOKS AT THE COMMONWEALTH INSTITUTE
**Kensington High Street, London W8 6NQ.**     **01-603 0754**

**Subjects:** General and Academic books about or published in Commonwealth Countries.
**Hours:** Mon - Sat 10.00 - 5.30. Sun 2.00 - 5.00.
**Services:** Special orders — Library (school supply). Exhibitions. Mail order (lists).

One large room in the Commonwealth Institute is made attractive with arts, crafts, posters and records to back their interesting stock of books concentrating on the Commonwealth countries. The stage exhibitions to coincide with events of the Institute with Black Literature, Women's Studies having their strong sections. Children have a large proportion of space with picture books in the five major India languages and many books not readily available in Britain, Africa, Canada, India and Australasia exhibit works from poetry and drama to fiction and religion making this bookshop unique in the support of these countries.

### 736 EARLY LEARNING CENTRE
225 Kensington High Street, London W8 6SA.   01-937 0419

**Subjects:** Educational books for young children, pre-school books.
**Hours:** Mon - Sat 9.00 - 5.30.
**Services:** Credit cards, newsletter, catalogue, mail order, a play area, discounts for playgroups, hospitals and handicapped children.

A shop with books for young children up to the age of 12 years. Brightly lit and coloured, with a small play area for toddlers while mother or father looks around the books and toys, most of which have a learning function. A very good idea and helpful to slower learning parents who should be able to launch their young J.S. Mill from here.


### 737 YOUNG WORLD
(Children's Book Centre Ltd.)
229 Kensington High Street, London W8 6SA.   01-937 6314

**Subjects:** Children's books.
**Hours:** Mon - Sat 9.30 - 6.00.
**Services:** Credit cards.

Children are well thought of south of the Park and here is another good book and toy shop for them. Books are on the ground floor and toys in the basement. The book sections are by age group and there are also ones on sport, crafts, etc. all well sign posted. There is a small selection of adult best sellers. Light and bright with the colours of optimism as it should be.

### 738 WATERSTONE'S BOOKSELLERS
### 193 Kensington High Street, W8 6SH.          01-937 8432

**Subjects:** General.
**Hours:** Mon - Fri 9.30 a.m. - 10.30 p.m. Sat 9.30 - 7.00.
Sun 12.00 - 7.00.
**Services:** Special orders. Mail order. Credit cards including a Waterstone credit card.

The high standard of both books and decor is carried by Waterstones to Kensington High Street where they have a corner site with three floors devoted to their excellent stock in general subjects. At ground floor level there is plenty of room to browse among fiction, biographies and their travel section. Downstairs more specialist subjects including the childrens department and on the first floor they have their very interesting art titles and a very knowledgeable staff in all departments.

### 739 MICHAEL WIMBLETON
### 16 Adam & Eve Mews, London W8 6UJ.          01-937 0513

**Subjects:** Art books, especially non-European, anthropology.
**Hours:** By appointment (but welcome to turn up).
**Services:** Catalogue - 10% discount booksellers' orders.

Although in a private house Mr. Wimbleton does have a comfortable room where the books are displayed and may be examined. He specialises in tribal art and anthropology and most of the books are those published since 1880 but out of print.

### 740 D. MELLOR & A.L. BAXTER
### (Antiquarian Booksellers)
### 121A, Kensington Church Street, W8 7LP.          01-229 2033

**Subjects:** Antiquarian, fine bindings, literature, science, medicine, travel and history.
**Hours:** Mon - Fri 10.00 - 6.30. Sat 10.00 - 5.00.
**Services:** Mail order, catalogue, credit cards, search service, binding, and book restoration on the premises.

An excellent antiquarian bookshop on ground and basement level. The less expensive books are in the basement and at ground level the rarer items are found and it is here, that the book restoration is carried out which adds interest ot a visit. The shop which was previously in Grays Antique Market deserves to flourish here on its own and I'm sure it will.

### 741 W. H. SMITH & SON LTD.
**132-136 Kensington High Street, London W8 7RP.    01-937 0236**

**Subjects:** General.
**Hours:**    Mon - Sat 9.00 - 6.00,  Thu 9.30 - 6.00.
**Services:** Credit cards, special orders.

This is a well managed shop run by Mr. Dunn who has been in the business for 31 years. There is a good book section in the basement of the shop which is in a rather upmarket area. On the ground floor there is a record department annexed to the main shop.

### 742 KANOUNE KETAB LTD. (Iranian Bookshop)
**2A Kensington Church Walk, London W8 9BL.    01-937 5087**

**Subjects:** Iran.
**Hours:**    Mon - Sat 9.30 - 12.30. 1.30 - 6.00.
**Services:** Mail order, Catalogue.

Down this small mews behind Kensington High Street in the Iranian bookshop selling books in the Persian language and in English about Iran. Many subjects are covered in new books with a very small secondhand section and a large mail order service is provided.

### 743 VANESSA WILLIAMS-ELLIS
**4 Warwick Place, London W9 2PK.                01-239 0071**

**Subjects:** General.
**Hours:**    Mon - Fri 10.00 - 6.00,  Sat 10.00 - 2.00.
**Services:** Special orders.

Just off Little Venice this attractive bookshop is a real find to those who discover it in this largely residential area. The stock is predominantly literary but with good children's and cookery sections. Hardbacks and paperbakcs are carried. Books one is directed to by the literary pages of the 'quality' Sunday newspapers are sure to be obtainable here.

## 744 GRASS ROOTS
71 Golborne Road, London W10 5NP.     01-969 0687

**Subjects:** Black books specialising in Africa, Asia and the Caribbean.
**Hours:** Mon - Sat 9.30 - 6.30.
**Services:** Mail order.

Books are in English but they are described as revolutionary literature. This shop is a co-operative with gifts and African crafts taking up the majority of space, but books are available on politics, race relations and black studies generally.

# W11-12

**745 BOOKS FOR COOKS**
**(The Cook Book Shop)**
**15, Blenheim Crescent, London W11 2EE.**          **01-221 1992**

**Subjects:** Cooking — new and secondhand.
**Hours:** Mon - Sat 9.30 - 5.00.
**Services:** Special orders, mail order, catalogue, wants list, book repair and fine binding service, educational supply.

A small gem of a shop just west of the Portobello Road. It has so many notable features that only some can be mentioned. A cleaning repairing and re-binding service in the basement; a sofa to slump in for the exhausted browser; a commissioned stained glass window portraying a chef carrying a casserole — most eye catching; and much else without even mentioning the stock. This ranges from recipes for apfelstrudel in Aachen to zebra in Zululand and all stops on the way. The catholicity of its geographical span is most impressive. One could obviously line the Charing Cross Road with cooking titles but here in two fairly compact rooms are approximately 2000 titles which is just the right side of anorexia nervosa.

## 746 THE TRAVEL BOOKSHOP
### 13, Blenheim Crescent, W11 2EE.    01-229 5260

**Subjects:** Travel (New, rare, secondhand).
**Hours:**   Mon - Fri 10.00 - 6.00. Sat 10.00 - 5.00.
**Services:** Catalogue, wants list, mail order, credit cards.

A unique shop run by Sarah Anderson just off the Portobello Road. It specialises in travel, but 'specialises' doesn't begin to describe the range and interest of her stock.

Old, new, hardback, paperback, secondhand, antiquarian, guides, maps, charts, travellers tales, and biographers make up a partial list. The books are arranged by continent and then by country, all hugger mugger, a pedestrian guide next to a monograph from the Hakluyt Society. Be it the exigencies of space or whatever, it is a private opinion that these are the arrangements most loved by the reading and browsing brotherhood. The shop endeavours to have some books on all countries and has all on some.

## 747 THE OLD LONDON 'L.P.C.'
### 21 Kensington Park Road, London W11 2EU.    01-229 1888

**Subjects:** General, Antiquarian and Secondhand specialising in old books of London and Dickens, Scott and 19th Century poets.
**Hours:** Mon - Sat 10.30 - 6.00.
**Services:** Book search from enormous stock.

Much photographed by tourists and still displaying its gaslights amongst the ivory, bronze and general miscellary of collectors this scarlet painted shop specialises in famous old photographs with an unlikely index system. Books range from Dickens to Colin Wilson and I am assured that the back up stock is in the region of 30,000 to 60,000 so it is advisable to telephone before if a special title is required. A visit must be made if only to see a shop as it was 100 years ago and browse through old Dickensian books and postcards of London.

### 748  ELGIN BOOKS
**6 Elgin Crescent, London W11 2HX.**            **01-229 2186**

**Subjects:** General, Poetry, Feminism, Children's Books.
**Hours:** Tue - Sat 10.00 - 6.00.
**Services:** Special Orders, Displays of Book reviews from major newspapers on a noticeboard.

It is a new attractive shop in the area, dark green throughout with wooden shelving and a scarlet blind, it's two floors linked by a spiral staircase on which books are displayed. It is a good general shop, strong on fiction, and they keep about 8,000 titles overall in stock.

With Portobello Road nearby, it is quite strategically located, helping to push forward the 'gentrification' of this frontier area.


### 749  MAN TO MAN
**57 Pembridge Road, London W11 3HG.**            **01-727 1614**

**Subjects:** Homosexual literature.
**Hours:** Mon - Fri 10.30 - 7.00.
**Services:** Special orders.

An exotic commerce behind blackened windows. The shop's name alone should filter out the unwary. Though if someone did enter for 'straight from the shoulder' advice about buying rugby boots I would like to be there.


### 750  MANDARIN BOOKS LTD.
**22 Notting Hill Gate, London W11 3JE.**            **01-229 0327**

**Subjects:** General.
**Hours:** Mon - Fri 10.00 - 6.30, Sat 10.00 - 6.00.
**Services:** Special orders.

A good, general bookshop but rather cramped. The principle of book arrangement is a little hard to discern, but one can get most non-technical books there and they are good on new titles which have been recently reviewed.

### 751 PETER EATON (BOOKSELLERS) LTD.
**80 Holland Park Avenue, London W11 3RE.    01-727 5211/5955**

**Subjects:** Antiquarian, secondhand, local history.
**Hours:** Mon - Sat 10.00 - 5.00.
**Services:** Library supply, mail order, new book supply to Universities.

An imaginatively designed shop with a tall front window the height of two floors. Above the ground floor is a gallery where the antiquarian books are kept, at a street level are books for collectors and in the basement is the secondhand department, restocked daily, where there are thousands of books, mostly under £5. The counter display usually has new books of topographical interest to Londoners.

### 752 BRITISH ESPERANTO ASSOCIATION INC.
**140 Holland Park Avenue, London W11 4UF.    01-727 7821**

**Subjects:** General (in Esperanto).
**Hours:** Mon - Fri 9.30 - 6.00.
**Services:** Mail order, catalogue, reference library, journals on subscription, 10% discount off their publications to schools and libraries.

It looks more like an office than a shop but one is welcome to look around, but unless one has the language, directions will be needed. As well as books cassettes in Esperanto are sold.

### 753 W.H. SMITH
**92, Notting Hill Gate, London, W11 8QB.    01-727 9261**

**Subjects:** General.
**Hours:** Mon - Sat 9.00 - 6.00.
**Services:** Credit cards, special orders.

What was once rather a disappointment is now a joy, a good, W.H.S. bookshop. The first floor is almost entirely made over to books, with generous wall shelving and tables scattered around displaying new titles and fast sellers. The area, bedsitland, needed it and it now serves the area well, most general book buyers will try a Smiths before much else and in this branch at least their book-buying expectations probably will be met.

### 754 BOOK BARGAINS
**14, Shepherds Bush Market, London W12 8DQ.**     **01-740 0873**

**Subjects:** Secondhand paperbacks.
**Hours:** Mon - Fri 10.00 - 5.00 (closed Thu)
**Services:** Exchange service.

This large stall in the centre of the market has been run for thirty years by the same owner, who will also exchange books.


### 755 BUSH BOOKS
**144 Shepherd's Bush Centre, London W12 8PP.**     **01-749 7652**

**Subjects:** General, Open University stockist.
**Hours:** Mon - Fri 10.00 - 6.00. Sat 9.30 - 5.30.
**Services:** Special orders, credit cards.

A smallish good general bookshop in this modern shopping centre. Subjects clearly defined and marked, with children's books being their largest section. Helpful staff will take orders for anything not in stock.


### 756 A. & L. BOOKS
**167 Percy Road, London W12 9QJ.**     **01-749 4098**

**Subjects:** General, Secondhand.
**Hours:** Mon & Wed 10-12. Fri 10 - 6. Sat 11 - 6. Tue and Thu closed.

This attractive secondhand bookshop adds character to an area badly needing it as it stands just off the Uxbridge Road. A black and white frontage to two rooms of a well ordered and wide selection of secondhand books. Art and Antiques are two of the favoured subjects but most general subjects and militaria are well represented.

**757 POLONEZ**                                                     **01-749 3097**
**129/130 Shepherds Bush Centre, London W12 8PP. 01-743 2391**

**Subjects:** Books published in Poland and books in Polish.
**Hours:** Mon - Fri 9.00 - 5.00 (Thu 9.00 - 1.00)
Sat 10.00 - 5.00.
**Services:** Mail order, catalogue, subscriptions to Polish journals.

Half this double roomed shop sells books and half Polish artifacts and there is a small gallery where more books are displayed. There are a few books in English about things Polish. Quite a surprise to find such a shop here, but then it is on the South Kensington-Eton/Slough axis.

# W13-14

**758 BASKETTS BOOKSHOP**
**201, Uxbridge Road,**
**West Ealing, London W13 9AA.**  **01-567 5356**

**Subjects:** General
**Hours:** Mon - Sat 9.00 - 5.30. Wed 9.00 - 1.00.
**Services:** Special orders.

A rather cramped little bookshop with little order but seemingly quite a good range of general books.


**759 W.H. SMITH**
**64, The Broadway, London W13 OSU.**  **01-579 3461**

**Subjects:** General.
**Hours:** Mon - Sat 9.00 - 6.00.
**Services:** Special orders, credit cards.

A very generous portion of this large one floor branch is given over to the selling of books which are ranged around on shelves and centre tables.


**760 WALTER RODNEY BOOKSHOP**
**Bogle — L'Ouverture Publications Ltd.**
**5A, Chignell Place, Ealing, London W13 OTJ.**  **01-579 4920**

**Subjects:** Black studies, Third World literature, West Indies.
**Hours:** Mon - Sat 10.00 - 6.00.
**Services:** Booklist, catalogue, special orders, mail order, school supply.

This shop specialises in radical West Indian politics, especially Jamaican. Walter Rodney is seen as a political martyr by some Jamaicans in the West Indies and here in London and the shop is named in his honour. Caribbean writings are well covered and I noticed in their catalogue a book by Bernard Coard (remember Grenada P.) which may become a collectors item.

## 761 ANY AMOUNT OF BOOKS
### 103-105, Hammersmith Rd., London W14 0QH.    01-603 9232

**Subjects:** Secondhand, antiquarian and modern first editions.
**Hours:** Tue - Sat 11.00 - 7.00 — The Art Shop Fri & Sat 12.00 — 6.00 or by appointment.
**Services:** Catalogue.

In this small shop near Olympia they have pressed a large number of books, arranged under their subjects. The specialist art bookshop next door is open only on Friday and Saturday unless an appointment has been made. A good place for 'finds'.

# WC1

**800 CAMBRIDGE HOUSE**
English Language Bookshop,
13 New Oxford Street, London WC1A 1BA.                01-242 5577

**Subjects:** English as a Foreign language.
**Hours:** Mon - Fri 9.00 - 6.00.
**Services:** Mail order, (International) Special orders. Cassettes, Videos.

A large stock of books from many publishers to enable people to learn English as a Foreign language with all the facilities and software to assist.


**801 NIHON TOKEN**
23 Museum Street, London WC1A 1JT.                01-580 6511

**Subjects:** Japanese art, history and culture.
**Hours:** Mon - Sat 10.00 - 5.00.
**Services:** Mail order, lists.

Books take second place to Japanese antiques in this shop. There is a small section of new books and the occasional secondhand bargain.


**802 BLOOMSBURY RARE BOOKS**
29 Museum Street, London WC1A 1LH.                01-636 8206

**Subjects:** General (secondhand) with medical sections.
**Hours:** Mon - Sat 10.30 - 6.00, Sun 12.30 - 6.00. Public Holidays please enquire.
**Services:** Catalogues, mail order, lists.

Mr. Page and Mr. Rhys Jones carry a good general stock, specialising in 17th Century English and other antiquarian books and manuscripts. Their books are quality secondhand and antiquarian on diverse matters scholarly, literary, scientific and musical.

### 803 M. AYRES
**31 Museum Street, London WC1A 1LH.**          **01-636 2844**

**Subjects:** Private press books, art reference, topography, natural history.
**Hours:** Mon - Sat 10.00 - 6.00.
**Services:** Mail order.

Dark red exterior to this shop displaying prints in the window. Inside more prints on view at the front but beyond those, high shelves of books, mostly collectors items. Quite a few limited editions from the private presses and childrens books.


### 804 RUDOLF STEINER BOOKSHOP
**38 Museum Street, London WC1A 1LP.**          **01-242 4249**

**Subjects:** Rudolf Steiner, children's books.
**Hours:** Mon - Fri 10.00 - 5.30, Sat 10.30 - 1.00.
**Services:** Mail order, small library.

A small shop stocking 50/50 soft and hardbacked books of Rudolf Steiner's work, also books by others relating to his philosophy and method of teaching. There is another Rudolf Steiner bookshop at 35 Park Road, Baker Street.


### 805 BOOKS FROM INDIA (U.K.) LTD.
**45, Museum Street, WC1A 1LR.**          **01-405 7226**

**Subjects:** The Indian Sub-continent.
**Hours:** Mon - Fri 10.00 - 5.30. Sat 10.00 - 5.00.
**Services:** Mail order (catalogue) credit cards, institutional supply.

The shop has a stock of books on or from Pakistan, India, Bangladesh and Sri Lanka. The stock is multi-lingual and has a back up of audio aids. The owner, who hitch hiked from India many years ago, and his wife, provide knowledgeable and helpful service to help guide one around their vast stock.

### 806 BLAKETON HALL LTD.
**41 Museum Street, London WC1A 1LX.**

**Subjects:** General, principally hardback remainders; maps/guides London/GB
**Hours:** 9.30 - 5.30 Mon - Sat
**Services:** Credit cards.

Still shaking into their premises when we called, this shop has modest space at the front but by way of a wide approach, one enters a larger showroom at the back. Display racks line the walls. Formerly occupied by E.J. Brill, it is good to see the book tradition maintained by the new occupier.


### 807 THE ATLANTIS BOOKSHOP
**49a Museum Street, London WC1A 1LY.**     01-405 2120

**Subjects:** Occult, Witchcraft.
**Hours:** Mon - Fri 11.00 - 5.30, Sat 11.00 - 5.00.
**Services:** Mail order.

Rather a spare window display belies the larger collection of new and secondhand books to be found inside. Tarot cards and crystal balls on sale for the initiates. Wouldn't care to visit it on a dark Halloween.


### 808 THE TIBET SHOP
**10 Coptic Street, London WC1A 1NH.**     01-636 5529

**Subjects:** Tibetiana.
**Hours:** Mon - Sat 10.00 - 6.00 (closed 12.00 - 1.00 each day).
**Services:** Mail order, catalogue, special orders.

Bright little shop selling handicrafts as well as books. Many of the products are made by refugees living in India and Nepal. Books on the Tibetan language and Tibetan-English dictionaries sold, as well as western books about that country.

### 809 ANDREW BLOCK
**20 Barter Street, London WC1A 2AH.**　　　　　**01-405 9660**

**Subjects:** Rare books connected with the entertaining arts, conjuring.
**Hours:** Mon - Fri 10.00 - 5.00.
**Services:**

Run by Mr. Block, a well known character in the book world, who is 89 years old and a member of the Magic Circle. There are many books on conjuring inside but it is rather difficult to look around, for the centre of the room is taken up with brown folders holding ephemeral prints.

### 810 BONDY BOOKS
**16 Little Russell Street, London WC1A 2HN.**　　　**01-405 2733**

**Subjects:** Miniature books, early printed books, early children's books and books on caricature.
**Hours:** Mon - Fri 10.30 - 6.30. Sat 10.30 - 5.15.

A small dark two roomed shop in a side street near the British Museum. The miniature books are displayed in attractive old cabinets. The remainder of the stock is mainly antiquarian with some modern first editions, D.H. Lawrence for instance and books on the art and history of caricature.

### 811 SKOOB BOOKS LTD.
**15 Sicilian Avenue, Southampton Row,**
**Holborn, London WC1A 2QH.**　　　　　　　　**01-404 3063**

**Subjects:** Antiquarian and second hand, specialising in literary scientific and technical books.
**Hours:** Mon - Sat 10.30 - 6.30.
**Services:** 10% discount for NUS members, books bought over the counter.

When Pooles in the Charing Cross Road closed, four members of the staff joined together again to start this shop in the attractive pedestrian arcade of Sicilian Avenue. Apart from the antiquarian section just inside the entrance, most of the books are second hand scholarly text books. The shop provides useful service to the thousands of students at nearby London University. The name SKOOB is an anagram which shouldn't tax the mind for too long.

## 812 GOLDEN COCKEREL BOOKSHOP
**25, Sicilian Avenue, WC1A 2QH.**  **01-405 7979**

**Subjects:** Academic books in all subjects.
**Hours:** Mon - Fri 9.30 - 5.30.
**Services:** Catalogue, institutional supply.

This shop is a front window for the Golden Cockerel Press, Associated University Presses and Cornwall Books but functions as a normal bookshop. The range of subjects covered is impressive with an emphasis on the humanities; the staff most helpful.

## 813 THEOSOPHICAL BOOKSHOP
**68 Great Russell Street, London WC1B 3BU.**  **01-405 2309**

**Subjects:** Those religions and philosophies outside the mainstream, alternative medicine.
**Hours:** Mon - Sat 9.30 - 5.00.
**Services:** Mail order.

The shop forms part of the worldwide Theosophical Movement, sometimes known as Esoteric Buddhism. Well ordered inside with linoleum floor and spotlights, it has an air of the reference library. The headings range from Astrology, through Krishnamurti to Zen.

### 814 TRIANGLE BOOKSHOP
36 Bedford Square, London WC1B 3EG.　　　01-631 1381

**Subjects:** Architecture.
**Hours:**　　Mon 11.00 - 6.00, Tues - Fri 10.00 - 6.00.
**Services:** Credit cards, mail order, catalogues.

The Triangle Bookshop is found at the bottom of an iron staircase at the Architectural Association. The books are well displayed and their range is broad enough to include related subjects such as photography, theatre and arts and crafts, though architecture predominates. A few remaindered books are sold, as well as journals.


### 815 THE CINEMA BOOKSHOP
13/14 Great Russell Street, London WC1B 3NH.　　　01-637 0206

**Subjects:** Books and magazines about the cinema.
**Hours:**　　Mon - Sat 10.30 - 5.30.
**Services:** Mail order.

The small window of this shop catches the eye of the passer by with glossy unmounted photographs of film stars. It concentrates on this one subject, the cinema, very thoroughly. At ground floor level are the new books and in the basement are secondhand books, stored away awaiting a request.


### 816 SOUVENIR PRESS LTD.
43 Great Russell Street, London WC1B 3PA.　　　01-637 5711/3
　　　　　　　　　　　　　　　　　　　　　　　　01-580 9307/8

**Subjects:** General, children's books, maps.
**Hours:**　　Mon - Fri 9.30 - 5.30.

A corner shop on the ground floor of a grey building opposite the British Museum. Not immediately apparent as a shop until you see a notice 'Bookshop now open'. It is mainly a showroom and offices for the Souvenir Press who publish a general range. There are children's books from other Publishers on sale too, and these are displayed in the window with some toys to attract attention.

## 817 BOSWELL BOOKS AND PRINTS
**44, Great Russell Street, WC1B 3PA.**  01-580 7200

**Subjects:** Oriental - antiquarian, secondhand and new.
**Hours:** Mon - Fri 10.00 - 6.00. Sat 11.00 - 4.30.
**Services:** Special orders, Credit cards.

Together with their large range of books on the orient they display some beautiful Japanese wood block prints and other attractive objects of art. The antiquarian section has fine illustrated natural history books and rare items from English literature.

## 818 LUZAC & COMPANY LTD.
**P.O. Box 157,**
**46 Great Russell Street, London WC1B 3PE.**  01-636 1462

**Subjects:** Oriental booksellers and publishers.
**Hours:** Mon - Fri 9.00 - 5.00, Sat - if convenient by appointment.
**Services:** Credit cards, suppliers to institutions.

The Knight-Smiths have been running this renowned Oriental bookshop since the beginning of the century. All their extensive stock is at ground floor level and enquiring customers are most courteously received. The shop is very strong on Islam and Buddhism and there is a counter devoted to natural healing, massage, herbal beauty and oriental cooking. There is rumoured to be a Scottish gentleman ghost about the place - hope it's not John Knox.

## 819 ARTHUR PROBSTHAIN
**41, Great Russell Street, London WC1B 3PH.**      **01-636 1096**

**Subjects:** Islam, Middle East and Art.
**Hours:** Mon - Fri 10.00 - 6.00, Sat 10.00 - 3.30.
**Services:** Lists, discount for Universities.

For those interested in the Orient and Africa, this is a renowned shop. Inside one is overwhlemed with the quantity of books but customers can quickly find what they want. There is a geographical arrangement of books one is told, but you probably have to be an orientalist to perceive it.

## 820 COLLETS CHINESE GALLERY AND BOOKSHOP
**40 Great Russell Street, London WC1B 3PJ.**      **01-580 7538**

**Subjects:** China.
**Hours:** Mon - Sat 9.45 - 5.45 (Gallery 11.00 - 4.00).
**Services:** Mail order, subscriptions to Chinese newspapers and magazines.

The shop certainly does have books on China but these take second place to an attractive range of Chinese bric-a-brac. Upstairs is a small gallery selling posters, embroidery and a few books on Chinese art. Collets are at the evangelical end of the world socialist movement and as China has not proved to be one of the two great centres of this 'struggle' one feels this little shop has been left to make its own way, (without the great helmsman), selling silks and satins. The books cover all things Chinese, from travel to archeology, medicine and dictionaries.

## 821 THE MUSEUM BOOKSHOP
### 36 Great Russell Street, London WC1B 3PP.           01-580 4086

**Subjects:** Archeology, classical studies, travel, history.
**Hours:** Mon - Fri 10.00 - 6.00, Sat 12.00 - 5.00.
**Services:** Mail order, library and University supply, occasional lists.

At ground floor level two rooms converted into one open showroom. The stock is well displayed and labelled clearly. Despite its name and location it is quite a good all round shop with literary and travel sections as well as scholarly ones. Old and new books live side by side on the shelves.


## 822 ARTS BIBLIOGRAPHIC
### 37 Great Russell Street, London WC1B 3PP.           01-636 5320

**Subject:** Modern art.
**Hours:** Mon - Fri 10.00 - 6.00.
**Services:** Mail order, credit cards.

Entered through a hallway and sidedoor is a well laid out spacious room with books on modern art. The books are subdivided into sections - sculpture, painting, individual artists - and there is a shelf of catalogues.


## 823 THE GOOD BOOK GUIDE
### Braithwaite and Taylor
### 91, Great Russell Street, WC1B 3PS.           01-580 8466

**Subjects:** General.
**Hours:** Mon - Fri 9.30 - 5.45. Sat 9.30 - 5.00.
**Services:** Special orders, credit cards, mail order, catalogue, The Good Book Guide.

The publishers of The Good Book Guide are true to their title and stock, discriminatingly chosen, the books of which they approve and have written up in their guide. They keep a log fire in winter and have a childrens corner with an attractive mural which all go to make a place well worth a visit. Subscribers to the guide are provided with a discerning selection of books which if ordered will be immediately dispatched anywhere. Braithwaite and Taylor have approached the book trade at rather an original tangent and that track can only but flourish because of them.

## 824 S.C.M. BOOKROOM
**58 Bloomsbury Street, London WC1B 3QX.**     01-636 3841/4

**Subjects:** Religion
**Hours:** Mon - Fri 9.00 - 5.00.
**Services:** Mail order, catalogue, special orders.

Number 58 is a protected Georgian building and the owners are not allowed to advertise their presence. Once you've passed into the building and then through a door marked 'Reception' you enter two well lit rooms which serve as a shop and publisher's showroom. All aspects of Christianity are covered under their various headings — there is one on church art and architecture. The staff are friendly and helpful.

## 825 BRITISH MUSEUM BOOKSHOP
**Great Russell Street, London WC1B 3RA.**     01-636 1544
Ext. 624

**Subjects:** Those relevant to the various departments of the Museum.
**Hours:** Mon - Sat 10.00 - 4.45, Sun 2.30 - 5.45.
**Services:** Mail order, lists.

Just inside the main entrance to the Museum is the bookstall and you can also purchase good replicas. All civilisations and all the disciplines by which we may understand them will probably have a book or pamphlet somewhere here. You could save the expense, like Marx, and write your own in the Reading Room — the great simplifiers are a boon to scholars and the book trade.

## 826 WATERSTONES
**62-64 Southampton Row, London WC1B 4AR.    01-831 901**

**Subjects:** General.
**Hours:** Mon - Fri 8.30 - 6.30.
**Services:** Special orders, credit cards, school supply, Faber list. Mail orders.

Waterstones is the wonder of the age. Their maroon awnings flutter in various parts of London now and are winning widespread recognition. Here on the western margin of Bloomsbury is another excellent shop stocking all that a man with 2 'O' levels or more to rub together, would hope to find.

## 827 H.K. LEWIS & CO. LTD.
**136 Gower Street, London WC1E 6BS.           01-387 4282**
**(7 lines)**

**Subjects:** Medical, science and technology
**Hours:** Mon - Fri 9.00 - 5.30, Sat 9.00 - 1.00.
**Services:** Mail order, lists, library, subscriptions to medical journals.

Impressive Portland stone fronted building with its history and dates engraved outside was erected for the company in 1930 and houses its medical books on two floors connected by stairs and an ornate lift. Part of the ground floor is a library with works of medical reference, useful to students at nearby University College Hospital. The shop has an atmosphere of a Victorian library and the range of medical books is extensive with excellent sections on nursing and psychology. Upstairs a large department of Sciences and Technology, all in heavy wooden bookshelves giving a solid well established background.

## 828 KNIGHTSBRIDGE (BOOKS) LTD.
**32 Store Street, London WC1E 7BS.            01-636 1252**

**Subjects:** New and Secondhand specialising in Oriental and African books, also Routedge and Kegan Paul publications.
**Hours:** Mon - Fri 9.30 - 5.30.
**Services:** Mail Order (catalogues), University supply, Credit Cards.

Just along from their old premises this bookshop has moved to a similar shop still specialising in Asian and African studies but now operating a secondhand section.

### 829 BUILDING BOOKSHOP LTD.
### 26 Store Street, London WC1E 7BT.   01-637 3151

**Subjects:** Building Trade, D.I.Y., Town Planning.
**Hours:** Mon - Fri 9.30 - 5.15, Sat 10.00 - 1.00.
**Services:** Mail order.

A modern open plan shop with two large display windows and an impressive glass domed entrance. Inside it is brightly lit by ceiling spot lights on white contemporary shelving. There are two rooms divided by the entrance door, the righthand one has technical drawing, town planning and all other aspects of the building trade, the lefthand one has D.I.Y. books.

### 829b HOUSING CENTRE TRUST BOOKSHOP
### The Update House (6th Floor),
### 33 Alfred Place, London. WC1E 7DP.   01-637 4202

**Subjects:** Housing.
**Hours:** Mon-Fri 10.30 - 5.00.
**Services:** Mail order, catalogue & lists, magazine. Special orders.

All aspects of housing are catered by books in paper and hard back including design, architecture and of particular interest is a section on housing for the disabled or elderly. They have a good mailing service and send a magazine to non-members of the Trust if required and this includes a list of recent publications.

## 830 DILLONS UNIVERSITY BOOKSHOP LTD.
**1 Malet Street, London WC1E 7JB.**　　　　　　　**01-636 1577**

**Subjects:** Academic, general, secondhand, antiquarian, computers.
**Hours:** Mon - Sat 9.00 - 5.30, Tue 10.00 - 5.30.
**Services:** Mail order, book lists, catalogues, Institutional supply, subscriptions for journals, records, Credit cards.

In the heart of London's main concentration of University colleges, this bookshop maintains the highest standard to which a bookshop can aspire. It is housed in a four storey turreted Edwardian building on the corner of Malet Street and Torrington Place. The bookshop was owned by London University until 1977 when it was acquired by the Pentos group who already had interests in the academic publishing and bookselling field.

The shop has 21 departments from astrology to zoology covering three floors of the building: science, technology, geography, and their new computer section are in the basement, the Humanities and general books are on the ground floor: more Humanities, foreign languages, anthropology and economics are on the first floor. Dillons has its own promotions department which produces catalogues and arranges joint promotions with publishers. The staff are expert and the departments are run by specialists in that particular field. Though Dillons is located in something of a by- way as far as the general working public is concerned, its reputation makes it a place to head for when book buying in London.

## 831 EUROPEAN SCHOOLBOOKS LTD.
**19 Store Street, London WC1E 7LA.**　　　　　　　**01-637 9491**

**Subjects:** English and Continental literature.
**Hours:** Mon - Fri 9.30 - 5.30.
**Services:** Mail order, University, school and library supply.

Opposite the Building Centre is this bookshop specialising in European languages with particularly strong sections of German and French books, resulting from a buy-out of the Learning Book Centre by Hans Preiss Ltd.

## 832 JEWISH MEMORIAL COUNCIL BOOKSHOP
**Woburn House/Floor 2**
**Upper Woburn Place, London WC1H OEP.**         01-388 0851

**Subjects:** Jewish Faith.
**Hours:** Mon - Thu 10.00 - 5.30. Fri 10.00 - 2.00 (Winter)
10.00 - 4.00 (Summer) Sun 10.30 - 12.45 p.m.
**Services:** Mail Order Catalogue, Discount for Students & Institutions.

You are asked to sign a visitors book as you enter this large rambling building. The bookshop is on the second floor above the museum. The books are for the community at large, but particularly the Jewish one.

Bibles, biographies, memoirs and books of general interest are well displayed and easily accessible. There is a good selection of Hebrew & Yiddish dictionaries. The service is helpful and attentive.


## 833 FRANK CASS (BOOKS) LTD. (The Woburn Book Shop)
**10 Woburn Walk, London WC1H OJL.**         01-387 7340

**Subjects:** Africa, Middle East, Politics, History, Economics & Education.
**Hour:** Mon - Fri 10.00 - 6.00.
**Services:** Catalogue available. Mail order in near future.

Mainly second hand with some new and some rare books. A small attractive in a Dickensian-looking pedestrian shoping area, built abour 1820. Respectable Professors of the Dismal Sciences at nearby London University are well looked after here.


## 834 FLINDERS
**45, Burton Street, WC1H 9AL.**         01-388 6080

**Subjects:** Australiana.
**Hours:** Mon - Sat 10.00 - 6.00.
**Services:** Mail order (catalogue). Book search.

A small shop opened recently specialising in books on and about Australia. Flinders has ideas to enlarge the present premises to hold the very large stock of titles from "down under" — maybe with a reading area in the front to make the customers feel relaxed and able to browse at leisure. The stock includes titles of recreated legendary characters, episodes from Australia's history, fiction and a childrens section.

### 835 MARCHMONT BOOKSHOP
**39 Burton Street, London WC1H 9AL.**  01-387 7989

**Subjects:** General (secondhand), modern first editions, illustrated books.
**Hours:** Mon - Fri 11.00 - 6.00, Sat 10.00 - 5.00.
**Services:** Mail order.

The books are mainly secondhand at reasonable prices, though there are review copies and modern first editions to be found here—with a little searching, as the order is rather haphazard.


### 836 TAVISTOCK BOOKSHOP
**86 Tavistock Place, London WC1H 9RT.**  01-837 9116

**Subjects:** Theology.
**Hours:** Mon - Fri 9.00 - 5.00.
**Services:** Mail order, church supply.

The only shop in sight in rather drab Tavistock Place, it relies more on supplying hymn books, etc. to churches than on passing trade. A well lit shop at ground floor level with over 7,000 titles on the Christian faith, all denominations.


### 837 BLOOMSBURY BOOK PLACE
**11 Grenville Street, London WC1N 1LZ.**  01-278 8496

**Subjects:** General subjects mainly secondhand with emphasis on academic.
**Hours:** Mon - Sat 11.00 - 7.00. Sun 1.30 - 5.00 (often later).

A very large stock of secondhand books with academic especially the social sciences playing a major role. Large sections of different facets of education are displayed and well divided with a large musty basement backing the ground floor stock. Clinical and technical medicines, social welfare and the unusual disability and handicapped section make up the large health stock. Some unusual new books are stocked at bargain prices which are not remainders.

### 838 GROWER BOOKS
#### 50 Doughty Street, London WC1N 2LP.    01-405 7134/5

**Subjects:** Books of interest to Commercial growers and gardening.
**Hours:** Mon - Fri 9.00 - 4.30.
**Services:** Mail order (Lists). Special orders. Credit cards.

An office atmosphere but the public are welcome to call and look at the titles of Grower publications and books from other publishers on glasshouse crops, field vegetables and nursery stock. This must be the place for commercial growers but amateurs could also benefit from the many titles from flowers and flower arranging to theories on weed control books, on poisonous plants and their effect in Britain — a wealth of information for gardeners.


### 839 CREATIVE CAMERA BOOKSHOP
#### 19 Doughty Street, London WC1N 2PT.    01-242 0565

**Subjects:** Photography.
**Hours:** Mon - Fri 10.30 - 6.00.
**Services:** Mail order, catalogue, credit cards.

Over 1,000 titles on the artistic, cultural and historical aspects of photography. They produce a comprehensive catalogue for £1, which is refundable when returned with an order valued £5 or more. Of course pigeons and cameras have come together in wartime — but perhaps I've already said more than I should. A fascinating shop.


### 840 RACING PIGEON PUBLISHING CO.
#### 19 Doughty Street, London WC1N 2PT.    01-242 0565

**Subjects:** Racing Pigeons.
**Hours:** Mon - Fri 9.00 - 5.15.
**Services:** Mail order.

Headquarters of Coo Press Ltd., the books share a room with those of the Creative Camera Bookshop. If London has any pigeon fanciers left after Trafalgar Square this is a must. A rare specialist.

## 841 JENNER
**19 Great Ormond Street, London WC1N 3JB.**  01404 4415

**Subjects:** Old and rare medical books.
**Hours:** Tue - Thu 9.30 - 6.30 (advisable to phone about other days).
**Services:** Special orders, catalogue.

A unique specialisation in antiquarian and rare medical books is is complimented by old medical instruments and prints. Well situated for the hospitals nearby.


## 842 ODYSSEY BOOKS LTD.
**30 Lambs Conduit Street, London WC1N 3LE.**  01-405 6735

**Subjects:** Alternative Health and Natural Healing and Astrology.
**Hours:** Mon - Fri 10.30 - 6.30. Sat 11.00 - 5.00.
**Services:** Mail order, Special orders.

Odyssey Bookshop which stocks Holistic Books for Mind, Body and Spirit is situated in the heart of Old Bloomsbury just 5 minutes walk from Holborn or Russell Square tubes. A sunny, light, airy shop with a peaceful atmosphere makes it ideal for quiet, relaxed browsing. A wide selection of Alternative Health and Natural Healing titles as well as Vegetarian Cookery, Eastern & Western Philosophies, Astrology, Psychology and much more. Mail order available and the owners are very happy to offer help and advice if needed.


## 843 BERNARD STONE
**THE TURRET BOOKSHOP**
**42, Lamb's Conduit Street, WC1N 3LJ.**  01-405 6058

**Subjects:** General, poetry, the work of Ralph Steadman.
**Hours:** Mon - Sat 10.00 - 6.00.
**Services:** Credit cards, mail order (catalogue)

A move from Covent Garden to Lamb's Conduit Street has given this bookshop brighter premises but Sigmund Freud, still glowers at the customers — a sculpture by Lyn Kramer made to promote one of the books by Ralph Steadman (the cartoonist) in whose work this shop specialises.

**844 WEST END BOOKS**
**82 Lambs Conduit Street, London WC1N 3LT.**     **01-405 3029**

**Subjects:** Medical.
**Hours:** Mon - Fri 9.30 - 6.00.

This shop is strategically located near several hospitals. Run by a helpful husband and wife team, it is well lit and spacious. They hope to expand their services to mail order, etc. soon.

**845 KINGS BOOKSHOP**
**17a Rugby Street, London WC1N 3QT.**     **01-405 4551**

**Subjects:** General.
**Hours:** Mon - Fri 9.30 - 6.00.

A large window enables one to comprehend most of the books in this small shop from the street. Their stock is in the general/popular range.

**846 VERMILION BOOKS**
**57 Red Lion Street, London WC1R 4PD.**     **01-242 5822**

**Subjects:** General (No fiction).
**Hours:** Mon - Fri 10.00 - 6.00.
**Services:** libraries sold at 25% retail price. Review copies bought and sold with up to 1/5 off Published Price.

Books on a bench on the pavement mark the spot. Warm and well lit inside. The books are carefully arranged by subject then alphabetically with all paperbacks one third off. Helpful service from the owner at a desk inside the entrance.

### 847 FINE BOOKS ORIENTAL LTD.
**Empire House (3rd Floor)**
**34/35 High Holborn, London WC1V 6AA.**   01-405 0650

**Subjects:** Oriental.
**Hours:** Mon - Fri 9.00 - 5.30.
**Services:** Mail order, catalogue.

If you are interested in Asia, from Turkey to Japan, this is the place for you, its comprehensive rare and secondhand stock is one of the best in London. It is well worth taking the lift or stairs to the fourth floor to inspect the facinatating stock or to obtain expert advice. Though most of the business is mail order it is well laid out to receive the browser. The Japanese section is probably the largest.

### 848 H.M.S.O. (HER MAJESTY'S STATIONERY OFFICE) GOVERNMENT BOOKSHOP
**49 High Holborn, London, WC1V 6HB.**   01-928 6977

**Subjects:** Government and Parliamentary publications.
**Hours:** Mon - Fri 8.30 - 5.00.
**Services:** Publishers and distributors of most official books and pamphlets.

This shop, established in 1786, has the busy atmosphere of a wholesale business. The rules and regulations of government and other established bodies can all be obtained here, the whole kept running by a large and knowledgeable staff. One can get Hansard hot from the Chamber and also excellent maps and guides to areas and walks in this country. It stocks the tourist range of Ordnance Survey maps.

### 849 PIPELINE BOOKS LTD.
**87 High Holborn, London WC1V 6LS.**   01-242 5454

**Subjects:** General.
**Hours:** Mon - Fri 9.00 - 5.30.
**Services:** Credit cards.

The first London retail bookshop of this well run distributing company. Starting up as we go to press, we hope to have fuller notes in our next edition.

Previous occupants here were Templar Books, whose record shop continues at No. 86.

**850 OYEZ STATIONERY LTD.**
**49, Bedford Row, WC1V 6RL.**  01-242 7132

**Subjects:** Law.
**Hours:** Mon - Fri 9.00 - 5.00.
**Services:** Credit cards, special orders.

Mostly red tape here but a small selection of legal books. Try and order a copy of Brief Lives here and you could confuse the staff.

**851 PARKS**
**244, High Holborn, WC1V 7DZ.**  01-831 9501/2

**Subjects:** Accountancy, banking, law and business studies.
**Hours:** Mon - Fri 9.00 - 6.00. Sat 9.00 - 1.00.
**Services:** Special orders, mail order, catalogue.

A well laid out shop covering their chosen field comprehensively, both for students and practitioners of these black arts — I mean if they wore red something would have gone wrong wouldn't it.

**852 JAMES SMITH**
**94 Grays Inn Road, London WC1X 8AA**  01-405 5697

**Subjects:** Remainders and New Books of general interest with an emphasis on Art.
**Hours:** Mon-Fri 8.00 - 6.00 Sat: Sometimes in winter
**Services:** Booksearch and export despatch.

A small well lit shop with an individual character. A willing staff to assist in locating or obtaining new or out of print books.
  Mr Smith says they've operated for some 20 years without a proper sign, but that he's thinking about having one put up!

**853 GEOGRAPHERS**  01-242 9246
**28 Grays Inn Road, London WC1X 8HX.**  01-405 7322

**Subjects:** Maps, guides, A-Z publications.
**Hours:** Mon - Fri 9.00 - 5.00.
**Services:** Mail order.

A small shop specialising in maps, guides, atlases and globes. They are the publishers of the A-Z Guides.

### 854 FOUR PROVINCES BOOKSHOP
### 244-246 Gray's Inn Road, London WC1X 8JR.   01-833-3022

**Subjects:** All aspects of Irish culture.
**Hours:** Tue - Sat 10.00 - 6.00.
**Services:** Mail order.

Incorporating the Irish Book Centre this shop in Gray's Inn Road stocks books relevant to Ireland. Art, Music, Children's books in Gaelic — Gaelic Language and Literature, History and Politics and a large selection of Irish Socialist writings and facsimile reprints of the Cuala Press are available. New and secondhand books are shelved in this small shop with pamphlets of Dublin Historical Association available.


### 855 CENTRAL BOOKS LTD.
### 37 Grays Inn Road, London WC1X 8PP.   01-242 6166

**Subjects:** General, politics (left wing), sociology, women's movement.
**Hours:** Mon - Fri 9.30 - 5.30, Sat 10.00 - 2.00.
**Services:** Mail order, bookstalls at Conferences given discount.

A brightly lit shop in down-at-heel Grays Inn Road, with a large clean window display. The books are arranged under subject headings but only the fiction section has alphabetical order. If you are of the party of 'our friends in the woods' this is the shop for you. Rather good on booklets from Chess Congresses, especially Russian ones.


### 856 McCARTA LTD.
### 122 Kings Cross Road, London WC1X 9DS.   01-278 8278

**Subjects:** Map and guide specialists.
**Hours:** Mon - Sat 9.30 - 5.30.
**Services:** Mail Order (Lists). Special orders. Credit cards.

If you want a guide or map it is worth the journey to the one way system opposite Kings Cross Station to this small shop with an excellent stock. Town plans in Europe and the Middle East as well as Britain are available and climbing, walking and waterway guides are well covered even details of the Alps for the enthusiast. It may be worth making use of their Mail Order service although they are open six days a week.

# WC2

**900 TEMPLAR BOOKS LTD.**     01-405 3189
**75/76 Chancery Lane, London WC2A 1AA.**     01-242 8669

**Subjects:** General, remainders, Law.
**Hours:** Mon - Fri 9.00 - 5.30.
**Services:** Credit cards, mail order, library supply.

Two shops in Chancery Lane, one stocking records and remainders and two doors away the smaller one stocking new titles with an emphasis on Law and Reference books. They endeavour to stock the complete Penguin list and those of other major paperback publishers.

**901 THE CHANCERY LANE BOOKSHOP**
**6 Chichester Rents,**
**Chancery Lane, London WC2A 1EG.**     01-405 0635

**Subjects:** Secondhand, antiquarian.
**Hours:** Mon - Fri 9.00 - 5.30.
**Services:** Mail order, catalogue, University and library supply.

In an intriguing alleyway off Chancery Lane, with a dark green front and a table of books outside. Inside the books are everywhere, some on the floor, a skylight helps to lighten the way a little and the antiquarian section specialising in topography and European travel gives the profit.

**902 LAW NOTES LENDING LIBRARY LTD.**     01-405 0780
**25/26 Chancery Lane, London WC2A 1NB.**     01-405 6151

**Subjects:** Law books.
**Hours:** Mon - Fri 9.30 - 5.00.

This is largely a library for the legal profession and law students but there is a retail section. Behind a heavy counter are dark shelves of books which form the library section, but on the customer side are the books, fewer in number, which are for sale — all legal books.

## 903 HAMMICK, SWEET & MAXWELL
### 116 Chancery Lane, London WC2A 1PP.      01-405 5711

**Subjects:** Law books.
**Hours:** Mon - Fri 9.30 - 6.00.
**Services:** Credit cards, mail order, catalogue, subscriptions to to journals.

An attractive looking shop with a bow window on each side of the entrance. Inside it is well lit and spacious with a good display of law books, including their own publications. They publish and sell loose leaf volumes of encyclopedias to help keep the practioners up to date with new cases, acts and orders. There is a small section of general books.

## 904 THE ECONOMISTS' BOOKSHOP LTD.
### Clare Market,
### Portugal Street, London WC2A 2AB.      01-405 5531

**Subjects:** Economics, politics, social sciences. anthropology.
**Hours:** Mon - Fri 9.30 - 6.00 (Wed 10.30 - 6.00),
         Sat 10.00 - 1.30 (only in college term time)
**Services:** Mail order, catalogue, credit cards, University and library supply.

The shop is jointly owned by the Economist magazine and the London School of Economics and is located a short step from the latter. It is a compact and comprehensive shop dealing fairly exclusively in its speciality subjects but there is a Penguin and Fontana paperback section at the far end. The notices in the shop warning against theft are presumably directed towards the Utopian school of economists. Mail orders and Accounts are at 43 Gloucester Crescent, NW1.

## 905 THE ECONOMISTS' BOOKSHOP
**(Secondhand Department)**
**Clare Market, Portugal Street, WC2A 2AB.**              **01-405 8643**

**Subjects:** Secondhand, remaindered and out of print works on all subjects stocked by The Economists' Bookshop next door.
**Hours:** Mon - Fri 9.30 - 6.00 (Wed 10.30 - 6.00).
**Services:** Special orders, mail order, credit cards, books bought.

These new premises are situated just inside the college, they throb with activity as they are much used by the students of the L.S.E. The stock is comprehensive and the staff helpful. The place seems to overflow with books.

## 906 WILDY & SONS LTD.
**Lincolns Inn Archway,**
**Carey Street, London WC2A 2JD.**              **01-242 5778**

**Subjects:** Law books.
**Hours:** Mon - Fri 8.45 - 5.15.
**Services:** Credit cards, mail order, valuation, institutional supply.

Beautifully situated in the old Archway at Lincoln's Inn. It is a family business owned by W.E. Sinkins whose father kept records in his head. Today there is a filing system with records of law books published from 1500 to the present day.

Established in 1830 this shop is for those who practise Law. At ground floor level the books are arranged alphabetically by subject, from Abortion onwards, and up a few stairs is a large room with antiquarian and secondhand books. Here also is an interesting little display of relics found in the building and newspaper cuttings of famous cases like that of Crippen.

### 907 MODERN LAW BOOKS
(Instant Companies Ltd)  
7 Bell Yard, London WC2A 2JR.

01-242 1705  
01-831 8581

**Subjects:** Company Law.  
**Hours:** Mon - Fri 9.00 - 5.30.  
**Services:** Mail Order.

This small shop is the trade counter for the Publishers Barry Rose, who produce books on company law: other publishers in the same field also have books here, all on the law.

### 908 BUTTERWORTHS LEGAL BOOKSHOP
9/12 Bell Yard,  
Temple Bar, London WC2A 2JR.

01-405 6900  
Ext 295 and 296

**Subjects:** Legal, tax.  
**Hours:** Mon - Fri 9.00 - 5.30.  
**Services:** Credit cards, mail order, catalogues, supply to the Legal profession, subscriptions to some legal magazines.

A modern well lit shop in a side road off Fleet Street next ot the Law Courts. Hard and softbacked books are stocked, and, of course, their own publications are well represented.

### 909 THE ROYAL SHAKESPEARE COMPANY BOOKSHOP
Aldwych Theatre,  
49 The Aldwych, London WC2B 4DF.      01-379 6721 Ext 45

**Subjects:** Theatre, plays.  
**Hours:** Mon - Sat 10.00 - 7.30.  
**Services:** Theatre vouchers for R.S.C., mail order.

A small shop selling books, theatrical photographs, T-shirts and other promotional material for R.S.C. The book selection is quite large and plays performed by the company can be bought.

## 910 B.B.C. WORLD
**Bush House, Strand, WC2B 4PH.**

01-240 3456
Ext 2575

**Subjects:** B.B.C. publications.
**Hours:** Mon - Fri 9.30 - 7.00.
**Services:** Special orders for B.B.C. publications, lists.

This ground floor shop is one of the several outlets where the B.B.C. sell their generally excellent publications. Bush House is the H.Q. of World Service which many would say was the most excellent of the many activities carried out by the corporation.

## 911 HORACE C. BLOSSOM, BOOKSELLERS
**36, Great Queen Street, London WC2B 5AA.**

01-831 0381

**Subjects:** Secondhand, general and remainders.
**Hours:** Mon - Fri 10.30 - 6.00. Sat 11.00 - 4.30.

A very attractive secondhand bookshop brightly coloured in pinks and green, a welcome change from what is too often a rather depressing ambience for browsing. The stock is excellent with an emphasis on the arts and natural history, and the remainders are carefully chosen.

## 912 THE CITY LITERARY BOOKSHOP
**22 Stukeley Street,**
**Drury Lane, London WC2B 5LJ.**

01-242 9872
Ext.22

**Subjects:** Educational.
**Hours:** Mon - Fri 12.00 - 7.45.
**Services:** Special orders.

The bookshop is in the foyer of the City Literary Institute and mainly serves the students there. Besides subjects related to the courses they have some popular quality fiction and a small secondhand section.

## 913 BRITISH INSTITUTE OF MANAGEMENT
**Management House,
43 Parker Street, London WC2B 5PT.** 01-405 3456

**Subjects:** Management.
**Hours:** Mon - Fri 9.30 - 5.00.
**Services:** Mail order, lists, catalogue.

This department of the Institute sells books, pamphlets and reports of interest to top management, much of the stock published by themselves. Next to the shop is an extensive library for members of the B.I.M.


## 914 W. H. SMITH & SON LIMITED
**11 Kingsway, Aldwych, London WC2B 6YA.** 01-836 5951

**Subjects:** General.
**Hours:** Mon - Fri 8.30 - 5.30 (Thu 10.00 - 5.30)
**Services:** Credit cards, special orders.

Until the opening of the Holborn Branch, this was the WHS flagship in these parts. There is a prominent book section on the ground floor at the back and the shop has an impressive range of monthly and quarterly magazines on display.


## 915 YOUTH HOSTELS ASSOCIATION SERVICES LTD.
**14 Southampton Street, London WC2E 7HY.** 01-836 8541

**Subjects:** Outdoor activities, travel.
**Hours:** Mon - Sat 9.30 - 5.30.
**Services:** Credit cards, discount for members.

A large area has been given to the book and map department with entry from the shop or from the street. All outdoor sports are comprehensively covered together with ancillary pursuits like bird watching and camping. The shop is open to non members. The change in the character of Covent Garden has brought this shop to the notice of many more people than formerly. Their own publications cover off the beaten track holidays in Europe and are ideal for the budget traveller.

### 916 HARRIS PUBLICATIONS LTD.
42 Maiden Lane, London WC2E 7LW.     01-240 2286

**Subjects:** Philately,
**Hours:** Mon - Fri 9.00 - 5.15, Sat 9.30 - 2.30.
**Services:** Mail order, catalogue, credit cards, subscriptions to philatelic magazines.

At street level more like an office, where they handle catalogues, but up a spiral iron staircase you are led to a gallery where the books are kept. They specialise in the one subject, international stamp collcting, and their expertise and service is most helpful.


### 917 INTERMEDIATE TECHNOLOGY PUBLICATIONS LTD.
9 King Street, London WC2E 8HN.

01-836 9434
(Ext 11 - mail order)
(Ext 14 - bookshop)

**Subjects:** Alternative approaches to development.
**Hours:** Mon - Fri 9.30 - 5.30.
**Services:** Mail order, catalogue (posted world-wide, free), journal subscriptions.

One goes through an office to a small room where the books and pamphlets are kept. The ideas behind this shop are those of the late Dr. Schumacher of nutty slack and 'Small is Beautiful' fame. The shop name is self-explanatory and is to help developing countries avoid the violent disruption of sudden industrialisation. The areas covered are agriculture, building, co-operative education, energy, etc. There is plenty of interest for indigines here too.


### 918 AFRICA BOOK CENTRE
38 King Street, London WC2E 8JT.     01-836 1973/4

**Subjects:** Africana
**Hours:** Mon - Fri 9.30 - 5.30.

This is chiefly an exhibition centre rather than a bookshop although there are a few books on sale which have a popular demand. The shop is in the same building as the African Centre which is an Educational Institute but independent of it. In future they hope to include Caribbean books too.

### 919 DORLING KINDERSLEY LTD.
9 Henrietta Street,
Covent Garden, London WC2E 8PS.        01-240 5151/5

**Subjects:** Reference works.
**Hours:** Mon - Fri 9.30 - 5.30.
**Services:** Mail order, catalogue.

Really a book packager, working closely with publishers to create quality illustrated reference books. The shop is to comply with Covent Garden rules, and they have an attractive showroom with works on sport, gardening, cookery, crafts, D.I.Y., photography and alternative life styles.

### 920 HAMMICKS
1 The Market,
Covent Garden, London WC2E 8RA.        01-379 6465

**Subjects:** General, children's books.
**Hours:** Mon - Sat 10.00 - 7.30.
**Services:** Credit cards, special orders.

This is an attractive shop in the old Floral Hall of Covent Garden. There are three floors to the shop, connected by a carpeted staircase, the top one has children's books. The pine shelving, colourful decor and the adaptation of the old structure with its arches and surprising recesses, make it most interesting to look around. They have a good general range well displayed.

### 921 THE PENGUIN BOOKSHOP
10 The Market,
Covent Garden, London WC2E 8RB.        01-379 7650

**Subjects:** General, art, literature.
**Hours:** Mon - Sat 10.00 - 8.00.
**Services:** Cards, special orders for Penguin, Allen Lane and Kestrel publications.

The shop is in the Central Avenue of the prettily refurbished Covent Garden and has kept much of the form of its market stall forebear with stone floors and an iron staircase to the basement room. Penguin books predominate but there are other paperback publishers and a few hardbacked books. The ground floor is a little cramped but downstairs where the mainly literary books are kept there is ample room to browse.

## 922 ALTERNATIVE BOOKSHOP
**3, Langley Court, Covent Garden, WC2E 9JY.**  01-240 1804

**Subjects:** Libertarianism, human rights, free market economics.
**Hours:** Mon - Sat 11.00 - 6.00. (Jun - Sep 11.00 - 8.00)
**Services:** Credit card, mail order, University supply, meeting centre for Libertarians.

The only bookshop of its kind in the country, this is the Capitalist Alternative.

Individual liberties are what count here, in both the classical liberal and non-socialist anarchist traditions. Its stock covers everything from race, sex and defence to free market economics. Pro-nuclear energy, anti astrology and generally anti-Marxist, it has taken its stand on the interstices of more general movements.

## 923 ARTS COUNCIL SHOP
**8 Long Acre**
**Covent Garden, London WC2E 9LG.**  01-836 1359

**Subjects:** Books on performing and visual arts, Arts Council publications.
**Hours:** Mon - Sat 10.00 - 7.45.
**Services:** Mail order, catalogue at Christmas, special order, credit cards.

Scarlet is the colour chosen by the Arts Council for its shop front. Inside it is carpeted, with centrally standing book cases. The walls house the more expensive books behind glass. There are sections on art, architecture, poetry, music, photography, etc. A table at the back has remainders and sale books and down a few stairs is a separate section with its own entrance from Garrick Street on all aspects of the theatre.

## 924 EDWARD STANFORD LTD.
### 12-14 Long Acre, London WC2E 9LP.     01-836 1321

**Subjects:** Maps, guides, travel, geological and maritime books and charts.
**Hours:** Mon - Fri 9.00 - 5.30 (often 7.00), Sat 10.00 - 4.00).
**Services:** Mail order, Catalogue, Credit cards, Stanford guide to maps available on request.

Part of the George Philip cartographic company and the largest map retailers in the world, Stanfords have a reputation second to none for their range of maps, charts and globes. From a large scale section of a British ordnance survey map through to maps of the world with all the scales and places between, they can all be obtained here.

Stanfords is the unique source for specialist international maps imported from Europe, Africa, Asia and the Americas, with world-wide guide books to match. Mounted maps for wall display are made up to order. The special sections on climbing, geology and sailing are probably the best in London.


## 925 BERTRAM ROTA LTD.
### 30/31 Long Acre, London WC2E 9LT.     01-836 0723

**Subjects:** First editions, antiquarian, private presses.
**Hours:** Mon - Fri 9.30 - 5.30.
**Services:** Mail order, catalogue.

An interesting looking shop outside and in. It has a glass panelled front with dark green surrounds and, inside, black pillars abound with a huge skylight at the rear. The shop was once a banana warehouse and was redesigned by John Prizeman. Books line the walls and above are galleried offices. Rotas have long been a mecca for the collector of modern first editions and their books range in value from £5 to £5,000.


## 926 BOOK BARGAINS
### 124, Long Acre, WC2E 9PE.     01-836 0625

**Subjects:** Remainders
**Hours:** Mon - Sat 10.00 - 8.00. Sun 2.00 - 6.00.

On the periphery of the new Covent Garden this shop has quite a good selection of quality remainders with Art and Photography featuring prominently, but the stock is varied, selling both hard and paperbacked books.

## 927 THE PHOTOGRAPHERS GALLERY
### 8 Great Newport Street, London WC2H 7HY.                01-240 5511

**Subjects:** Photography
**Hours:** Mon - Sat 11.00 - 7.00, Sun 12.00 - 6.00.
**Services:** Mail order, catalogue, credit cards.

The reception area is given over to books and beyond there is a large gallery exhibiting photographs. This specialist shop/gallery has new, out of print and rare books on photography, technical as well as artistic angles.


## 928 GUANGHWA COMPANY
### 9 Newport Place, London WC2H 7JR.                01-437 3737

**Subjects:** China.
**Hours:** Mon - Sat 10.30 - 7.00, Sun 11.00 - 7.00.
**Services:** Mail order, Catalogue, Special Orders, A library & Institutional Supply, and subscriptions to Chinese and Hong Kong Magazines.

This shop has a large booklined room devoted to books on China with texts in the Chinese languages and teaching aids such as cassettes and records for help in learning them. The shop is in the heart of London's Chinatown and serves as a sort of cultural centre. Besides the books which range from childrens to scholarly texts, they also sell attractive prints and artifacts from China.


## 929 RAY'S JAZZ SHOP
### 180, Shaftesbury Avenue, WC2H 8JS.                01-240 3969

**Subjects:** Jazz.
**Hours:** Mon - Sat 10.00 - 6.30.
**Services:** Mail order, credit cards, discount system for cheques and cash.

Primarily for the aural senses — records, tapes and cassettes, the shop does have some jazz books but they are behind the counter and not generally accessible.

### 930 POPULAR BOOK CENTRE
**218 Shaftesbury Avenue, London WC2H 8EB.**          **01-240 2210**

**Subjects:** Secondhand.
**Hours:** Mon - Sat 10.00 - 6.00.
**Services:** Exchange of books, one-third allowed.

The window displays old copies of Picture Post, which are now probably collector items. Inside are more magazines and secondhand books which can be exchanged, or bought. Many of the magazines could be described as risqué.


### 931 FORBIDDEN PLANET 2
**58, St. Giles High Street, WC2H 8LH.**          **01-379 6042**

**Subjects:** Cinema.
**Hours:** Mon - Sat 10.00 - 6.00 (Thu 10.00 - 7.00).
**Services:** Special orders, credit cards.

A special shop for the movie addict with magazines, movie stills and posters, film track records and shelves devoted to books about films, the producers, actors and any other aspect of the cinema. It is only a few steps away from their science fiction shop and very near Tottenham Court tube station.


### 932 ZENO
**6 Denmark Street, London WC2H 8LP.**          **01-836 2522**

**Subjects:** Classical and Modern Greece.
**Hours:** Mon - Fri 9.30 - 6.00, Sat 9.30 - 5.00.
**Services:** Mail order, catalogue, library supply, magazine subscriptions.

They have a large selection of books, new, second hand and rare, on Greece and the Hellenic World of about 350 BC. There are two rooms crammed with stock, and the shop is a centre for the Greek community resident and passing through London.

### 933 FORBIDDEN PLANET
23 Denmark Street, London WC2H 8NA.   01-836 4179

**Subjects:** Science fiction, comics.
**Hours:** Mon - Sat 10.00 - 6.00, Thu 10.00 - 7.00.
**Services:** Mail order, catalogue, subscription to magazines.

Here Sci-Fi buffs have their own shop. Large collection, new and old, hard or soft covers, with many American publications not easily obtainable elsewhere. Posters records and film stills from Dr. Who, Satr Wars, etc. are also on sale. Unique in its specialisation.

### 934 CORNER HOUSE BOOK SHOP
14 Endell Street, London WC2H 9BD.   01-836 9960

**Subjects:** Radical and alternative education. Feminist movement.
**Hours:** Mon - Sat 10.00 - 6.00.
**Services:** Mail order, catalogue for sale, Conference supply.

Books, pamphlets and magazines on feminism, race, etc. There is a section of non-sexist, non-racist children's books. Racialist non-sexists and vice versa proceed with caution. The bookshop is a co-operative venture, and is an inner London example of the new growth area in bookshops.

### 935 THE ART BOOK COMPANY
18 Endell Street,
Covent Garden, London WC2H 9BD.   01-836 7907

**Subjects:** Art, design, graphics.
**Hours:** Mon - Fri 9.30 - 5.30.
**Services:** Credit cards, mail order, catalogue, Institutional supply.

Having to ring a bell rather indicates that mail order is the chief method of selling here. Rather office-like atmosphere but books well arranged and lit, and customers are welcome to inspect. Books on design and graphics, new and old, are their speciality.

### 936 CHAPMANS PROFESSIONAL BOOKSHOP
**20, Endell Street, Covent Garden, WC2H 9BD.**     **01-240 5011**

**Subjects:** Books for the professions and business studies.
**Hours:** Mon - Fri 9.00 - 6.00.
**Services:** Special orders, Mail order, booklists.

Another new bookshop for Covent Garden. This one specializes in accountancy, finance, taxation, banking and other business studies. They have a very efficient special order service with, in some cases, same day delivery.

### 937 THE ALBANIAN SHOP
**3 Betterton Street, London WC2H 9BP.**     **01-836 0976**

**Subjects:** Books related to Albania and paperbacks.
**Hours:** Mon - Fri 12.00 - 6.00. Sat 3.00 - 6.00.
**Services:** Mail order.

This is also known as the Gramophone Exchange so there are many thousands of records with handicrafts from Albania also prominent. There is a selection of paperbacks and a stock of books related to Albania. Music, travel, and poetry are popular. Titles are mostly in English although books in Albanian are available here. Art, archaeology and current affairs of that country are among the subjects stocked.

### 938 MYSTERIES
**9 Monmouth Street, London WC2H 9DA.**     **01-240 3688**

**Subjects:** New books on Psychic, Paranormal and Esoteric subjects.
**Hours:** Mon - Sat 10.00 - 6.00.
**Services:** Credit cards, Special orders, Mail order (Lists), Psychic readings.

All the paraphernalia and metaphysical research equipment is on sale here with an excellent range of books on all associated subjects with Psychic readings available by resident Clairvoyants. Books are well orgainsed in shelves to enable the customer to browse without obstruction from the many oils, candles, jewellery, crystal balls, music tapes, etc.

### 939 A. ZWEMMER LTD.
24, Litchfield Street, WC2H 9NJ.                           01-836 4710

**Subjects:** Artistry and Architecture new and out of print.
**Hours:** 9.30 - 6.00. Sat 9.30 - 5.30.
**Services:** Credit cards, Special orders, Mail order (lists).

This family firm is well known throughout the Art world and as well as their rare and out of print books, they have a good range of inexpensive books for the student on the history of Art and Architecture. Two floors in which to browse and a third for the antiquarian department for which it is advisable to make an appointment.

### 940 GREENWICH BOOK COMPANY
37, Neal Street, WC2H 9PR.                                 01-240 3319

**Subjects:** General.
**Hours:** Mon - Fri 10.00 - 7.00. Sat 10.00 - 6.00.
**Services:** Credit cards, special orders.

Well, the new Covent Garden is certainly pulling them in. Here we have a good general bookshop, recently opened, with clear lines brightly lit and with a good range of books. I do hope all those late night wine bibbers or those just after a rare lentil soup appreciate the quality of the commerce in these parts.

### 941 NEAL STREET EAST
5, Neal Street, WC2H 9PU.                                  01-240 0135-6

**Subjects:** China and Japan.
**Hours:** Mon - Fri 10.00 - 5.45 (Wed 10.00 - 7.00) Sat 10.00 - 5.00.
**Services:** Credit cards, special orders.

An unusual shop on several levels with the books just inside the main entrance. All the oriental arts of cooking, calligraphy design and so forth are well represented and there are also a few books which deal with the Indian experience in these things.

## 942 READS
**48A, Charing Cross Road, WC2H 0BB.**　　　　**01-379 7669**

**Subjects:** Antiquarian and general secondhand, travel, topography.
**Hours:** Mon - Sat 10.00 - 10.00. Sun 12.00 - 8.00.

A good basic secondhand bookshop with some specialisation in travel and the performing arts.

## 943 S. SOLOSY LTD.
**50 Charing Cross Road, London WC2H 0BB.**　　　　**01-836 6313**

**Subjects:** Militaria, aeronautical, maps and guides.
**Hours:** Mon - Fri 7.00 - 6.15, Sat 7.00 - 6.00.
**Services:** Special orders, magazine subscriptions.

The hours kept give the clue to this being principally a newsagent. The redevelopment in the Charing Cross Road has kept the owner's circumstances cramped but he keeps a few shelves on his specialised subjects.

## 944 COLLETS PENGUIN BOOKSHOP
**52 Charing Cross Road, London WC2H 0BB.**　　　　**01-836 2315**

**Subjects:** Penguin publications, new and secondhand.
**Hours:** Mon - Sat 10.00 - 6.30.
**Services:** Mail order, credit cards.

Collets have been selling Penguin books since the time they were sold for sixpence. This small shop aims to stock every one of the series in print, which is a great boon for those who can never find the one they want at most shops. This Penguin shop was opened in 1962.

## 945 HENRY PORDES BOOKS LTD.
**58-60 Charing Cross Road, WC2H 0BB.**　　　　**01-836 9031**

**Subjects:** Antiquarian, secondhand and remainders, Judaica, topography.
**Hours:** Mon - Sat 9.15 - 7.00.

All power to this fairly new bookshop. While many other shops have taken flight from this famous books street. Pordes have arrived and quite handsomely too. None of the stock is 'new', but as aficionados know, there is fine grading amongst the rest, and it is all here. A feature worth mentioning is a secondhand German section.

### 946 ANY AMOUNT OF BOOKS
**62 Charing Cross Road, London WC2H OBB.**       01-240 8140

**Subjects:** Secondhand and Antiquarian.
**Hours:** Sat 10.30 - 7.30. Sun 12.00 - 6.00.
**Services:** Catalogue.

The interesting stock of books at Hammersmith has expanded to premises in Charing Cross Road which will be more convenient for visitors to London to browse among the secondhand books held in most general subjects.


### 947 COLLETS LONDON SHOP
**64/66 Charing Cross Road, London WC2H OBB. 01-836 6306**

**Subjects:** Politics (orthodox marxist), economics, social sciences, general, secondhand.
**Hours:** Mon - Fri 10.30 - 6.00 (Thu 10.00 - 7.00), Sat 10.00 - 6.00.
**Services:** Mail order, credit cards, library supply, magazine subscriptions.

Certainly the principal left wing bookshop in London but with a good general range too of fiction, poetry, etc. There is also an interesting secondhand department. The Soviet umbilical is fairly strong and here in 1930 the author of 'Quiet Flows the Don', Mikhail Sholokov, was signing copies for a then untraumatised public.


### 948 SILVER MOON
**68 Charing Cross Road, London WC2H OBB.**       01-836 7906

**Subjects:** Feminism and Women's writing.
**Hours:** Tue - Sat 10.30 - 6.30.
**Services:** Café. Disabled access.

This shop has devoted its stock to writings for, about and by women — with a café run by women. Women's art and music are part of the stock with Feminist books lining the shelves with the object of making this a meeting place as well as a bookshop.

## 949 IAN SHIPLEY (BOOKS) LTD.
**70, Charing Cross Road, WC2H OBB.**  01-836 4872

**Subjects:** Visual arts.
**Hours:** Mon - Sat 10.00 - 6.00.
**Services:** Mail order (catalogue), search service.

Moved from Floral Street to the Charing Cross Road, Ian Shipley specialises in the visual Arts, which extends to books on the medium of advertising including Photography and Fashion. A specialist shop with Art, Architecture, Typography, Graphics, Aesthetics and Interior design, Japan and the Orient and their excellent stock of Exhibition catalogues, some costing as much as £20. Plenty of helpful expertise here for consultancies and individuals who wish to buy reference books.

## 950 AL HODA
**76-78 Charing Cross Road, London WC2H OBB.**  01-240 8381/2

**Subjects:** All aspects of Islam.
**Hours:** Mon - Sat 9.30 - 6.00.
**Services:** Special Orders, Educational Institutional Supply, Mail Order (Catalogue) Language Courses.

Three roomed bookshop segregated into English, Arabic and downstairs, Persian and Urdu.

A wide range of subjects is covered from Art and Architecture, Medicine, Third World and a comprehensive educational section backed by records and cassettes.

## 951 ZWEMMERS OXFORD UNIVERSITY PRESS BOOKSHOP
**72 Charing Cross Road, London WC2H OBE.**  01-240 1559

**Subjects:** O.U.P. publications.
**Hours:** Mon - Fri 9.30 - 5.30.
**Services:** Mail order, catalogues.

This is a shop window for one of the world's leading publishing houses. The books are mainly academic and educational, and it is of course a good place to buy a dictionary. They are also strong on children's books, legends and fairy tales.

### 952 A. ZWEMMER LTD.
**80 Charing Cross Road, WC2H OBE.**  01-836 4710

**Subjects:** Photography, Cinema and Graphic Design.
**Hours:** Mon - Fri 9.30 - 6.00. Sat 9.30 - 5.30.
**Services:** Mail order (Lists). Credit cards. Special orders.

Since the Art and Architecture sections have moved across the road this branch of Zwemmers has more room for its excellent stock of books on films, photography and graphics. The sections are clearly marked and they have some reduced books in their specialist subjects.

### 953 LOVEJOYS
**(Winart Publications Ltd.)**
**99A Charing Cross Road, WC2H ODP.**  01-437 1988

**Subjects:** Remainders and New paperbacks.
**Hours:** Mon - Sat 10.00 - 10.30.

A respectable shop selling remainders but with a warning to customers as it has a sex shop downstairs.

### 954 WATERSTONES
**121-125 Charing Cross Road, WC2H OEA.**  01-434 4291

**Subjects:** General.
**Hours:** Mon - Fri 9.30 - 7.30. Sat 9.30 - 7.00, except Thu - 9.30 - 8.00.
**Services:** Credit cards also own Credit card. Mail Order International. Book Lists. Literary Diary.

Selling books to Londoners at night is the basis of the Waterstone Group of Bookshops with the one in Charing Cross road next to Foyles as the main branch. The decor is excellent with black shelves on four floors with sections clearly marked in general subjects. Academic, Philosophy and Religion are strong sections but Art, National History. Childrens, travel best sellers are all extremely well covered with music backed by a classical record department. The staff appear to delight in the job and a very professional atmosphere prevails.

The travel department is so well stocked that it appears to have its own shop but it is inter-connected to the main area, although known as Waterstones Travel Bookshop. Literature on most aspects of travel can be found here with many titles on different countries and a separate section of London books. It upholds the excellent reputation the Waterstone stores have earned.

## 955 W. & G. FOYLE LTD.
**113-119 Charing Cross Road, London WC2H OEB.   01-437 5660**

**Subjects:** General, secondhand, bargain books, etc.
**Hours:**     Mon - Sat 9.00 - 6.00 (Thu 9.00 - 7.00)...
**Services:** Comprehensive — they do everything!

Probably the world's largest bookshop, Foyles, with a little patience on the customer's part, will locate any book he wants. It would be a cartographer's task to delineate the labyrinthine departments and to list all their sections. It is best to stalk one's quarry here rather than take it at a rush: the stock is so comprehensive that individual members of the staff can sometimes be only marginally less baffled than the customer. The several floors are linked by a stone staircase and a caged lift of some antiquity but escalators will soon supplement them. Always a busy and bustling shop, the one tranquil spot is the secondhand department where there is a good range of books and also a section of fine bindings. The remarkable Foyle family line has decidedly not thinned out with the current owner, Christina, whose running of this aircraft carrier of a shop is formidable and effective.

## 956 THE BOOK INN
**17 Charing Cross Road, London WC2H OEP.          01-839 2712**

**Subjects:** General, 'Adult' books and films in basement.
**Hours:**     Mon - Sat 9.00 - 11.00, Sun 11.00 - 10.00.
**Services:** Credit cards, special orders.

A spacious bookshop catering for the general popular taste with maps and guides for tourists. In the basement is the 'Adult' section.

### 957 COLLETS INTERNATIONAL BOOKSHOP
129/131 Charing Cross Road, London WC2H OEQ.

01-734 0782/3

**Subjects:** U.S.S.R., children's books, records.
**Hours:** Mon - Fri 10.00 - 6.30, Sat 10.00 - 6.00.
**Services:** Mail order, catalogue, library and university supply, credit cards, magazine subscriptions, special orders.

This shop in the Charing Cross Road, next to Foyles, is the most recent and ambitious of Collet's shops. Opened in 1976 it is an attractive brick building with plenty of space inside. The majority of the books come from the U.S.S.R., in many languages, but predominantly English and Russian. There is an extensive section of Soviet art books and posters, and a general stock of British books. In the basement classical and popular records are sold, with the Russian Melodiya label prominent, as well as Eastern European folk art.

### 958 NATIONAL PORTRAIT GALLERY
2 St. Martin's Place, London WC2H OHE.    01-930 1552, Ext 23

**Subjects:** Art.
**Hours:** Mon - Fri 10.00 - 5.00, Sat 10.00 - 6.00, Sun 2.00 - 6.00
**Services:** Mail order, catalogue.

A generously large shop just inside the entrance, with books relating to the pictures exhibited within. Also more general books on art, artists, the Royal Family and a table of remaindered books, all accessible and attractively displayed.

### 959 HOLBORN BOOKS LTD.
14 Charing Cross Road, London WC2H OHR.    01-240 2337

**Subjects:** Second Hand and New Penguin Books at reduced prices.
**Hours:** Mon - Sat 10.00 - 8.00. (Sundays 11.00 - 6.00)

This is a small busy shop at the southern end of Charing Cross Road usually crowded with lunch time bargain hunters. All books in the shop and those in boxes and shelves on the pavement outside are priced at under £2.

### 960 THE THEATRE SHOP
### 110 Charing Cross Road, London WC2H OJP.     01-836 4207

**Subjects:** Theatre.
**Hours:** Mon - Sat 10.00 - 6.00.
**Services:** Theatre ticket agency.

A small selection of books on the theatre here which they hope to expand soon, they also have a marvellous selection of old prints, posters and programmes. Books and theatres are the life blood around here (we won't mention the side streets) and this shop should blossom, though it lacks any window display.


### 961 BOOKS ETC.
### 120 Charing Cross Road, WC2H OJR.     01-379 6938

**Subjects:** General with Computer section including software.
**Hours:** Mon - Sat 9.30 - 8.00.
**Services:** Credit cards, Special orders.

Paperback fiction is one of the stronger subjects of this main branch of Books Etc. with cinema, travel, *science fiction* and computer sections well covered. In fact they have a very comprehensive stock in all general subjects and clear headings and sub-sections to guide the customers to the exact point of interest. Their travel department is extensive including maps and guides and software to back their computer section. Certainly a place to visit while in this area of many famous bookshops with easier access to the various departments than many.


### 962 HELLENIC BOOKSERVICE
### 122 Charing Cross Road, London WC2H OJR.     01-836 7071

**Subjects:** Greece and the Islands including Cyprus and Turkey. New, Secondhand and Antiquarian
**Hours:** Mon - Sat 9.00 - 6.00.
**Services:** Mail order, catalogue, special orders, University and library supply, subscriptions to magazines.

A small shop opposite Foyles but every inch is stacked with their specialist stock and there is no lack of enthusiasm from the three generations running this enterprising business. Every subject connected with Greece has its place, Art, Sculpture, Geology, Travel are just a few of the subjects with classics in Latin and educational sections with classes for everyone learning Greek, even the owners are surprised they can have so much under one roof.

### 963 THE BOOKSMITH
**148 Charing Cross Road, London WC2H OLB.**   01-836 3032

**Subjects:** General, bargain books.
**Hours:** Mon - Sat 9.30 - 8.00.

At the Tottenham Court Road end of Charing Cross Road, this is one of a number of shops in the chain. It stocks best selling paperbacks and hardback remainders and bargains. Art, cookery and the children's sections are the best represented.


### 964 THE GREEN KNIGHT BOOKSHOP
**34 St. Martins Court, London WC2N 4AL.**   01-836 3800

**Subjects:** Antiquarian - Out of Print books.
**Hours:** Mon - Fri 10.00 - 6.00 (flexible).
**Services:** Credit cards, mail order, catalogue.

A small shop with black panelled windows primarily serving collectors and dealers, in next street to Cecil Court.


### 965 MOTORBOOKS   01-836 5376
**33 & 36 St. Martins Court, London WC2N 4AL.**   01-836 6728

**Subjects:** Motor cars, motor cycles, railways, aviation, militaria.
**Hours:** Mon - Fri 9.30 - 5.30, Sat 10.30 - 5.30.
**Services:** Credit cards, mail order, subscriptions to motor magazines.

Two shops in St. Martins Court. Number 33 has the motor books including workshop manuals normally obtainable only from dealers, and in the basement there is a railway section, newly opened. At number 36 they have the military, naval and aviation sections. Most of the stock is in hardback as it tends to be in specialist fields.

### 966 J.B. CRAMER & CO. LTD.
**99 St. Martins Lane, London WC2N 4AZ.**        **01-240 1612**

**Subjects:** Music.
**Hours:** Mon - Fri 9.30 - 6.00, Sat 10.00 - 5.00.
**Services:** Mail order, lists, credit cards, subscriptions to musical magazines.

Musical instruments and books are on display in the window of this rather austere looking shop. Inside there is a large selection of song books and sheet music, mainly classical, but also a fair leavening of books on popular music, rock and music of the Thirties and Forties, Elvis Presley song books etc. Around the walls books and instruments are displayed and there is a central table with the more sumptuous music books on show.

### 967 THE BOOKSMITH (BSC REMAINDERS LTD.)
**36 St. Martin's Lane, London WC2N 4ER.**        **01-836 5110**

**Subjects:** Bargain books.
**Hours:** Mon - Sat 9.30 - 8.00.

A long, narrow, bright shop with bargain books arranged rather like piles of colourful vegetables at market. They also stock full priced paperback bestsellers, and downstairs bargain paperbacks at 4 for £1.

### 968 COLISEUM BOOKSHOP
**31, St. Martin's Lane, London WC2N 4ES.**        **01-836 0111**

**Subjects:** Opera & General Music.
**Hours:** Mon - Sat 10.00 - 7.30.
**Services:** Credit Cards, Special Orders.

The London Coliseum has opened a bookshop next door with appropriate architecture and plenty of space for opera buffs to browse among the books and scores, particularly of those relevant to the performances of the English National Opera Company. Biographies of composers and singers are prominent but other aspects of music are covered. There are also opera related records, cassettes and video cassettes.

### 969 STAGE DOOR PRINTS
1 Cecil Court, London, WC2N 4EZ.　　　　　　　01-240 1683

**Subjects:** Second hand books on Ballet, Opera and Theatre.
**Hours:**　　Mon - Fri 11.00 - 6.00. Sat 11.30 - 6.00.

A small shop specialising in antique prints of ballet, opera and the theatre with a small selection of secondhand books on these subjects, makes an interesting addition to the very special atmosphere of Cecil Court.


### 970 HAROLD T. STOREY
3 Cecil Court, London WC2N 4EZ.　　　　　　　01-836 3777

**Subjects:** General, Antiquarian and Secondhand.
**Hours:**　　Mon - Fri 10.00 - 6.00.
**Services:**　Sat 10.30 - 5.30.
　　　　　　Credit cards.

At first glance you may feel this shop is only dealing in prints but inside they do have a wall of books concentrating on fine buildings rather than any particular subjects


### 971 BELL, BOOK AND RADMALL　　　　　　　01-240 2161
4, Cecil Court, WC2N 4HE.　　　　　　　　　01-836 5888

**Subjects:** Modern first editions.
**Hours:**　　Mon - Fri 10.00 - 5.30.

In its new site Bell, Book and Radmall have maintained their excellence. Very much a collectors shop, with most of the books classifiable as 'literature'. The books are arranged alphabetically by author, which finally is probably the most sensible thing to do as it is these we love and the various effusions of their minds,, and any other taxonomy fragments our endeavours to hunt down a beloved writer.

### 972 REG AND PHILIP REMINGTON
**14 Cecil Court, London WC2N 4HE.**                     **01-836 9771**

**Subjects:** Antiquarian and Secondhand specialising in Voyages, Travel and Natural History.
**Hours:** Mon - Fri 10.00 - 5.00.
**Services:** Book search.

An ideal situation for a bookshop specialising in antiquarian books on travel backed by maps and prints. They have German and French translations and have offices at 26 Charing Cross Road (Suite 33) if the shop is closed.


### 973 DANCE BOOKS LTD.
**9 Cecil Court, London WC2N 4EZ.**                     **01-836 2314**

**Subjects:** Dance, Ballet, Human Movement, folk and ballroom. (New, secondhand and out of print).
**Hours:** Mon - Sat 11.00 - 7.00.
**Services:** Credit cards, mail order, catalogue, subscriptions to Dance magazines. Special orders. Records for ballet class.

Photographs and posters in the window proclaim their speciality. Ballet to Ballroom is covered and the shop is ideally located in the heart of theatreland. Run by the owners who are dedicated to the dancing world and publish their own books, they stock all books currently published in this country on dancing, plus a good selection of American material and a sprinkling of Continental. A central table holds files of unframed glossy photographs of famous dancers — a marvellous shop for the dance fanatic.


### 974 TRAVIS & EMERY
**17 Cecil Court, London WC2N 4EZ.**                     **01-240 2129**

**Subjects:** Music.
**Hours:** Mon - Fri 10.00 - 6.00, Sat 10.00 - 1.00.
**Services:** Mail order, catalogue, special orders.

The owner has unquestionable expertise on books and music. The shop is much visited by famous musicians. New and secondhand books line the walls and the antiquarian ones are kept under lock and key at the back for security. There is a large basement for stock which can be produced on enquiry. Again a special shop adding to the atmosphere of Cecil Court.

### 975 QUEVEDO
**25 Cecil Court, London WC2N 4EZ.**               01-836 9132

**Subjects:** Secondhand, antiquarian, Spain.
**Hours:** Mon - Fri 10.00 - 5.30.
**Services:** Mail order, catalogues.

Specialises in rare and secondhand books on Spain and in Spanish and has a large selection on English and Continental literature published before 1830.


### 976 H.M. FLETCHER
**27 Cecil Court, London WC2N 4EZ.**               01-836 2865

**Subjects:** Rare and secondhand books.
**Hours:** Mon - Fri 10.00 - 5.30.
**Services:** Special orders.

Mr. Fletcher has been in Cecil Court since 1937 and runs this collectors shop with his family. He keeps a rack of secondhand books outside and inside, has a spacious shop which the owner is proud to claim avoids subject specialisation but concentrates more on the book itself. The books can range in price from 20p to £2,000.


### 977 HAMBLING'S (MODELS) LTD
**29 Cecil Court, London WC2N 4EZ.**               01-836 4704

**Subjects:** Railway and model railway books, trams, buses.
**Hours:** Mon - Fri 9.00 - 5.30. Sat 10.00 - 4.00. Oct to Mar.
**Services:** Credit cards.

Apparently a shop selling model railways and accessories. There is one wall at the side, with books on the real thing with the emphasis on British railways. Decades of expertise available.

## 978 PLEASURES OF PAST TIMES
**11 Cecil Court, London WC2N 4HB.**               **01-836 1142**

**Subjects:** Entertainment, Music Hall, Circus, children's books.
**Hours:** Mon - Fri 11.00 - 6.00 (closed 2.30 - 3.30),
Sat (1st in month) 11.00 - 2.00.
**Services:** Hire for film and TV studios.

A marvellous place to see, full of early children's books, valentines, old postcards and playbills. All the thrills and chills of Victorian ephemera are here. Besides children's books there are many out of print works on the world of entertainment - the theatre, conjuring, etc. Mr. Drummond, the owner, started his collection as a hobby when he was on the stage and has made this charming byway very much his own.


## 979 WATKINS BOOKS LTD.                           01-836 2182
**19-21 Cecil Court, London WC2N 4HB.**           **01-836 3778**

**Subjects:** Mysticism, occultism, astrology, new age and oriental philosophy.
**Hours:** Mon - Sat 10.00 - 6.00. Wed 10.30 - 6.00.
**Services:** Mail order, catalogue.

One of the larger premises in Cecil Court, with two shops knocked into one. There is a secondhand section at the back of the shop. A mecca for browsers interested in the shop's subjects.


## 980 ANGLE BOOKS LTD.
**2 Cecil Court, London WC2N 4HE.**               **01-836 2922**

**Subjects:** English, local history and topography.
**Hours:** Mon - Fri 10.30 - 6.00.
**Services:** Mail order, credit cards and an occasional catalogue.

Drawings and watercolours are to be found in the basement while topography and English local history, arranged by counties are on the ground floor. The bookselling community in Cecil Court certainly seem to cover all fields between them.

### 981 ROBERT CHRIS BOOKSELLER
8, Cecil Court, WC2N 4HF.      01-836 6700

**Subjects:** Nutrition, natural therapies and holistic health.
**Hours:** Mon - Sat 11.00 - 5.30.
**Services:** Mail order.

Two ladies run this bookshop who are committed to the idea of a positive approach to health. Peggy Last works as a nurse in one of five N.H.S. homoeopathic hospitals and is well read and knowledgeable about the subject while Val Chris, wife of the late owner's nephew is interested in nutrition, relaxation and Yoga, so the shelves in this bookshop are crammed with advice on special diets, sensible ways to eat, the control of stress and homeopathic medicine etc. In short, the emphasis is on practicality and a positive attitude towards mind and body. It is good to see Cecil Court being kept as a special bookselling area in London.

### 982 IMAGES
Peter Stockham Ltd.,
16 Cecil Court, London WC2N 4HE.      01-836 8661

**Subjects:** New, antiquarian, children, miniature books, reference, art, illustrated books.
**Hours:** Mon - Closed. Tue - Fri 11.00 - 6.00, First Sat in month 11.00 - 2.00. Other times by appointment.
**Services:** Mail order, catalogue, special orders, consultancy service, magazine subscription.

The owner here stands in a pulpit-like structure looking down inside this small shop. Every inch of space is taken up with a fascinating collection of books, which probably number about four thousand. Art, illustrated books, children's books, miniature books, scholarly monographs, and collectors items are only part of the range here. There is also room for old toys and dolls to give the place the excitement of a Christmas stocking.

## 983 FROGNAL RARE BOOKS
18 Cecil Court,
Charing Cross Road, London WC2N 4HE.          01-240 2815

**Subjects:** Antiquarian, rare, specialising in Law, economics and business histories.
**Hours:** Mon - Fri 10.00 - 6.00.
**Services:** Mail order, catalogue, University and library supply.

A small premises in Cecil Court with the less expensive items near the door working back to less accessible complete sets, but a ladder is provided for the browser. Mrs. Finer who has been in the trade 25 years, gives expert advice to callers.

## 984 ALAN BRETT LTD.
24 Cecil Court, London WC2N 4HE.          01-836 8222

**Subjects:** Antiquarian, topography.
**Hours:** Mon -Sat 9.00 - 5.30.
**Services:** Special order.

A small shop with a gallery to the rear with prints. Old books on topography together with maps, globes and other ephemera realting to their speciality.

## 985 SOUTH AFRICA HOUSE BOOKSTALL
8 Duncan Street,
Trafalgar Square, London WC2N 5DP.          01-930 4488
                                              ext. 164

**Subjects:** Information on South Africa.
**Hours:** Mon - Fri 10.00 12.00. 2.00 - 4.00.
**Services:** Mail order, Special order.

Books about South Africa including maps and guides are displayed in a room on the third floor at Golden Cross House. Books can be ordered from South African publishers.

### 986 JOHN MENZIES (HOLDINGS) LTD.
40 The Strand, London WC2N 5HZ.                           01-930 0033

**Subjects:** General.
**Hours:** Mon - Fri 8.00 - 6.00, Sat 9.00 - 6.00. Sun 12.00 - 6.00.
**Services:** Credit cards.

One wall of this shop is lined with paperbacks and there is a table of bargain books. Quite good on maps, gardening books, and ones of general reference. John Menzies is a large chain of shops and station stalls, currently much stronger in the North and Scotland, where they tend to concentrate their book-selling activities. This type of shop is useful to tourists.

### 987 W.H. SMITH
**Charing Cross Mainline Station,**
**London WC2N 5HS.**                                      01-839.4200

**Subjects:** General.
**Hours:** Mon - Sun 7.15 a.m. - 9.00 p.m.
**Services:** Credit cards.

Open bookstall accommodating the travellers and selling books, mainly paperbacks, with a good reference section and maps and guides.

### 988 GRANT & CUTLER LTD.
**11 Buckingham Street, London WC2N 6DQ.**                01-839 3136

**Subjects:** Books in the major European languages.
**Hours:** Mon - Fri 9.00 - 5.30, Sat (April-August) 9.00 - 1.00, (September - March) 9.00 - 12.30.
**Services:** Mail order, institutional supply.

There seem dozens of inter-connected rooms packed with books in the major European languages, French being best represented, but the others amply so. Excellent foreign dictionary section. There are no English language books here.

**989 CLAUDE GILL BOOKS**
**140 The Strand, London WC2R 1HH.**　　　　　　Ex Directory
　　　　　　　　　　　　　　　　　　　　　　　　　　　　(240 0376)
**Subjects:** General.　　　　　　　　　　　　　　　　　　　　3042
**Hours:**　　Mon - Fri 9.30 - 6.00, Sat 10.00 - 5.30.
**Services:** Special orders.

A modern shop near Waterloo Bridge. The stock is general but slightly 'up-market', hard and soft backed. The proximity of Kings College gives the shop a bias towards English literature and the classics. The stock is arranged by subject and there is a small remainder section. Friendly and helpful staff.


**990 ESSEX HALL BOOKSHOP**
**1 Essex Street, Strand, London WC2R 3HY.**　　　　　01-836 0525

**Subjects:** General, cookery, sport, Unitarian Church publications.
**Hours:**　　Mon - Fri 9.30 - 5.30.
**Services:** Mail order, special orders, supplies Unitarian Church bookstalls.

The shop is affiliated to the Unitarian Church but keeps a good general stock too. It is to be found in a narrow street off the Aldwych, and its display of books is well lit and given plenty of room. Maps and cards are also sold.


**991 AUSTRALIAN GIFT SHOP**
**Western Australia House,**
**115 The Strand, London WC2R OAA.**　　　　　　　　01-836 2292

**Subjects:** Australiana, travel.
**Hours:**　　Mon - Fri 9.00 - 5.30, Sat 9.00 - 1.00.
**Services:** Mail order, special orders for Australian publications, issue of book tokens for use in Australia.

The entrance to the shop is in Savoy Street, just off the Strand, down a few steps. All the major Australian Publishers are represented and the books are arranged by subject. National, State and City maps are here together with government publications. Besides books you can buy Aboriginal artifacts, postcards and the like in a friendly setting.

# Subject Index

Academic 54 708 812 830
Africa-Natural history (old & Ant) 465
African 828
African & Caribbean lit 484
Africana 119 143 333 670
Alternative Medicine 26 118
  Tech 222
  Books 482
  Energy 118
  Life styles 456
  Medicine 464 485
American 242
Americana 119
Anarchism 112 6
Anti Imperialist 120
Antiquarian 45 58 102 210 223 230 236 237 263 317 318 330 331 425 432 436 445 447 498 501 503 507 616 639 640 669 670 671 672 680 740
Antiquarian & S-hand
  Australiana 675
  Central Asia 701
  Chess 675
  India 701
  London books 747
  M.East 701
  N.Africa 701
  Tibet 701
  Modern first 761
  London Hist 751
Antiquarian, Secondhand 712 718 703 729
Antiquarian Maps & Prints 439
Antiquarian Travel & Exploration 435
Antiquarian Travel & Maps 448
Antiques 109 473

Antiques, Ref Bks 443
Arabic 262 705
Archeology 821
Architecture 100 617 671 728 814
Armies, British & Indian 442
Art 100 103 229 264 341 413 434 469 470 472 634 666 671 722 739 819
Art & Crafts 473
Art Reference 802
Art, Modern 822
Arts 231 430 489
Arts, Contemporary 668
Asia 462
Asian languages from India 632
Assorted Horse racing lit 681
Astrology 485
Atlases 56
Australiana 674
Autographs 432
Aviation 123 137 150

B.B.C publications 613 57 401
Baedeker guides 679
Banking 38 51
Bargain Books 644
Bengali 1
Best sellers 607
Bibles 53
Bibliography 669
Black Books 744
Black Culture 13
Black studies 155 760
Black Womens Lit 101
Books on & from France 643
Books relating to
  Commonwealth ctrs 735
Boxing 257

British Travel 36
Brownies 423
Bruce Lee specialists 625
Buddhism 652
Building 829
Business 29 38 51 208 246
Business & home computers 624
Business Studies 36 720 509

CND 155
Caribbean 119 333
Caricature 810
Catering 720
Catholic 319 405 406
Charts 39 41
Childrens Books 232 348 349 425 427 490 518 519 601 804 1 9 10 20 103 135 225 241 249 263 264 321 326 327 348 352 418 458 499 521 510 603 605 647 649 665 673 677 680 704 725 726 737 748 816
China 820
Chinese 120
Christianity 300 356 460 47 334 353 506 522 604 709 23 50 57 221 408 419
Church History 410
Churchilliana 670
Cinema 219 815
Cinema & theatre 661
Classical studies 821
Clothing trade & pattern books 621
Coins & Medals 437
Community Politics 155
Community issues 492
Computers 323 636 830 21 632 635
Conjuring 809
Continental Lit 831
Cookery 19 249 259 647
Cookery, Whole Food 611 464

Cooking New & second hand 745
Crime Thrillers 726

DIY 352 829
Dance 219
Dentistry 316
Design 428
Dictionaries 341
Discount Books 407
Drama 252

Earls Court life 456
Early Childrens Books 810
Early English lit 672
Early Printed Books 810
Early travel 440
Ecology 118
Economics 17 432 720
Education 141 147 218 18 115 224 228 323 338 346 483 509 521 606 711
Educational Childrens Books 736
Electronics 702
Energy 118 431
Engineering 467 702
English FLT 312 800
English Language 218
English Language teaching 706
English Lit 247 432 680 831
Entertaining Arts 809
Environmental Studies 431 655
Exams 265

Family planning 620
Fantasy 130 499
Feminism 101 105 112 118 155 222 250 255 339 430 500 609 733 748 13 20
Fiction 416
Fine & Applied Art 728

Fine bindings 616 669 670 680 740
First Editions 45 450
First Editions (modern) 229 263 487 603
Fishing 104 433
Folk Dance 214
Folk Music 214
Food 440
Foreign Languages 201 239
French 475 477
French antiquarian books 446

Games 249
Gardening 427
Gay 105 112 222
Genealogy 438
General medicine 620
Geology 468
Germany 236
Girl Guides 423
Globes 56
Graphic Design 303
Greek 200
Guides 56 104 124 259 403 415 479 723
Guides & Maps 8 40 475 521 663
Guns 16

Health 464
Hebraica 4 267 273 270
Heraldry 438
Hi-Fi 625
Historical 680
History 17 247 740 821
Hobbies 416
Homosexual lit 749
Horror 130 240
Horses 422
Housing 431 829b

Illustrated 241 603 616 639 677 487 671
Indian 333

Indian Sub-Cont 805
Industry 402
Iran 742
Ireland 121 255
Islam 116 204 819 705

Japanese 216 646
Japanese Art 801
Japanese Culture 801

Kent 326

Language teaching (new & s-hand) 466
Languages 224 673
Law 31 48 720
Left wing 117
Lesbianism 101
Limited editions 234
Literary 811
Literature 740
Literature (Modern) 231
Lithuania 106
Local 20
Local Community 340
Local History 1 40 103 210 232 494
London 35 45
London History 327
London Info (inc. current & hist) 660
Management 509 720
Manuscripts 432 640 672
Maps 9 56 104 124 259 403 415 609 723 816
Maps/Guides (see Guides/Maps)
Marine Insurance 52
Maritime 2 28 39 41 329
Martial Arts 662 461
Marxist 247
Marxist-Leninist 120
Medical 24 301 618 631 702 802 827 316 432 740
Medicine, Alternative 813

Mental Handicap 27
Micro technology 636
Middle East 641 819
Militaria 137 142 306 357
Military 123
Military Equipment 232 233
Military History 233
Minerology 468
Minature Books 810
Missionary Work 307
Models 704
Moslem World (New, S-hand, O/P) 707
Mothers Union 412
Motoring 663 723
Music 222 308 476 608 629 651 653 657 682
Music, Sheet music 612
Mysticism 485

National History 357
Natural childbirth 611
Natural history 469 481 679 803
Nautical 137
New & Secondhand paperbacks 513
New Zealand 429
Nuclear Debate 107
Nursing 24

Occult 807
Oriental 215 263 817 818 828
Orientalist 444
Ornithology 669
Orthomolecular medicine 611
Out of print books 436
Own publications 654

Pacifism 112
Paperbacks 30 129 146 322 332 342 493 733
Performing Arts 357
Philosophy 17 609
Photography 609 702

Poetry 250 455 748
Poland 727
Polish books 453 757
Politics 20 627 17 222 247 344 500
Popular 266
Popular best sellers 457
Popular fiction 726
Pottery & Ceramics 656
Printing 303
Private Press 803
Private Presses 234 263 670
Pschotherapy 253
Psychiatry 609
Psychoanalysis 480
Psychology 222 252 253
Psychotherapy 480

Quakerism 202

Rabbinical 144
Radical 13 105
Railways 16 111
Railways & transport 610
Rare books 450 639 640 671
Rare maps 440
Readers Digest publications 673
Records 604
Reference 57 124 348 518 619 673
Religion 156 209 411 732 824
Religions, minor 813
Religious 207
Religious Educ 412
Remainders 43 49 113 458 470 471 493 623 626 642 733
Remainders (H/B) 806
Remainders, Secondhand 730
Review copies 58
Road Transport 111

Sacred Music 156
Sailing 5
Scholarly Secondhand 331

School 21
Sci-Fi 130 240 499
Science 3 124 432 467 469 740 827 811
Secondhand 10 58 121 210 212 220 226 230 236 237 317 318 330 336 358 404 447 450 491 498 501 503 516 678 756 452 507 425
Secondhand Art & Lit 614
   Biography 667
   Cookery 667
   Golf books 676
   Illustrated 676
   Juvenile 676
   Paperbacks 508 721 754
   Transport 676
   Travel 667
Sheet Music 653
Shipping 52
Shooting 433
Slavonic studies 453
Social Science 231
Socialism 105 339
Spain 228
Spiritual development 26
Spiritualism 426
Steiner 213 804
Student 20

Tech 124
Technical 811
Technology 3 827
Theatre 219 633
Theatres in book form 628
Theology 206 140 410
Theology (Inc Secondhand) 619
Third World 125 155
Tibetiana 808
Topography 438 802
Tourist Books 42
Town Planning 829
Toys 628 704
Transport 470 431

Travel 25 115 122 128 131 133 141 222 236 252 255 259 352 354 401 414 416 490 607 609 619 647 665 672 673 679 702 734 740 821 427 429
Travel new, rare, secondhand 746
Turkish 145

Vehicles 713
Victoriana 677

Wars 302
Wine 259 440
Witchcraft 807
Womens press 654

# Shop Index

A&L Books 756
Abbot 22
Academy Bookshop 728
Acton 708
Addison 493
Afford 343
Africa 918
Agentrose 266
Aisenthal 267
Al Hoda 950
Al Saq'i 707
Albanian 937
Allen & Co 422
Alternative 922
Ambassador 356
Angel Bookshop 109
Angle 980
Any Amount W14 761
Any Amount WC2H 946
Apex 23
Arcade 323
Archive 210
Archway 125
Arms & Militaria 142
Army & Navy SE1 3 335
Army & Navy SW1 401
Arnots 9
Art Bk Co 935
Art Stat. 348
Arts Biblio 822
Arts Council 923
Ash 45
At the Sign 499
Athena W1R 0XF 638
Athena W1V Troc 659
Athene 201
Atlantis 807
Atoz 662
Austen-Parish 124
Australian Gift 991
Australiana 674

Automobile Ass W1-V 663
Automobile Ass W6 723
Aviation Bookshop 150
Ayres 803
BBC Pubns 613
BBC World 910
BEC 509
Balham 492
Barbara Stone 264
Barbican Business 38
Barbican Centre 37
Bargain 132
Barker & Howard 2.
Barkers 731
Barn 121
Barnes 496
Basharen 145
Basilisk 234
Basketts 758
Battersea Arts 489
Bayswater 703
Belgravia 421
Bell, Book 971
Bellman 247
Belsize 235
Benedicts NW1 224
Benedicts SW6 466
Bentalls 716
Berger 414
Bible Soc 53
Bibliopola 263
Blaketon 806
Block 809
Bloomsbury Rare 802
Bloomsbury Bk Pl 837
Blossom 911
Bolingbroke 490
Bonanza SW1P 407
Bonanza W1N 623
Bonaventure 122
Bondy 810

Book Addict 460
Book Bargains W12 754
Book Bargains WC2E 926
Book Boat 327
Book Centre (FPA) 620
Book Club Assoc 630
Book Gall 676
Book Inn 956
Book Mart 226
Bookcase 49
Bookend W1P Goodge 626
Bookends W1R Regent 642
Bookmarks 117
Bookplace 340
Books Asia 462
Books Plus 339
Books etc EC4 55
Books etc SW1 400
Books etc W1P 635
Books etc WC2H 961
Books for Cooks 745
Books from India 805
Books for Blackheath 313
Bookshop SE1 305
Bookshop, Blackheath 315
Booksmith W8 733
Booksmith WC2H 963
Booksmith WC2N 967
Bookspread 510
Boosey 651
Booth 446
Boots N22 153
Boots NW4 244
Boots W1R 650
Boswell 817
Bransdon 711
Brett 984
Brit Esperanto 752
Brit Inst Man 913
Brit Museum SW7 481
Brit Museum WC1B 825
Brown & Perring 28
Building 829
Bunch 625

Bush 755
Business Bkshp 208
Buttersworths 908
C&L Bksllrs 243
CND Bkshp 107
Caissa 675
Camberwell 318
Cambridge 800
Campion 497
Cannings 341
Canonbury 103
Cass 833
Cassidy 211
Catholic Truth 405
Cavendish Rare 435
Centerprise 13
Central Bks 855
Chain Lib. 30
Chancery 901
Changes 253
Chapmans Prof 936
Chappell 682
Chapter One 108
Chapter Travel 259
Chelsea Rare 450
Chener 354
Childrens N10 135
Childrens SW19 519
Chimes 612
Cholmeley 123
Chris, Robt 981
Christian Lit. 50
Church Hse 408
Church Lit. 410
Church Miss 307
Cinema 815
City Bksllrs EC2V 34
City Bksllrs EC3V 44
City Lit 912
Clarke-Hall 58
Cobb 501
Coliseum 968
College 303
Collets Chinese 820

Collets Internat 957
Collets London 947
Collets Penguin 944
Collins 351
Commissariat 350
Compendium 222
Comyns 148
Connoisseur 713
Constant Reader 463
Cook Hammond 403
Corner Hse 934
Craftsmen 656
Cramer 966
Creative Camera 839
Crompton 461
Crouch End 131
Dance Books 973
Dar el Dawa 705
David & Chas 610
Daybreak 334
Debenhams 600
Dennys EC1M 24
Dennys SE1 301
Deptford 321
Design Cen 428
Dillons 830
Dillons QMS 3
Ditchfield 14
Dorling 919
Dulwich 352
Ealing 717
Early Learning 736
Early Music 608
East Asia 215
Eaton 751
Economists 904
Economists 2nd hand 905
Edmonds 639
Edna Whiteson 136
Elgin 748
Elys 517
English Cont. 242
Essex Hall 990
Eurocentre 312

European School 831
Evangel 709
Evans 622
Faculty N3 115
Faculty NW4 246
Fagins 141
Fanfare 21
Fantasy 130
Farlows 433
Faulks 147
Fen Books 40
Festival Hall 308
Fielders 521
Fine Books 847
Finlay 347
Fisher & Sperr 127
Fitzjohns 237
Flask 229
Fletcher 976
Flinders 834
Folk Shop 214
Forbidden Planet 933
Forbidden Planet 2 931
Foss 609
Foster E6 10
Foster W4 712
Four Provinces 854
Foyle 955
Foyles Educ 606
Franks 621
Freedom 6
French Bkshp 477
French's 633
Friends 202
Frognal 983
GLC London Tourist 660
Gabriels 228
Gallery 349
Game Advice 249
Genesis 26
Geographers 853
Geographia 56
Geolog Mus 468
Gilberts 258

Gill W1M Jas 615
Gill W1R Oxf 637
Gill W1V Pic 665
Gill W5 Eal 719
Gill WC2R Str 989
Girl Guides 423
Glendale 677
Golden Cockerel 812
Goldsmiths 338
Golub 4
Good Book Guide 823
Gordons 495
Grant & Cutler 988
Grass Roots 744
Green Knight 964
Greenwich SE1 311
Greenwich SE10 328
Greenwich WC2H 940
Greenwood 668
Grower 838
Guangwha 928
HMSO 848
Hachette 643
Halter 257
Hambling's 977
Hamleys 649
Hammick Sweet 903
Hammicks W6 725
Hammicks WC2E 920
Hamstead Village 231
Harrington 448
Harris 916
Harrods 425
Harvey Nichols 424
Hatchards 664
Hebrew 144
Hellenic 962
Heraldry 438438
Heywood Hill 680
High Hill 232
Higham 206
Highgate 128
Hill Bkshp 518
History Bkshp 137

Holborn Books 959
Holloway 129
Hollywood Rd 485
Holy Cross 319
Hoppen 440
Hosains 701
Houndsditch 342
Housing Cen 829b
Housmans Bkshp 112
Howe 126
Hudsons 720
ISO Pubns 306
Il Libro 445
Images 982
Imp College 467
Imperial War 302
Inst Contemp 430
Intermed. Tech 917
Islamic 204
Jay Vee 710
Jenner 841
Jerusalem 270
Jewish Chronicle 46
Jewish Mem 832
John Lewis 601
Jones & Evans 51
Joseph 616
Kanoune 742
Karnac 480
Kelly 443
Keltic 706
Kelvin Hughes 39
Kens Bk Shop 476
Kilburn 255
Kimon 200
Kimptons W1N 618
Kimptons W1P 631
Kings 845
Kingsbury 265
Kirkdale 357
Knightsbridge 828
Ksiegarnia 727
Labour Party 344
Lally 503

Lamley 469
Lavells 271
Law Notes 902
Lester 444
Lewis 827
Liberty 647
Library Bkshp 106
Lion Micro 636
Little Bkshp 515
London Bkmkt 644
London City 300
London Toy 704
London Visitor 415
London Yacht 5
Lovejoys 953
Luzac 818
Maggs 672
Man to Man 749
Mandarin 750
Manna 506
Marcet 330
Marchmont 835
Marlborough 671
Martin NW11 269
Martin SW11 488
Martin SW18 512
Martin W6 726
Martins N3 114
McCarta 856
Medici Gall 472
Mellor 740
Mencap 27
Menorah 273
Menzies EC2M 29
Menzies EC2V 33
Menzies NW1 203
Menzies SE3 314
Menzies SW7 474
Menzies W2 700
Menzies WC2N 986
Mercury 346
Methodist Miss. 209
Miles N1 104
Miles, AA NW1 212

Model Railway 111
Modern Bk 702
Modern Law 907
Morgans 152
Mothers Union 412
Motorbooks 965
Mowbray 619
Museum Bkshop 821
Museum of London 35
Music Bk Cen 629
Muslim Info 116
Mustard 221
Muswell Hill 133
Mysteries 938
NEDO 402
NSS E4 8
NSS SW5 457
Nat Book Ex 508
Nat Poetry 455
Nat Portrait 958
Nat Schizo 514
Nat. Army 442
Neal St E. 941
New Beacon 119
New City 43
New Era 120
Nihon 801
Notting Hill 730
O'Callaghan 678
OCS 216
Oakhill 140
Observation 332
Odyssey 842
Offstage 219
Old London 747
Operation Headstart 143
Oppenheim 470
Orbis 453
Other Bkshop 105
Owl 248
Oyez Stat EC2M 31
Oyez Stat EC4A 48
Oyez Stat WC1V 850
Paddington 605

Pan SW10 486
Paperback Cen E13 17
Paperbacks SW9 483
Paperbacks Cen W1P 627
Paperchase 634
Parents Centre 18
Parks 851
Passage 316
Penguin SW3 451
PenguinW1A 602
PenguinWC2E 921
Penguin/Lib 648
Periera 261
Peter Jones 418
Peters Music 657
Petersfield 729
Phase One 239
Photographers Gall 927
Pickering & Chatto 432
Pickering & Inglis 57
Pilot 624
Pipeline 849
Planning Bkshp 431
Pleasures of Past
Plus Books SE27 358
Plus Books SW19 513
Poland St 655
Pollocks 628
Polonez 757
Popular Bk Cen SE13 336
Popular Bk Cen SW1P 404
Popular Bk Cen SW11 491
Popular Bk Cen WC2H 930
Popular Bks 146
Pordes 945
Potter 41
Primrose 223
Probsthain 819
Protestant Truth 47
Pulteney 471
Quaritch 640
Quartet 654
Quevedo 975
RIBA 617

Racing Pigeon 840
Ram 658
Ray's Jazz 929
Razzall's 494
Readers Digest 673
Readers Matters 155
Reads 942
Reads of Maryleb 614
Reedmore 240
Regent 217
Remington 927
Response 456
Richard Worth 500
Riverside 722
Robinson 603
Rogers Turner 331
Rota 925
Round About 12
Rowland Ward 465
Roy Hayes 325
Royal Academy 666
Royal Shakespeare 909
Rushworth 156
S. London Christian 353
SCM 824
SPCK 207
STA Trav 479
Sahara 484
Sandoe 441
Sanford 447
Sawyer 670
Scholabooks 475
Schott 653
Script Union 604
Seal 718
Selfridges 607
Shapero 679
Shipley 949
Shorouk 641
Sifton 439
Silver Moon 948
Simmonds EC4 54
Simmonds SE10 329
Sims, Reed 436

Sister Write 101
Skola 218
Skoob 811
Sky 721
Slaney 449
Smith & Fawkes 230
Smith, Jas. 852
Solosy 943
Soma SE11 333
Soma W8 735
Sotheran 669
South Africa 985
Souvenir 816
Spink 437
Spiritualist 426
Spreadeagle 326
St Geo Gall 434
St John's Wood 262
St Paul 732
Stage Door 969
Stanford 924
Star Bks 632
Steiner NW1 213
Steiner WC1A 804
Stevens 250
Stokes 420
Stone 843
Stone Trough 317
Storey 970
Strathmore 260
Sunpower 118
Swans 322
Swans Bookstall 511
Swiss Cott. 252
Take 5 516
Tate Gall 413
Tavistock 836
Templar 900
Tetric SW4 452
Tetric SW6 459
Theatre Shop 960
Theosophical 813
Tibet 808
Tokamine 646

Tower Bkshp 42
Tower Hamlets 1
Trailfinders 734
Travel Bkshop 746
Travis 974
Triangle 814
Trotman 233
Truslove 427
Tudor 7
Turf 681
Uajmaa 482
Unicorn 241
United Soc 411
University Bkshps 113
Upper St Bkshp 100
Vandeleur 498
Vanes 15
Vermilion 846
Vic & Alb 473
Village NW3 236
Village SW16 507
Vintage Mag 661
WHS E15 19
WHS E6 11
WHS EC1N 25
WHS EC2 32
WHS EC2Y 36
WHS N1 110
WHS N10 134
WHS N12 138
WHS N13 139
WHS N18 149
WHS N22 154
WHS NW1 205
WHS NW11 268
WHS NW11 272
WHS NW2 227
WHS NW3 238
WHS NW4 245
WHS NW6 254
WHS NW7 256
WHS SE1 304
WHS SE1 309
WHS SE1 310

WHS SE13 337
WHS SE18 345
WHS SE22 355
WHS SE6 320
WHS SE9 324
WHS SW15 502
WHS SW16 504
WHS SW19 520
WHS SW1V 416
WHS SW1W 417
WHS SW5 454
WHS W4 714
WHS W5 715
WHS W6 724
WHS W8 741
WHS W11 753
WHS W13 759
WHS WC2B 914
WHS WC2N 987
Walden 220
Walford 102
Walter Rodney 760
Waltons 505
Waterstones SW7 478
Waterstones W1R 645
Waterstones W8 738
Waterstones WC1B 826
Waterstones WC2H 954
Watkins 979
Well 419
West End Bks WC1N 844
West End Green 251
West London 458
Westmin Abbey 409
Westmin Cath 406
Whetstone 151
Whitcoulls 429
Whole Thing 20
Wholefood 611
Wildy 906
Willen 16
Williams-Ellis 743
Wimbledon Evang 522
Wimbleton 739

Windmill 464
Wisdom 652
Witherby 52
Words etc. 487
World of Bks 667
Writers & Readers 225
YHA 915
Young World 737
Zeno 932
Zwemmer WC2H 939
Zwemmer/Photo 952
Zwemmers OUP 951